Beyond Accommodation

Thinking Gender
Edited by Linda J. Nicholson

Also published in the series

Feminism/Postmodernism
Linda J. Nicholson

Gender Trouble
Judith Butler

Words of Power
Andrea Nye

Femininity and Domination
Sandra Bartky

Beyond Accommodation

ETHICAL FEMINISM, DECONSTRUCTION, AND THE LAW

DRUCILLA CORNELL

ROUTLEDGE

NEW YORK AND LONDON

Published in 1991 by

Routledge
An imprint of Routledge, Chapman and Hall, Inc.
29 West 35 Street
New York, NY 10001

Published in Great Britain by

Routledge
11 New Fetter Lane
London EC4P 4EE

Copyright © 1991 by Routledge, Chapman and Hall, Inc.

Printed in the United States of America

Library of Congress Cataloging in Publication Data

Cornell, Drucilla.
    Beyond accommodation / [Drucilla Cornell]
        p.   cm.—(Thinking gender)
    Includes bibliographical references and index.
    ISBN 0-415-90105-7.—ISBN 0-415-90106-5 (pbk.)
    1. Feminist theory. 2. Feminist criticism. 3. Women—Legal status, laws, etc. I. Title. II. Series.
HQ1190.C67   1991
305.42'01—dc20   91-8554
                                                        CIP

British Library Cataloguing in Publication Data

Cornell, Drucilla
    Beyond accommodation : ethical feminism, sexual difference, & utopian possibility. — (Thinking gender)
    I. Title   II. Series
    305.42

    ISBN 0415901057
    ISBN 0415901065 (paperback)

For Maureen
In admiration and friendship

Contents

Introduction: Writing the Mamafesta:
The Dilemma of Postmodern Feminism   1

1.   The Maternal and the Feminine:
      Social Reality, Fantasy and Ethical Relation   21

2.   The Feminist Alliance with Deconstruction   79

3.   Feminism Always Modified:
      The Affirmation of Feminine Difference Rethought   119

4.   Feminine Writing, Metaphor and Myth   165

Conclusion: "Happy Days"   197

Notes   207

Index   235

Acknowledgments

I want to thank Judith Butler, Jacques Derrida, and Sam Weber for their valuable editorial suggestions. I also want to thank my two assistants, A. Collin Biddle and Deborah Garfield, for their devotion and tireless effort in seeing my work to fruition. Maureen McGrogan, my editor at Routledge, has been a continuous source of support for me throughout the writing of this book. She has been a constant reminder of how important an editor can be to an author. Her combination of friendship and editorial skill has been invaluable to me. My thanks are in the dedication of the book.

Introduction
Writing the Mamafesta: The Dilemma of Postmodern[1] Feminism

Who in his heart doubts either that the facts of feminine clothiering are there all the time or that the feminine fiction, stranger than the facts, is there also at the same time, only a little to the rere? Or that one may be separated from the other? Or that both may then be contemplated simultaneously? Or that each may be taken up and considered in turn apart from the other.

—James Joyce, *Finnegans Wake*

Something of the consummation of sexual difference has still not been articulated or transmitted. Is there not still something held in reserve within the silence of female history: an energy, morphology, growth or blossoming still to come from the female realm? Such a flowering keeps the future open. The world remains uncertain in the fact of this strange advent.

—Luce Irigaray, *Sexual Difference*

The need to let suffering speak is the condition of all truth.

—Theodor Adorno, *Negative Dialectics*

Throughout *Finnegans Wake*, Annah Allmaziful's letter, an "untitled mamafesta memorialising the Mosthighest has gone by many names at disjointed times" is renamed and rewritten, put aside and passed on, analyzed by perplexed masculine observers and discarded in dismay, only to be picked up again, reread and reworked.[2] Annah the Allmaziful's we read, but if it is hers, it is not hers alone. She is not the origin of the letter. Nor is she the inventor.

[W]ho in hallhagal wrote the durn thing anyhow? Erect, beseated, mountback, against a partywall, below freezigrade, by the use of quill or style, with turbid or pellucid mind, accompanied or the reverse by mastication, interrupted by visit of seer to scribe or of scribe to site, atwixt two showers or atosst of a trike, rained upon or blown around, by a right-down regular racer from the soil or by a too painted whittlewit laden with the loot of learning?[3]

The discovery of the letter is a rediscovery. The letter is always, already being written. The ultimate proclamation of the mamafesta is anticipated but never finally delivered. Even so, the letter circulates between generations of women—and perhaps more importantly—is put into circulation, so the story goes, by Woman. The writing goes on and on and on. The destiny of the letter is that it is to be rewritten and recirculated. The revelation of her

1

reality cannot be separated from the letter and the letter is only as it is rewritten. The letter does not, then, present an unchanging feminine "reality." Feminine "reality" is instead brought from the "rere" to the fore in the writing of the letter. The feminine is in the writing. As the letter is renamed and rewritten, in "disjointed times" and places, feminine "reality" *is* differently.

Writing the mamafesta, as I rewrote it here, is a fable for the elucidation of Her-story such that feminine "reality" can be written. In the fable as I have rewritten it, the opposition between the literal and the textual is undermined. Undermined, but not obliterated. The material suffering of women is not being denied in the name of a process of writing that continually transforms the representation of the feminine as if the rewriting itself could put an end to patriarchy. Instead, the fable emphasizes the deconstruction of a reality that stands in as the unshakable, literal truth, so that the more that has yet to be written from the side of the feminine is not shut out as non-existent. No woman can claim that hers is the ultimate reality excluding all others, based on a concept of gender identity or on the uncovering of the essence of Woman. Thus, the writing of the mamafesta does not attempt to resolve the riddle of femininity once and for all, by locating women's specificity in a pregiven nature of sexual difference.

If there is a central tenet in this book, it is that the condition in which the suffering of all women can be "seen" and "heard," in all of our difference, is that in which the tyranny of established reality is disrupted and the possibility of further feminine resistance and the writing of a different version of the story of sexual difference is continually affirmed. Put somewhat differently the more (*mère/mehr*), not as what *is there* in the actual, but as what has yet to be rendered at all, as the repressed, as the disruption of the unconscious, as the explosive force of an imaginary that cannot be completely shut out, is the feminine as written in the letter. One of Jacques Lacan's central insights is that the explosive power of *jouissance*, as what cannot be captured of lived feminine sexuality by the current, hierarchical gender divide, can also not be separated from what shifts in language. But I give a new twist to Lacan's insight by stressing that what shifts in language cannot in turn be understood without appreciating the role of metaphor and the process of re-metaphorization in feminine writing. Agreeing, in other words, with his formulation, I disagree with his ethical and political pessimism—that the problem of the subjection of woman is insoluble. Nor is feminine as written and rewritten within the continual shifting of a "reality" presented in metaphor; it is not reducible to the subversion of the unrepresentable. The rewriting of the feminine can, in other words, be transformative, not merely disruptive.

Writing, of course, cannot stand in for political activity. But political activity, if it is to avoid the ever present danger of the restoration of the masculine-dominated world feminism seeks to dismantle, demands that we write the feminine that has been pushed to the "rere" so that we can enact a critical standpoint by which to judge "their" world as false, precisely because it pretends to be the "whole."

The feminine as it is written and affirmed in the letter, in other words, is not simply "there" to be imposed upon the women who live and dream of the feminine differently. This is the motivation behind the separation of the affirmation of feminine sexual difference as an ethical and political positioning, and the attempt to resolve the riddle of femininity in a pregiven sexual nature. The feminine "is" only in and through the letter as it is written and rewritten, circulated and recirculated. But the feminine is also not just a name, merely a nominalist category to be shrugged off when it is strategic to do so, as opposed to the fundamental empirical reality of *actual* women. To pit "materialist" feminism against feminine writing is to fail to heed the performative power of language and, more specifically, metaphor. We cannot, in other words, get behind the letter to find the "real truth" of individual women's experience which only then is represented in language. Woman and women cannot be separated from the fictions and metaphors in which she and they are presented, and through which we portray ourselves. The letter is Her-story, and Her-story is the letter. Feminine "reality" is as "fici-fact."

The central purpose of this book is to give further body to this fable and to demonstrate how its ethical and political power helps us to orient ourselves differently toward a central dilemma of feminism. That dilemma can be summarized as follows: If there is to be feminism at all, we must rely on a feminine "voice" and a feminine "reality" that can be identified as such and correlated with the lives of actual women; and yet at the same time all accounts of the feminine seem to reset the trap of rigid gender identities, deny the real differences between women (white, heterosexual women are repeatedly reminded of this danger by women of color and by lesbians) and reflect the history of oppression and discrimination rather than an ideal or an ethical positioning to the Other to which we can aspire. To avoid misunderstanding, I must put in a caveat here.

I put the word "voice" in quotation marks deliberately. As already told, the fable of the mamafesta is a fable of writing, not of speaking. I am not, therefore, addressing here the privileging of speaking over writing that Jacques Derrida has argued is crucial to Western metaphysics. I use "voice" in contrast to muteness that makes feminine "reality" disappear because it cannot be articulated. Muteness not only implies silencing of women, it also indicates the "dumbness" before what cannot be "heard" or "read" because it cannot be articulated.[4]

But let me return once again to the opening quotes to trace the web in which we have become ensnared. We seem forced to choose between the confirmation of gender identity, or what is unique in female sexuality, as the basis of any account of feminine difference, or the suspicion—that seemingly risks political indifference to the suffering of women—of any statements that indicate the specificity of feminine sexual difference, including those that cover the "empirical" condition of women or the construction of Woman within a particular context such as law. I choose my words carefully. In the recent debate between essentialist and supposedly anti-essentialist feminisms, different philosophical positions are often run together because what would constitute an essentialist account of either Woman as general conceptual form, or Woman as a set of identifiable properties which identify her unique "being," is not precisely defined. In turn, a biological and/or naturalist account of feminine sexuality has not been adequately separated from an essentialist rendering of feminine or of women's "reality." The result has unfortunately been that any attempt to write feminine difference, or even to specify the construction of Woman or women within a particular context, has been *identified* as essentialist and then, depending on one's position on essentialism, either affirmed or rejected. It is important to note here that both sides of the debate have implicitly concluded that there is some kind of *necessary* relationship between essentialism, the possible specification of feminine sexual difference as feminine, and the elaboration of the suffering of women as unique to women. The central tenet of this book is that once we understand what is entailed by the deconstruction of essentialism, we will be able to show why there is no such necessary relationship. Once we understand that there is no such necessary relationship, we will then be able to free "feminine" writing and the evocation of the feminine as uncontainable by the current gender hierarchy from the charge of essentialism, as well as from the charge made by some Lacanians of reliance on a prelinguistic, specifically female, libido. We will then be able to distinguish the attempts to elaborate the specificity of Woman or women as constructed by a particular context—my focus will be law—from either essentialist or naturalist accounts.

Of course, one crucial aspect of feminism as it developed as a political movement in the late Sixties and early Seventies was to break the silence of women so as to articulate *their* suffering as women; to give us, in other words, another recourse than that of muteness.[5] This breaking of the silence and the solidarity it made possible was associated with consciousness-raising groups. To raise consciousness was to understand the self as a woman, to know suffering collectively so as to grasp its basis not only in gender, but in a system of gender that subordinates women. The truth of women was precisely in letting our suffering speak, to understand what was happening to each one of us not individually, but as women. Two of the writers I discuss in this book, Robin West and Catharine MacKinnon, both of whom continue to advocate consciousness-raising as *the* feminist method, take essentialist positions, West explicitly, MacKinnon implicitly. I begin with West because her account of the identity of Woman, which at times slides between essentialism and naturalism, forcefully puts forward the *political* appeal of such accounts, if one assumes that there is a necessary relationship between breaking the silence that surrounds our suffering and the uncovering of the *truth* of women's "reality."

The question becomes: How does one *tell* the truth of our suffering without such an account? From this point of view, what is called "postmodern" philosophy can seem to be either just another patriarchal excuse for indifference to the crushing of women's lives and hopes, or the rampant illusion of individualism with its pretense that "a person" can be freed from the designations imposed by context and simply rise above gender. Indeed, if Heidegger taught us anything in *Being and Time*,[6] the opposite conclusion would seem to follow. We are thrown into a pregiven context we do not control and which shapes us. Our "throwedness," *Geworfenheit*, belies the illusion of the transcendental subject that supposedly can pull itself up out of its empirical designations, and therefore, center itself. The decentered "subject" is precisely the subject who cannot pull herself up by her own boot straps so as to completely escape the designations imposed by context, by language and by the others who "see" us within our context. (A recent study showed that in the first *seconds* of an encounter, the viewed person is identified first by "race" and then by "sex.")

Technically, the accurate philosophical statement is that "they" have constructed "me" as a woman. Politically, within "consciousness-raising," the imposition of "they" is turned in on itself to become the recognition "I" am a woman, not just myself or a person. Without this recognition, so the argument goes, there would be no feminist solidarity based in "genderized" identification, if not in identity. The further affirmation, "I am" a feminist, was and is understood as a political stance against a shared and gender-based subordination. Even within this framework, the statements "I am a woman" and "I am a feminist" are not identical, nor, if we read through Heidegger, do such statements necessarily imply a transcendental or centered subject. MacKinnon emphasizes the erasure of the woman's "I" as a political aspect of her subordination. Women are not free to say "I," because they are identified as women who as "fuckees," objects, by definition cannot be subjects.

I emphasize in this account that how "I am" as a woman is "to be" identified as such by "them," because the "essentialism" of either West or MacKinnon has an explicit political motivation that must not go unnoticed in the philosophical dispute. The motivation in both cases is to first emphasize the basis of shared genderized "reality" of subordination, and in West, if certainly not MacKinnon, of a different female morality. It is driven also to locate the specificity of female subordination within our current legal system. In 1990, as we are in the process of watching some of the most important legal gains of the Sixties and Seventies made by women be undermined, when not directly overruled, we should not take the political motivation lightly. The intensity in the debate over essentialism is, to my mind, best explained by the political implications that seem to flow from an anti-essentialist position.

But as we will see, once the deconstruction of essentialism is correctly understood, the political danger of seeming indifference to the specificity of the suffering of women can be successfully avoided. I will argue that we do not need to have an essentialist account of Woman to specify the conditions of subordination in a particular context. Such specification obviously demands that we look at different historical and cultural conditions. Within American law we can also meet West's aspiration for a "feminist" jurisprudence that would allow unnoticed harms to women to be translated into the legal system in such a way as to recognize their sex- or gender-specific construction. We can do so by putting West's reconstructive jurisprudence within the framework of Jean-François Lyotard's writing on "the differend."[7]

West, implicitly at least, relies on the American version of object relations theory, which distinguishes the genders on the basis of women's maternal role and the corresponding socialization of women to be mothers. As we will see, for MacKinnon, West's affirmation of women's "different voice" is condemned for perpetuating our oppression. We will return to the way in which MacKinnon's own *unmodified* feminism represents the violence of a conceptual, supposedly all-inclusive definition of what feminism is and must be. Under her analysis, feminism becomes a series of normative injunctions, hidden behind a supposedly materialist analysis. Those who do not abide by the analysis do not obey and by definition are not feminists. It is precisely this imposition of one conceptual definition of what feminism is and must be that has been ethically and politically critiqued, not only by deconstruction, but by other trends in philosophy that are labelled "postmodern."

Yet, the more far-reaching critique of MacKinnon is that she reinstates the very gender hierarchy that she supposedly condemns. West, on the other hand, attempts to displace the gender hierarchy that necessarily repudiates the feminine, by affirming not only woman's difference, but her value. She does so through an analysis of the maternal role and women's reproductive capacity more generally. Even freed of her own essentialist analysis, there remain serious problems with West's attempt to base sexual difference on mothering, either as a role or as a particular bodily capacity. I begin with West's discussion because it gives us an account of the ethical, legal and political significance of the American version of object relations theory.

The attempt to locate the specificity of feminine sexual difference in the maternal is not only embodied in the literature of object relations theory, but holds the same attraction in other frameworks, including French Lacanian "feminine" writers. Thus, I contrast West's analysis with the writing of Julia Kristeva, who also, at least in her early writings, locates feminine sexual difference in the repressed maternal and, more specifically, in the maternal body as an alternative relation between subject and Other. Although her Lacanian background keeps Kristeva from making West's essentialist or naturalist justifications for woman's difference, her own analysis falls prey to a similar difficulty, in which Woman is once again reduced to her maternal role or function. The maternal role becomes one more container that curtails feminine sexual difference and ultimately re-legitimates the imaginary masculine fantasy of Woman as Mother. Indeed, I will argue that in spite of her reliance on Lacan, Kristeva ultimately retrogresses because of her failure to fully heed the implications of this identification of Woman as mother. Kristeva, in other words, comes close in some of her more sentimental writings on mothering to endorsing the psychical fantasy of Woman in which the "good" mothers are separated from the "bad," unstable disrupters.

Thus, in her later writing, it should not surprise us that she has turned away from her own earlier work, in which the repressed maternal, as the imaginary symbiotic relationship of the mother/child dyad—or the ethical appreciation of heterogeneity metaphorically implicit in the maternal body, not the actual maternal role—operated with utopian force through what Kristeva called the semiotic. Kristeva's emphasis on the semiotic and the utopian force marked her "break" with Lacan. The tension, however, in the early Kristeva between the semiotic as the disruptive power of the repressed feminine that could not be known and thus fully captured by the masculine symbolic, and her attempt to locate feminine difference in the actual maternal role so as to give some stability to "herethics," has been resolved in favor of the more conservative positioning. The result is her turning away from any attempt to write the repressed maternal or the maternal body as a counterforce to the Law of the Father. We are left instead with the maternal *function* as it is allowed its proper place in the established gender hierarchy of the masculine symbolic. But we are also forced, according to Kristeva, to reject the imaginary maternal, as a regressive fantasy that can only lead women into the mire of depression, melancholy, and even suicide. Matricide, in this specific sense, is the price we pay for survival within the established conventions of the existing order. Women achieve proper differentiation, in other words, only at the cost of accepting their castration. In the end, Kristeva leaves us with a very traditional Freudian analysis of woman's proper place in the maternal function which, once obtained, stabilizes women.

Thus, as we will see, Kristeva leaves us with what Luce Irigaray has beautifully described as *"derelection,"* in which feminine difference cannot be expressed except as signified in the masculine imaginary or the masculine symbolic. *Derelection*, which Irigaray systematically deconstructs within the

Freudian framework, is precisely the inability to express either the repressed maternal, or the actual, libidinal relationship to the mother, as other than phallic, the longing to be in the place of the man so as to also satisfy "Mommy." Yet Irigaray also warns against the identification of feminine sexual difference with the maternal *function* as usually defined within gender hierarchy. The attempt to symbolize the imaginary mother/child dyad, or even the mother/daughter relationship, as important as this is, is not the ultimate "solution" to *derelection*, as if there could be one solution. This symbolization, if posed as the solution to *derelection*, would just be another container, and thus another containment of feminine sexual difference. To quote Irigaray:

> The/a *woman never closes up into a volume*. The dominant representation of the maternal figure as volume may lead us to forget that woman's ability to enclose is enhanced by her fluidity, and vice versa.[8]

Irigaray's is a political warning against Woman's identification with the maternal *function*. Yet, the writing of the repressed maternal, the maternal body as the evocation of a subject "which is not one," and the representability of the mother/daughter relationship beyond the reduplication—one becomes the other—imposed by phallogocentrism (the daughter's fate is to become her mother), are viewed as embodiments of the feminine as a counterforce against the reign of the masculine symbolic. Especially in the writing of Hélène Cixous, the maternal, as the repressed and as the imagined ethical expression of another mode of being with the Other which recognizes the heterogeneity within the subject, is given play as the embodiment of an explicitly utopian longing.[9] But in her work, this writing of the maternal is clearly not identified with the symbolization of the actual, virtual relationship of mother to daughter, or of the daughter, in any direct way, to her own "origin." Thus, if there is to be a place, and an important place, for such writing to challenge *derelection*, the status of the maternal must be understood and then distinguished from the reduction of feminine sexual difference to the maternal function or role. The imagined unity of mother and child is, of course, not the story from the woman's point of view, which is why feminine writing, even of the maternal body, celebrates the experience of heterogeneity, not of an idealized unity.

The writing of the mamafesta is the challenge to the containment of woman, not a reinstatement of her proper place. But such writing, of course, also necessarily challenges the erasure of the mother as other than the idealized function or role. In Irigaray's sense, the writing overflows the limits imposed by any rigid conceptual definition. As a result, the writing of the maternal remains important for its refusal of the devaluation of the feminine upon which gender hierarchy rests, and also as an evocation of a subject not centered in itself against the "outside" world.

I have already suggested that West's legal program need not rely on her essentialist explanation of women's difference. But the more fundamental point is not simply to show how this can be done, but to argue that we cannot separate our actual existing legal system from the law of the replication of existing gender identity. In other words, if we are to challenge the situational sexism women endure within our own legal system, we must also challenge the current gender divide as it is implicated in the limits we have experienced on the possibilities of legal reform and transformation. The further argument in this book is that the struggle against the enforcement of the gender divide in law or in other contexts cannot be separated from the affirmation of feminine sexual difference—which is not to be identified with the properties "correlated" within current conventions with actual women—as a crucial movement in the displacement of gender hierarchy. But to indicate why this is the case let us return to the opening quotes.

In the quotation from Luce Irigaray, the "female blossoming that keeps open the future of sexual difference," and at the same time allows us to judge the past of the "silence of female history" in which our suffering was inexpressible, is dependent upon the affirmation of the specificity of the feminine as *difference* beyond the established system of gender identity (and more generally of any pregiven identity). If the feminine is repudiated, if "feminine reality" is once again pushed to the "rere" and pushed under, no matter how or why we justify doing so, we will be left in the masculine arena in which the old games of domination are played out. There will only be repetition, no re-evolution to the future. Irigaray is ultimately a thinker of change.

Without the feminine there is only the masculine, at least if we accept the basic feminist proposition that human "being"—being as constructed by patriarchal culture, not as an empirical entity or substance or as a set of inborn, universalizable properties—is currently marked and marred by the gender dichotomy that defines each one of us as locked into one gender or the other. Nor are the sides of the dichotomy equalized. The feminine is pushed to the "rere" and under. The masculine dominates—more specifically, in the guise of being identified as what is truly "human." On this understanding of the constitutive force of the gender divide, violence to feminine "being" inheres in the very act of the repudiation of the feminine. This repudiation, *where there is gender hierarchy*, is considered to be cross-cultural if not erected in the same manner. As a result, it does not need to deny historical differences, including the different forms gender hierarchy takes.[10] This position only affirms that a repudiation necessarily shuts us into a reality that is phallogocentric, at least in the sense that the world is not given to us neutrally, but is instead constructed through the masculine realm of the symbolic. Cut off from a feminine in which we could seek in Woman a different contact with our "sex," we are all to easily forced back into the model of femininity established by the gender hierarchy. Woman is reduced to the signifier of masculine desire as fantasy objectification.

This is Catharine MacKinnon's position on the feminine and femininity, which is why she rejects the recent American version of object relations theory. As already indicated, for MacKinnon, in our circumstances of male domination, the feminine is only as it is made to be by our victimization. We must not rewrite the feminine, but reject "it" completely as the justificatory apparatus for our subordination. For MacKinnon, the identification of femininity with the feminine, and as a result with the masculine vision of us as an object they have made us into, is inevitable and completely inescapable within patriarchal culture—which for MacKinnon is culture. "Theirs" is a pornographic reality in which women are pushed to their knees and then forced to like it because that is what it means to be female. Femininity is a *culturally* imposed, inescapable role if we are to survive. As a result, it becomes identified as femaleness. Femininity, in other words, in all its distortion, is what sexual difference comes to be identified as, at least within our male-dominated cultural context. As such, femininity is ironically and tragically reduced to the ideology that justifies the perpetual crushing of women by the weight of the world. An imposed femininity lays us down before the very omnipotence of their system. Femininity can only "be" collaboration. When we affirm feminine difference we confirm femininity as objectification. Within this system of gender hierarchy we are only rattling our chains.

As MacKinnon herself has written, "femininity as we know it is how we come to want male dominance, which most emphatically is not in our interest."[11] MacKinnon's objection to the supposed affirmation of difference is obviously political. For MacKinnon, difference within the legal system *is* useful only as a justification for discrimination. The difference between the two contrasting positionings *vis à vis* the feminine of MacKinnon and Irigaray is not, however, as MacKinnon would have it. It is not that Irigaray argues that the current *conception* of the feminine within the gender dichotomy is not domination. Indeed, for Irigaray, femininity as the conception of sexual difference and as an imposed gender identity is just that, domination. A crucial aspect of Irigaray's project is the deconstruction of the phallogocentric identification of the feminine as the symmetrical Other, with feminine sexual difference. For Irigaray, the phallogocentric order establishes femininity as relational and subordinate to the masculine within a pregiven system of ideals. As a result, difference from the current conceptualization of gender is erased, in the sense that difference remains captured in the categories of opposition that serve as the basis of the gender hierarchy. The categories of opposition and contradiction are interpreted to have political and ethical significance because of the privileging of the masculine in which femininity is reduced to contradiction with them or our mere opposition to them. Put more broadly, the Idealism that culminated in Hegel and which comprehends difference within identity, is challenged—as in Derrida's writings—as inadequate to and indeed, ethically violative of sexual difference.

Within the terms of the debate on essentialism, Irigaray's deconstruction of phallogocentrism does not proceed to expose the logic of sameness defined by Naomi Schor as "the denial of the objectified Other to the right of difference"[12]—as opposed to de Beauvoir's exposure of the logic of otherness—the attribution of difference that seems to justify women's oppression. De Beauvoir, in this particular aspect of her writing, is very close to MacKinnon. For Schor, however, these are two separate if correlated logics. I would argue instead that Irigaray, from within her own confrontation with Lacan—and I would add here, his lingering Hegelianism—deconstructs the premise that there are two logics. What is deconstructed is precisely the *conceptualization* of femininity as the *truth* of feminine difference. The exposure is of the logic of gender identity that reduces feminine difference to its conceptualization within the system of patriarchal culture, and therefore marks it as the same, in the sense of merely the Other to the established characteristics of Man. The logic of otherness as described by Schor is, in this sense, dependent on the logic of sameness as Irigaray would understand it. Woman's "identity" is only as what is different, other to them. Irigaray, in other words, only risks "universalism" to expose the logic that, indeed, defines the feminine as one "thing" for them. As we will see, this is not her positioning *vis à vis* the writing of her "sex," but only her positioning within the deconstruction of phallogocentric logic of gender identity.

Moreover, MacKinnon's failure to heed the full implications of Irigaray's deconstruction has implications for her own critique. The difference between the two positionings involves the disagreement over the condition in which "liberation" for women, and indeed, even legal transformation could be achieved. The difference ultimately has to do with how one intertwines the ethical relationship to the other that protects heterogeneity and feminine difference as the threshold to an elsewhere not governed by gender hierarchy, with the struggle for political change for actual women, in all their cultural diversity. The politics of revenge, as I call the program of MacKinnon, can only reverse the gender hierarchy, not displace it. Such a reversal would not be liberation, but only perpetuation, even if women were to finally be on top. From within the position that affirms feminine sexual difference as a necessary movement within feminism, there is a tragic flaw in MacKinnon's position.

Without the affirmation of the feminine, we can only identify with "Daddy" in a genderized system of identity such as our "own." The abjection of the phallic mother undermines the appeal to any feminine identification that is not given by Daddy because it is only through an imaginary identification with the father that women can successfully enter the symbolic. The cruel irony is that within the patriarchal order of the symbolic, this imaginary identification with the father cannot be separated from the abjection of the repressed mother. As already suggested, Kristeva advocates that this is an irony that we must live with if women are to avoid crippling depression. Obviously I reject her accommodation to the patriarchal order of the symbolic. If the feminine is rejected as we enter "their" world, we are left with only our masochism and our self-contempt. The terrible psychic cost for women of the abjection of the mother—with which the later Kristeva also leaves us—and the corresponding repudiation of the feminine, is portrayed in Sylvia Plath's poem "Daddy."

> You stand at the blackboard, daddy,
> In the picture I have of you,
> A cleft in your chin instead of your foot
> But no less a devil for that, no not
> Any less the black man who
>
> Bit my pretty red heart in two.
> I was ten when they buried you.
> At twenty I tried to die
> And get back, back, back to you.
> I thought even the bones would do.
>
> But they pulled me out of the sack,
> And they stuck me together with glue.
> And then I knew what to do.
> I made a model of you,
> A man in black with a Meinkampf look
>
> And a love of the rack and the screw.
> And I said I do, I do.[13]

Very simply put, repudiation of the feminine within a genderized world can only come from the side of the masculine in which we make a model of the imaginary father who, as imagined, pushes the feminine under. MacKinnon does not write in psychoanalytic terms. Yet her feminism, in spite of its intent, turns into restoration because resistance to the reinscription of the masculine demands an affirmation of feminine sexual difference. The need for the feminine as resistance to domination and a different contact to the other explains the insistence, in what has come to be labelled the New French Feminism, on the affirmative writing positioned as feminine. This affirmation is meant to protect the threshold of sexual difference from being appropriated to the same old story of masculine domination. The affirmation of feminine difference, irreducible to being their Other, is understood as "truly new under the sun," a future not identifiable as the evolution of the same. This understanding of the affirmation of the feminine as itself necessary for the displacement of gender hierarchy gives us a different take on what has often been identified as a contradiction within French feminine writing. That contradiction is thought to be between the recognition of an inherent bisexuality in both sexes or, in more precise Lacanian terms, the impossibility of the full and secure achievement of sexual identity, and the celebration of the feminine.[14] But it is mistakenly thought to be a contradiction for two reasons. The first is that the slippage inherent in the so-called achievement of sexual identity—because this identity takes place within mythical fantasy projection and is not given in biology—is what makes possible rewriting from the position of the feminine that denies its current definition as the whole truth. The feminine, if it were simply given, could not be disruptive of the imposed categories of the gender hierarchy. The feminine would be unshakable as a given reality. Second, if the displacement of gender hierarchy based on imposed gender identity is affirmed as ethically and politically desirable because it expands the possibilities of lived sexuality, such a displacement, if it is to be displacement and not mere repetition, demands the affirmation of feminine sexual difference that phallogocentrism blocks by its own structures of definition.

Within a strand of feminist theory in the United States and in England, discomfort with the supposedly essentialist or naturalist overtones of even this affirmation of the feminine as the beyond to the masculine world irreducible to his Other, has led to a continuing uneasiness with the feminine, not only as a literary strategy to disrupt imposed femininity, but even when the psychic cost of MacKinnon's position is recognized. The feminine, as a result, if it is affirmed at all, is only affirmed abstractly as one figure of difference that disrupts all claims to identity, including feminine identity. Within this frame, the feminine is to provide a service, to stand in for the uncontainable heterogeneity that undermines the logic of identity. Ethically, Woman symbolizes the difference that cannot be grasped by any established systems of ideals. Politically, however, the feminine can also function as a matter of strategic necessity. Gayatri Spivak, for example, has argued that the struggle *against* sexism and *for* feminism demands an appeal to the feminine in the form of strategic "essentialism."[15] The appeal, however, is consciously strategic since there *is*, under this reading of the feminine, no stabilized feminine identity which could philosophically justify the appeal to Woman as a universal. There *are* only women, of many different cultures, nationalities, races and sexual identities. As a result, on a philosophical plane at least, there can only be feminisms, not one, unmodified feminism. But the need for an alliance between women, as well as the need to avoid MacKinnon's dilemma, justifies the strategic reliance on the feminine within a particular context at a particular time.

As we will see, Spivak's mistake is to label her approach strategic "essentialism," as if *any* appeal to the feminine must inevitably involve essentialism. As I have already suggested, to see why this is indeed a mistake, we will have to look more closely at the technical, philosophical "basis" for essentialism. Yet her recognition that, at least on the level of strategy, an appeal to the feminine is necessary is a significant step forward. Done in the way Spivak envisions, an appeal to the feminine, since it is strategy, would not erase differences between women by establishing the feminine once and for all as a universal identifiable "reality" necessarily shared by all women. It protects the recognition of the other woman. Without such an appeal we are seemingly left with an abstract difference which, through its very abstractness, potentially erases the specific contours of feminine difference, and by so doing reinscribes the repudiation of the feminine, and even indifference to women's suffering. If we want to recognize that the play of sexual difference is not captured by the stereotypes of any gender hierarchy, we do not want to deny the tragedy of women's suffering as we also do not want to pretend that all women endure the *same* level of oppression. The privileges of class, race, nationality and heterosexual identity are realities feminism has continually run up against in its effort to create political solidarity between women as women.

There is a second understanding of the affirmation of the feminine only as a strategy. This understanding would insist on exposing the genealogies of the power structures that have constituted women as Woman. Such exposures do not pretend to be beyond power; they are within power, for the purpose of its redistribution. To affirm the feminine might be politically useful. If it is, do it. If not, reject it. But whatever else is to be done, the warning is against the romanticization and the essentialization of the feminine as politically retrograde. Such a critique, it should be noted, is also implicitly connected to the rejection of utopian possibility if that possibility is conceived as being beyond power and the strategies of instrumental reason. Feminism is itself understood as a power discourse, but within the specific Nietzschean-Foucaultian framework in which there can "be" no beyond to power discourses.

French feminine writing on this version of postmodern feminism is suspect for its "as it were" romanticism, outdated utopianism and simplistic universalism. "Oh Woman! Oh, Woman! She is different. *She is different.*"[16] Her difference instead should be understood only within the actual political battles.

The insistence that genealogical exposure is the *only* approach consistent with the critiques of identity logic including gender identity, assumes that feminist theory has mistakenly asserted that there must be some existing *identity* for the category of woman beyond the discourses of power. As already suggested, Irigaray does not affirm the identity of the feminine as femininity, even if she affirms a politics of identification. Even so, she does not seek an identity for Woman. Rather, she deconstructs the identification of femininity within the logic of sameness, and dreams of an identification between women that logic blocks.

However, in spite of my caveat, the "metaforeplay"[17] of French feminine writing stands accused as just one more reinscription of identity even if done in high literary style. Metonomy is instead preferred as the literary strategy consistent with genealogy against the "gushiness" of the metaphoric affirmation of Woman. We are again returned to the repudiation of the feminine. Why is it so bad to gush? Because gushing is identified as a "feminine" characteristic? French feminine writing, as part of its affirmation of the feminine, may well appear "gushy," but as against what? Can one construct a stabilized subject identified as Woman and represented as such from within the gush? Is not the "gush" exactly what overflows the very boundaries of subject, understood as held apart, an erect self against the other, Lacan's illusionary consolidated entity, the one? The gush, of course, is a metaphor, but a metaphor associated with the female "sex," not as a neatly constructed gender category, but as *sex*, if not a sex. The gush figures the undermining of the illusion of the subject to be one with itself. Irigaray is constantly evoking fluidity as the overflow of the barriers of identity, gender or otherwise. To quote Irigaray:

> *Fluid* has to remain that secret *remainder*, of the one. Blood, but also milk, sperm, lymph, saliva, spit, tears, humors, gas, waves, airs, fire . . . light. All threaten to deform, propagate, evaporate, consume him, to flow out of him and into another who cannot be easily held on to. The "subject" identifies himself with/in an almost material consistency that finds everything flowing abhorrent.[18]

Of course, it is precisely this evocation of fluidity as itself Other, and supposedly associated with a property of the female body, that is accused of flagging Irigaray's essentialism. Essentialism, in feminist circles, does not usually return us to the technical discussions of Husserl or of Hegel. Again to quote Schor, who has succinctly conceptualized the understanding of essentialism within current feminist circles,

> Essentialism in the specific context of feminism consists in the belief that woman has an essence, that woman can be specified by one or a number of inborn attributes which define across cultures and

> throughout history her unchanging being and in the absence of
> which she ceases to be categorized as a woman.[19]

As Schor continues, in practical terms, essentialism maps the feminine onto femaleness.

But for Irigaray, from within the Lacanian framework she deconstructs, there can be no femaleness upon which femininity could be mapped. Femaleness is only femininity as defined within a cultural, symbolic, masculine order. Her rebellion against Lacan's own conclusions about femininity is ethical and political. But more importantly, in her innumerable discussions of fluids and the gush, Irigaray makes it all too evident that in her writing she is attempting only to refigure sexual difference by evoking the metaphor of her "sex" as a difference that overflows any rigid logic of definitions and the illusion of a unified, compact subjectivity. As we move through my own book, we will come to understand why it is a mistake to identify metaphoric refiguration in any simplistic way with a new conception of the essence of Woman. Irigaray may refigure the feminine, but she does not define or describe femaleness as a pregiven nature of sexual identity upon which the feminine could be mapped. Her aspiration is to disrupt gender hierarchy, not to cement it by resolving the dilemma of femininity.

Because of her refiguring of sexual difference, Irigaray has been falsely accused of once again understanding anatomy as destiny. But this accusation only makes sense if Irigaray is understood as *describing* the female body and then drawing conclusions about what women *are* from this description. Instead, the second aspect of her deconstruction should be understood to undermine the identification of gender with her "sex," now in the name of feminine desire. Sexual difference, in other words, reaches into the definition of desire itself. Irigaray, in effect, challenges Lacan's own writing of the split subject as a masculine version of desire. Perhaps women desire differently? Who's *to know*? But if we cannot know her desire within the structures of phallogocentrism, we have to be true to the implications of that insight. What cannot be known, cannot be designated. Here again, we are returned to the reinterpretation of Lacan's insight that the concept of *jouissance* cannot be separated from the concept he calls "significance," or what shifts in language. Irigaray's writing, positioned from within the re-metaphorization and ethical affirmation of the feminine "sex"—but not as a universal *description* of our gender which maps the feminine onto the female—can only be understood in the context of the Lacanian framework she seeks to undermine as an *accurate* account of the truth of Woman. In Lacan, Woman's lack of the phallus within the phallogocentric order reduces her to a ghost, without substance, without essence, without self. She only signifies man's desire. That is her significance in the masculine symbolic. Her "sex" is her gender, her identification is as Woman. In this sense, even if this identification is a "sham" meaning not given in the nature of anatomical sex itself, but only enforced by the current phallic order, it still is "there" for us. Lacan is very close to MacKinnon in his understanding of femininity as defined by the masculine symbolic.

But *is* "it," the female "sex," lack or so much more? Can it be reduced to its significance within gender identity? Can we not instead play with our significance to them? Is our desire reducible to the symmetry of male fantasy, where what we desire is to be desirable objects for them, so as to make their *jouissance* possible? Irigaray's feminine "sex" is correctly understood when it is read as the so much more remembered within the feminine imaginary that can never be completely excluded at the same time that it cannot be grasped in "their" knowledge of us.

Do we know there is a feminine imaginary? Of course not. The imaginary, if it is "there" at all, is only indicated as it is written and lived in protest, and in the process of transformation. Our "sex," in other words, is irreducible to the definitions of the established gender hierarchy, once we deconstruct the logic of gender hierarchy that seems to define us. Her *jouissance* overflows any attempt to confine her or to designate her desire. The feminine "sex" is now affirmed, not rejected, because rejection, or more technically, repudiation, is part of the logic of sameness in which Woman's desire is supposedly captured by "the old dream of symmetry"[20]—that is, we desire what they want us to desire. And this affirmation is both ethical and political, and done in language through the shifts made possible by re-metaphorization.

The politics of Irigaray's affirmation of her "sex," in all the ambiguities implied by "sex" and not by gender, can only be understood if we remember our context as one in which bulimia and anorexia have reached epidemic proportions. To reduce Irigaray's positioning *vis à vis* the "sex" of feminine specificity to description of gender identity or of biological femaleness is to fail, as we will see, to heed the specificity of Irigaray's literary language and its performative powers to crack open what "is."

But if the affirmation of feminine difference is not just the reinstatement of gender identity for an explicit political purpose, if this affirmation instead dreams and then refigures the feminine as the difference that undermines gender identity and the logic of gender identity, why not just return to the position that celebrates the feminine as the stand-in for heterogeneity? For Irigaray, the answer is obviously that the affirmation of feminine desire is a good "in itself," a resistance to the silencing of our "sex," our desire. The call to desire is itself a call to live differently and to keep open the infinite possibilities of feminine *jouissance*. As I have also indicated, if one understands the repudiation of the feminine as fundamental to gender hierarchy, then to defend the purpose of such affirmation as other than affirmation can itself be understood as an aspect of repudiation. The feminine is good only for some other purpose. The feminine, in other words, is useful if functional.

But if feminine desire is to be affirmed, rather than rejected as in MacKinnon, it may well demand the end of the *use* of the feminine.

We seem to be constantly returned to the either/or I stated in the opening of the Introduction, but now in a new form: either genealogy which exposes the constitutive power constructs that have made Woman and women, or the feminine writing that re-metaphorizes Woman.

In order to overflow the boundaries of this either/or, we have to think explicitly of the utopianism that so-called postmodernism does not foreclose, but instead makes possible, and indeed necessary, if we are to think differently about the status of the feminine as written. We have to dance differently with the old distinctions, distinctions that have indeed been displaced by "postmodern" philosophers. But the political and ethical significance of this displacement has unfortunately gone unnoticed. For this book, when we trace the utopianism of deconstruction, we do so with an emphasis on the importance of the unerasable moment of utopianism that deconstruction guards, and its alliance with the "feminine" writing of sexual difference. And what exactly is the unerasable moment of utopianism that deconstruction guards? Obviously, I cannot adequately summarize it in a sentence. But I can indicate here that the ethical commitment of deconstruction is to break open the prison of what has been called ontology, which becomes a prison precisely because it seems to shut out all our other possibilities as "unreal." Derridean deconstruction exposes the limit of any system of ideality established as reality, whether that limit be evoked as the supplement, the margin, the logic of parergonality,[21] or indeed as *Woman*. Crucial for this book is Derrida's undermining of the hierarchization of gender identity which has become "second nature" to us. The idea that we are hostage to the way things are now, to a human matrix constructed through gender hierarchy, is belied as an illusion that fails to understand the full significance of the Derridean insight that reality *is* only "there" as textual effect.

Derridean deconstruction operates on many levels to undermine the rigid gender divide, Lacan's "world" of wimps and ghosts. But as we will also see, this intervention is itself explicitly ethical, done in the name of a dream of a new choreography of sexual difference. Deconstruction, then, will not be read as a metalinguistic theory of the construction of the impossibility of meaning, but through Derrida's allegorization of Lacan's supposed truth of Woman, even if that truth be imposed, not given. This allegorization, however, returns us to the performative power of language in which Woman is presented. Woman "is" only in language, which means that her "reality" can never be separated from the metaphors and fictions in which she is presented. Derrida's allegory of the feminine, in spite of his own caution before this reading, allows for the affirmation of Woman, and not just as the truth of lack or the absence of truth—a misinterpretation of deconstruction frequently evidenced in feminist theory—but as the possibility of restylization that cannot be obliterated by the current framework in which she is given meaning.

But can we put together the Derridean allegory of the feminine, with the French feminine writing that relies more directly on myth? As we will see, we can if we understand the significance of fantasy for feminine writing, and for the evocation of a different way of being together that challenges gender hierarchy. This writing is explicitly utopian in that it evokes an elsewhere to our current system, in which sex is lived within the established "heterosexual" matrix as a rigid gender identity which creates our separation and identifies us as girls and boys. As we will see, feminine writing twists and turns through different motifs and writing strategies through the positioning, *vis à vis* the feminine, of what Irigaray has called *mimesis*. *Mimesis*—for our purposes here in the Introduction; I will discuss different dimensions of *mimesis* throughout my later discussion—is the affirmation of the feminine as performance, as a role that can be restyled, played differently. This playing cannot be understood as fully conscious or deliberate with a definite goal in mind. But as affirmation, rather than repudiation, this positioning is different precisely because it is affirmation of what has been repressed, as the negative to "their" positive, the absence to their presence. We cannot just announce a new beginning, we must begin anew from where we are in gender hierarchy, unable to confirm or state exactly where we are. As we will see, I will argue that *mimesis* should be interpreted to include engagement with myth. Once we understand that the Derridean "double gesture" or "double writing" puts itself under erasure for the sake of clarity about the philosophical status of what is written *about* Woman, we can understand how it is possible, indeed, inevitable, to combine allegory with myth, and to defend feminine writing from the charge of essentialism, particularly if essentialism is understood to map the feminine onto femaleness.

But if we can resolve the seeming philosophical difficulty of the return to essentialism, or at least romanticism, if we rewrite the feminine—in affirmation, as a positioning, as a performance, rather than of Woman as a description of reality—we still must confront the political challenge that such writing erases actual differences between women in the name of the norm of the white, middle-class, heterosexual woman who is hailed as Woman. In order to even begin to address that question, which is undoubtedly the central political question of feminism, I will discuss the use of myth and allegory in the writing of Afro-American women, and specifically the use of myth in Toni Morrison's novel *Beloved*.[22] We work within myth and allegory to bring the feminine from the "rere" to the fore.

To bring the feminine from the "rere" to the fore is itself a question of justice. Law denies any rigid dichotomy between so-called utopian feminism and materialist feminism. As Lyotard reminds us, "injustice is the crime combined with the perpetuation of silence that erases it."[23] Injustice is itself material, in that harm happens. But it becomes known as injustice in the naming. Feminist jurisprudence seeks to make harms to women that do not "exist"—as a harm that adequately expresses the experience and the actual suffering of women—within the current legal system. An abuse cannot be fought until it is understood as an abuse. We see this graphically in the case of "date rape." The name gave the crime a legal "reality." But also, such a project necessarily engages utopian possibility, as it incites a beyond to the current gender hierarchy, "the flowering that keeps the future open." Indeed, it does so as a way to understand the harm of discrimination as an enforced limit on lived sexuality, and the possibilities of a life not imprisoned in rigid gender identity. Feminine writing also has to do with the evocation of the truly new, the elsewhere, in which "human beings" would not be scarred by gender hierarchy. We understand discrimination as being against this possibility. It is only if we see the inevitable intertwinement of justice, politics and utopian possibility in feminism, that we can understand the promise and the necessity for the affirmation of the feminine, even if as a transition, as a threshold. But let me begin to spin the different story in which the either/or I have described no longer need ensnare us.

1

The Maternal and the Feminine: Social Reality, Fantasy and Ethical Relation

Introduction

Feminists have looked to maternity as the maternal role, to the maternal body as the evocation of a subject not united in itself against the Other, and to reproductive capacity more generally to uncover the irreducibility of the feminine as a basis for a shared female identity and also for an expression of the potential within womanliness as it is lived, for a different and better way of being human. In this chapter, I discuss the accounts of maternity, the maternal body and reproductive capacity which have been developed by Julia Kristeva, Robin West and Hélène Cixous. As we will see, their accounts rest on two divergent psychoanalytic frameworks. While West is explicitly *naturalistic* and *essentialist*, the reason to begin with her is that, in spite of the philosophical weaknesses of her approach, she has shown the political and ethical power of the affirmation of feminine difference within the field of law. West has shown us, in other words, why we need to give expression to the feminine if we are to articulate the harms to women that literally disappear within our legal system because they are not seen as harms, but just the way of the world. For West, if we are to bring those harms into view, we must challenge the predominance of the masculine viewpoint and we can only do so by validating the uniqueness of woman's own point of view and experience. While disagreeing with her approach, I agree with her ethical and political conclusion that feminine sexual difference must find expression if feminism is not to find itself in collaboration against its own ends. Although from a very different philosophical tradition, Kristeva's writing on the material and the maternal body allows for the affirmation of feminine sexual difference. The contrast between the accounts exposes the weaknesses inherent in this approach to the feminine, both as a described, natural reality, as in West, and as a basis for a "herethics" in Kristeva. I will argue that even in her early writings, there is a tension in Kristeva between her writing on semiotics and her explorations of maternity which has ultimately been resolved in favor of the "conservative" position that rejects the value of the fantasy figure of the phallic mother as the only way to express the repression of the feminine. I will then discuss the explicit appeal to the repressed maternal as fantasy, as used to evoke the specificity of the feminine imaginary and the feminine as an unforeclosable utopian possibility which is affirmed by Hélène Cixous.

In conclusion, I will argue that the goal of the recognition of the mother is not so much to develop a feminine symbolic in which the vertical mother/daughter relationship could be represented, but instead to challenge the rigid divide between the imaginary, the symbolic and the real, and to challenge the traditional Freudian hierarchization of the Oedipal and the pre-Oedipal period. In one sense, as we will see, it is a technical impossibility, if one accepts the Lacanian or even the Freudian framework, to represent the mother/daughter relationship in the symbolic as a beyond to the phallic order because the symbolic forecloses the expression of the daughter's libidinal relationship to the mother. But the deeper problem with this solution to the meaning given to *derelection* is that once again women are at least partially reduced to the maternal function as it is defined as their truly proper role within gender hierarchy. Moreover, such a feminine symbolic, if it is described as symbolic in Lacan's sense, undermines the utopian power of the feminine imaginary. In its place is the imagined unity of mother and child, expressed within the symbolic as the fantasy projection of the masculine imaginary. Feminine writing, on the other hand, evokes not the unity of mother and child, but the heterogeneity within the subject herself and the tie that indicates *both* separation and connection in the mother/daughter relation, without denying the value of the identification between women as women that could be at its base. This writing, whether of the maternal body or of maternity as a relation between the generations of women, emphasizes the otherness of the child, even of the female child, which belies the illusion of symbiosis as the lost paradise. The pregnant body has an *other* within that is non-identical to herself. The writing of the maternal (and the writing of the mother/daughter relationship) is indeed important to overcome the repudiation of the feminine, but only once its status is specified. But let me turn first to West's "phenomenology."

West's Phenomenology

West develops a conception of woman's hedonic experience which is correlated with her reproductive capacities, resulting in the separation of the female's identity from that of the male. For West, the central goal of feminist theory is to develop a "phenomenology" of women's difference that allows her experience to come into view. It is only within the context of a "phenomenology" of women's experience that feminists can critique the values of the current legal system as male dominated. As West explains:

> This abandonment by feminist legal theorists of the phenomenological realm of pleasure and desire is a function of legalism, not true feminism. It reflects the extent to which we have embraced the ideals of legalism—whether we regard those ideals as substantive equality, liberal tolerance, privacy or individual autonomy—rather than the methodology of feminism—careful attention to phenomenological narrative. It reflects the extent to which we have allowed liberal and radical norms drawn from non-feminist traditions to become the criteria by which we judge the narratives of our lives that emerge from consciousness-raising, *instead of the other way around.*[1]

West gives us example after example of how the experiences of women go unnoticed by the law. This lack of notice perpetuates tremendous suffering in the lives of actual women, precisely because it denies their experience. Within the legal sphere, the identification of the human with the male keeps our claims from being heard, let alone from being justified.

> Just as women's work is not recognized or compensated by the market culture, women's injuries are often not recognized or compensated *as injuries* by the legal culture. The dismissal of women's gender-specific suffering comes in various forms, but the outcome is always the same: women's suffering for one reason or another is outside the scope of legal redress. Thus, women's distinctive gender-specific injuries are now or have in the recent past been variously dismissed as trivial (sexual harassment on the street); consensual (sexual harassment on the job); humorous (non-violent marital rape); participatory, subconsciously wanted, or self-induced (father/daughter incest); natural or biological, and therefore inevitable (childbirth); sporadic, and conceptually continuous with gender-neutral pain (rape, viewed as a crime of violence); deserved or private (domestic violence); non-existent (pornography); incomprehensible (unpleasant and unwanted consensual sex) or legally predetermined (marital rape, in states with the marital exemption).[2]

In West's view, liberal feminism's central mistake is its attempt to justify women's injuries as legally redressable by translating them into a framework which inevitably only further distorts the "real" experience of women. West argues that the norms of the legal system itself (e.g., autonomy) make translation impossible, because they reflect male rather than female experience. We get legal redress in our current system only by denying or at least distorting the truth of female "reality." For West, a reconstructive feminist jurisprudence must face this dilemma directly; otherwise, the supposed solution of legal reform will only perpetuate the ultimate harm done to women: the silencing of our own voices.

> "Reconstructive feminist jurisprudence," I believe, should try to explain or reconstruct the reforms necessary to the safety and improvement of women's lives in direct language that is true to our own experience and our own subjective lives. The dangers of mandatory pregnancy, for example, are invasion of the body by the fetus and the intrusion into the mother's existence following childbirth. The right to abort is the right to defend against a particular bodily and existential invasion.[3]

For West, this process of translation of the harms suffered by women into legally established rights should reflect woman's fundamental experience of her body, which stems from her reproductive capacity. As a result of our unique bodily structure, we relate to the world differently than men do. According to West, we value intimacy rather than individuation because of our connection to birthing and child rearing; but we are also vulnerable to invasion because of our bodies. For example, we are susceptible to crimes such as rape, and we may also face unwanted pregnancies. West believes the right to abortion should be justified as the right to defend against "a particular bodily invasion," precisely because the fetus is other to the woman. Only on the basis of such a justification will the right reflect the experience of women. If our legal system is to overcome its masculine bias, the experience of bodily vulnerability, the protection against it and the recognition of the value of intimacy and love in public life must be introduced into the law. But we can only understand the legal system as masculine if we first grasp the basis for women's unique relationship to the world which we share with one another simply because we are women. West's account of women's bodies is the "foundation" for both her critical and her reconstructive project. As West explains:

> Underlying and underscoring the poor fit between the proxies for subjective well-being endorsed by liberals and radicals—choice and power—and women's subjective, hedonic lives is the simple fact that women's lives—*because of our biological, reproductive role*— are drastically at odds with this fundamental vision of human life. Women's lives are *not* autonomous, they are profoundly relational. This is at least the biological reflection, if not the biological cause,

of virtually all aspects, hedonic and otherwise, of our "difference." Women, and *only* women, and *most* women, transcend *physically* the differentiation or individuation of biological self from the rest of human life trumpeted as the norm by the entire Kantian tradition. When a woman is pregnant her biological life embraces the embryonic life of another. When she later nurtures children, her needs will embrace their needs. The experience of being human, for women, differentially from men, includes the counter-autonomous experience of a shared physical identity between woman and fetus, as well as the counter-autonomous experience of the emotional and psychological bond between mother and infant.[4]

There is a tension in West's work as to the causality of the biological in the formation of female identity. At times, West indicates that it is because of our biology that women are, and have been, different from men. Biology, in other words, determines our particular psychic structure. Our reproductive capacities shape our psychic identity by making us value intimacy and connection rather than autonomy and separation. Yet West also recognizes that our biology may be experienced in the way she describes because it is given expression and lived in a particular system of gender representation. Here, the system of gender representation, not the underlying biological "facts," engenders female identity. Correspondingly, it is not biology, but the system of gender representation that is the basis for women's shared experience. Citing those feminist theorists who have focused on the problem of woman's difference, West explains:

> [M]aterial biology does not *mandate* existential value: men *can* connect to other human life. Men can nurture life. Men can mother. Obviously, men can care, and love, and support, and affirm life. Just as obviously, however, most men don't. One reason that they don't, of course, is male privilege. Another reason, though, may be the blinders of our masculinist utopian visionary. Surely one of the most important insights of feminism has been that biology is indeed destiny when we are unaware of the extent to which biology is narrowing our fate, but that *biology is destiny only to the extent of our ignorance.*[5]

Although she recognizes the limits of biologically determined explanations of feminine difference, West nevertheless continues to maintain that there is a connection between a woman's identity, her experience, and her biology. Indeed, she defends the need to root feminist theory in a theory of female *nature* that cannot be completely severed from an account of how biology functions in the acquisition of a female identity. West believes that without a theory of female *nature*, it is impossible to develop a "phenomenology" of women's unique and shared experience; and that without such a "phenomenology," there is no basis for feminism if it is to be founded in the unique experience of women. Thus, in order for feminism to exist, we must have a naturalist or essentialist view of the feminine, for it is this view that provides us with a "female reality" that all women can, at least potentially, come to understand as their own. Women, in other words, are differentiated from one another; but as *women*, we share a common biological structure which affects our psychic identity. Individual identity remains, in this sense, a female identity. Thus, because there is a female nature, there can be shared experience. West is an "essentialist" in the sense defined by Naomi Schor.[6] She clearly maps the feminine onto femaleness.

Yet it is precisely essentialist and naturalistic accounts of the feminine that have been philosophically rejected as inconsistent with postmodern philosophy.[7] It is not a coincidence that many of the works that are often labelled as "postmodern" grew out of the critique of Husserl's phenomenology. West's project, however, is not based on French or German phenomenology. West wants to root the feminine in a natural account of women's reproductive capacity. She believes the "essence" of women is fundamentally linked with women's actual reproductive capacities, and therefore, the ultimate reality of woman is to be found in her biological structure. By so doing, West collapses woman's essence into her nature. In Husserl, on the other hand, "essences" are irreducible to the "factual" or to the natural. Husserlian phenomenology is concerned with essences that are eidetically abstracted, pure phenomena. Yet West's insistence on a feminine "reality," "there" as women's nature, is still subject to the postmodern deconstruction of the philosophical basis of phenomenology.

The Feminist Dilemma Restated

Derrida's deconstruction of Husserl's metaphor of the interweaving of the "pre-expressive" noema with the "expressive" power of language illuminates West's philosophical error and its ethical and practical significance within feminist theory. Derrida, with others, has deconstructed the rigid divide between *Sinn* and *Bedeutung*, roughly translated as reference and meaning. Derrida shows us that reference involves a context of pregiven meaning, which makes pure revelation impossible because we cannot wipe out the performative aspect of language. In his "Form and Meaning" Derrida demonstrates that although Husserl recognizes the productivity of language as expression through the inevitable "use" of metaphor in the revelation of pre-expressive noema, he continually seeks a mirror writing that would ultimately cancel out the metaphoricity of language. To quote Derrida,

Thus, the pre-expresive noema, the prelinguistic sense, must be imprinted in the expressive noema, must find its conceptual mark in the content of meaning. Expression, in order to limit itself to transporting a constituted sense to the exterior, and by the same token to bring this sense to conceptual generality without altering it, in order to express what is already thought (one almost would have to say written), and in order to redouble faithfully—expression then must permit itself to be imprinted by sense at the same time as it expresses sense. The expressive noema must offer itself, and this is the new image of its unproductivity, as a blank page or virgin tablet; or at least as a palimpsest given over to its pure receptivity.[8]

This attempt to achieve mirror writing which ultimately erases its own metaphors, and with metaphor the performative power of language, is, for Derrida, the very definition of metaphysical language which could be true to the things themselves. As we will see, for Derrida such a language is impossible; but for Husserl, it is necessary for the revelation of *essence* as a conceptually generalizable form. Crucial to Husserl's project is the "purification" of the concept of form, and with it of essence, from the metaphysical tradition which had "corrupted" it. But as Derrida explains this "purifying" critique continually gets bogged down by the very productivity of language in which it must be carried out and explained, which undercuts its own claim to "cut" through to the "essence" of the form of things themselves. This is why Derrida states "Form 'Is'—Its Ellipsis,"[9] because the interrelationship between the two strata cannot be described other than through expression which involves metaphors. It would only be possible to achieve phenomenology's stated goal of revealing the form of the things themselves if expression did nothing more than transport a constituted sense to the exterior, and by so doing merely reissue a noematic sense by providing access to conceptual form.[10] But just as Husserl is trying to explain how this purification is to take place, he gets strung up in the expression of the interlacing of the two strata, the pre-expressive and linguistic expression.

The *interweaving* (*Verwebung*) of language, the interweaving of that which is purely language in language with the other threads of experience constitutes a cloth. The word *Verwebung* refers to this metaphorical zone. The "strata" are "woven," their inter-complication is such that the warp cannot be distinguished from the woof. If the stratum of the logos were simply *founded*, one could extract it and bring to light its underlying stratum of non-expressive acts and contents. But since this superstructure acts back upon the *Unterschicht* in an essential and decisive manner, one is indeed obliged, from the very outset of the description, to associate a properly *textual* metaphor with the geological metaphor: for cloth means *text. Verweben* here means *texere.* The discursive is related to the nondiscursive, the linguistic "stratum" is intermixed with the pre-linguistic "stratum" according to the regulated system of a kind of *text.*[11]

Thus, Derrida shows us in his deconstruction of Husserl's problematic that the interweaving of *Sinn* and *Bedeutung* is regulated by its textuality and *mode* of expression, which is not to say that there is no distinction between *Sinn* and *Bedeutung*, but only that the distinction is itself dependent upon textuality.

We can now begin to understand what Derrida means and does not mean by his famous statement, "There is nothing outside of the text." He does not mean that deconstruction suspends reference, as if such a suspension would be possible. Indeed, language implies reference. If we can say that without *Bedeutung*, there would be no *Sinn*, we could also say that without the postulation of reference (*Sinn*), there would be no *Bedeutung*. We will return to the relationship of this postulation of reference to undecidability, which within the context of Husserl's philosophy indicates the impossibility of purifying form so as "to know" through eidetic abstraction the essence of things themselves. More importantly, we will return to how undecidability plays a necessary role in the reconceptualization of feminism as ethical feminism. For now, I simply want to note that deconstruction's insistence that the real world is "there" as textual effect does not mean that there is no "real" world to which we refer. The "real world" cannot be erased precisely because it is there as textual "effect." Deconstruction reminds us, in other words, how the real world "is"; it does not deny its pull on us, even as it insists that it is a pull, which in turn implies the possibility of resistance. This reminder of how the real world "is" as textual effect does reinstate a transcendental aspect in Derrida's thought, which is why Derrida himself is careful to remind us that deconstruction is neither anti-foundationalist nor foundationalist. However, the transcendental moment is itself called into question as the relationship between *Sinn* and *Bedeutung* is continuously problematized.

To say, in effect, that the description of the infrastructure (of sense) has been guided secretly by the superstructural possibility of meaning, is not to contest, against Husserl, the duality of the strata and the unity of a certain transition which relates them one to the other. It is neither to wish to reduce one stratum to the other nor to judge it impossible completely to recast sense in meaning. It is neither to reconstruct the experience (of sense) as *language*, above

all if one takes this to be a *discourse*, a verbal fabric, nor to produce
a critique of language on the basis of the ineffable riches of sense.
It is simply to ask questions about *another relationship* between
what are called, problematically, *sense* and *meaning*.[12]

To summarize, Derrida has deconstructed the attempt to establish language as a pure medium that transposes sense by bringing it to conceptual
form. The discourse of phenomenology cannot free itself from the productivity of *Einbildung* because of its own use of images, figures, etc.

West does not speak directly to the issue of the status she wants to give
to her phenomenology. But to the degree that she wants to get back beyond
language to the *very essence of form or Woman*, she is ensnared in the
phenomenologist's dilemma. An essentialist theory of Woman would have
to reveal Woman for what she truly is, beyond the trappings of culture and
the "false consciousness" of patriarchy. This attempt necessarily demands
that we "purify" language so that it is only a medium which would allow
the "true" form of Woman to at last be self-evident in its meaning. West
fails to understand just how her own essentialist project necessarily replicates
the attempt to cleanse language of its productivity.

It is in this sense that the deconstruction of the rigid divide between *Sinn*
and *Bedeutung* is relevant to recent feminist debates over the question of
essentialism. Essentialism in the strong sense does demand a particular view
of language. Even West's belief that women lie implies something like an
appeal to a known interiority in which "our experience" is safely enclosed.
In other words, consciousness-raising, if one takes West's phenomenology
literally, would end this lying, by bringing "our experience" to the exterior
and giving it conceptual form through expression. I believe that West herself
has a more expansive concept of consciousness-raising than making explicit
the true form of what was already "there." But I also want to suggest that
to the degree that West continues to advocate essentialism, she is in danger
of limiting the role of consciousness-raising.

Again we are returned to Derrida's analysis of philosophical language as
necessarily involving the aspiration to effectively erase the metaphors in
which it is enclosed. The goal of phenomenology, as we have seen, is to
achieve a pure conceptual knowledge through the constant cleansing of
language so as to reveal the form of the thing to be known. This aspiration
inevitably involves a suspicion of metaphor as the "contamination" of mirror
writing. Yet metaphor is inevitable to the description of the metaphysical
project itself. To quote Derrida:

Metaphor, therefore, is determined by philosophy as a provisional
loss of meaning, an economy of the proper without irreparable
damage, a certainly inevitable detour, but also a history with its

sights set on, and within the horizon of, the circular reappropriation of literal, proper meaning. This is why the philosophical evaluation of metaphor always has been ambiguous: metaphor is dangerous and foreign as concerns *intuition* (vision or contact), *concept* (the grasping or proper presence of the signified), and *consciousness* (proximity or self-presence); but it is in complicity with what it endangers, is necessary to it in the extent to which the de-tour is a return guided by the function of resemblance (*mimesis* or homoiosis), under the law of the same. The opposition of intuition, the concept, and consciousness at this point no longer has any pertinence. These three values belong to the order and to the movement of meaning. Like metaphor.[13]

Derrida seeks to show us that there is "no reassuring opposition of the metaphoric and the proper"[14] at the same time that he also seeks to demonstrate that it is through metaphor that we assign what is "proper" to a given thing. As we have seen, Derrida deconstructs the possibility of reaching the essence of the form of the thing itself through eidetic abstraction. But there is still the aspiration in philosophy to know the "essence" of the real, so that one can decisively separate the real and the literal from fantasy, illusion, and fiction.

Let us for the moment define the "literal" rendering of the real as that which most clearly respects the properties of things. If we cannot escape language or render it a transparent medium, we are forced to attribute properties through the "de-tour" of metaphor. Figuration through metaphor is a tool that must eventually be thrown away if it is to achieve its function of taking us to the "literal." This fundamental ambivalence inheres in the relationship Derrida describes between metaphor and philosophy. Put very simply, philosophy needs metaphor to reach the real, and yet metaphor always takes us away from "it" by performing on "it." Metaphorical transference, in other words, is a mechanism by which we attempt to reach the literal, understood as the necessary or essential properties of things. But ultimately, we must discard it as a mechanism if we are to achieve "mirror writing," and therefore, know the essence of the things themselves.

To quote Derrida's description of the conditions "necessary" for metaphoric transportation:

> The transported significations are those of attributed properties, not those of the thing itself, as subject or substance. Which causes metaphor to remain mediate and abstract. For metaphor to be possible, it is necessary, without involving the thing itself in a play of substitutions, that one be able to replace properties for one another, and that these properties belong to the same essence of

the same thing, or that they be extracted from different essences. The necessary condition of these extractions and exchanges is that the essence of a concrete subject be capable of several properties, and then that a particular permutation between the essence and what is proper to (and inseparable from) it be possible within the medium of quasi-synonymy. This is what Aristotle calls the *antikategoreisthai*: the predicate of the essence and the predicate of the proper can be exchanged without the statement becoming false. . . .[15]

Essence and property are not identical. The point is that without "direct" access to the essence of the thing, we reach that "essence" only through the metaphorical transference of properties. Metaphors, however, must ultimately be re-collected. If this cannot be done, and it cannot be done if the trail of metaphor never comes to an end, then we are left with a *prescriptive* transference through metaphor of the properties supposedly essential to the thing. In the myth that we can ultimately re-collect metaphor, it is precisely this *prescriptive* moment in metaphorical transference that is supposedly erased. In other words, there is the myth that I am not speaking of what is *proper* to the thing as it should be, I am only indicating what it is truly in its essence. Otherwise, we are left with a prescription of properties that cannot erase its normative underpinnings. We prescribe these properties as the essence of the thing because that is how we know the thing, or more precisely how we think the thing should be. If we cannot know the form of the thing through purified expression, we are always *prescribing* its properties. It is this moment of prescription in metaphorical transference which assigns the proper that makes Derrida himself suspicious of metaphor. (We will return to the political and ethical significance of Derrida's suspicion of metaphor later.)

I want to return now to the way in which the appeal to the essence of Woman, since it is not possible in any pure sense, leads to reification of so-called properties of femininity, and with it the proper place of women. What gets called the essence of Woman is precisely this metaphorical transport of the so-called proper. Therefore, what one is really doing when one states the essence of Woman is reinstating her in her proper place. But the proper place, so defined through her essential properties of what women can be, ends by shutting them in once again in that *proper* place. In this special sense, the appeal to the essence of Woman, since it cannot be separated completely from the *prescription* of properties to her, reinforces the stereotypes that limit our possibilities. We will return to whether or not metaphorical prescription, in this sense of reinforcing what is proper, can ever escape this danger of essentialism with its concomitant danger of once again shutting us into our proper place. For now, I want to emphasize how West's own essentialism misses its prescriptive reinstatement of the proper, precisely to the degree that it claims to have reached the "essence" of Woman.

This essence for West, as we have seen, carries within it our "should be," in the sense that women are potentially "better" because of their essence or nature. There are two ethical presentations of the view that the female voice should count as an expression of feminine difference that appear in the literature, sometimes without a clear line of demarcation between them, one stronger and one weaker. The weaker is that women's voices should count because all voices should count. The stronger is more explicitly rooted in the feminine as a different way of being human. Women's experience should count because it is ethically superior and, therefore, can provide us with a standard for judging this world. To paraphrase the argument: we, unlike men, know what it means to care and to love others. As a result, as we bring our voice into the public realm, the ethical and political reality of all of our lives will be changed. West embraces as her own the stronger rather than the weaker version of the story that tells of the *value* of taking into account female difference. For West, the rejection of the relevance of love as fundamental in public life is a reflection of masculine values. Moreover, this exclusion has severely crippled even the most radical of masculine political visions.

> Indeed, I can't imagine any project more crucial, right now, to the survival of this species than the clear articulation of the importance of love to a well-led public life. We not only need to show that these values are missing from public life and not rewarded in private life, but we also need to show how our community would improve if they were valued.[16]

When West makes statements about the ethical significance of our difference she is very close to Aristotelian naturalism—indeed, closer to Aristotelian naturalism than she is to Husserl's phenomenology—although no "modern" Aristotelian would embrace her conception of love as necessary to public life. But the structure of her argument echoes Aristotelianism. Women *are* x. A *good* woman is true to what she is. This description of the true woman carries within its own properties. We know what a *good* woman is because we can know what a woman is and therefore what it means to be "true" to our own nature. To be "good" is to live up to the potential that is "there." (Again, I do want to note here that this is not West's language when she speaks of the need for consciousness-raising. When she does so, she indicates that we must, at the very least, create as well as "uncover" the nature of woman.)

Yet, as with her essentialism, when West wants to ground woman's difference in her nature, she, in spite of herself, limits consciousness-raising to revelation. "True consensus," in other words, is ultimately possible between women, even if we currently disagree, because we can *use* consciousness-raising to take us back to our nature. Once we know what our true nature is, we can also assess whether our nature is "better" than theirs by comparing the properties that inhere in our "true" nature to those of men. The prescriptive moment in this argument demands the ascription of properties to women. It is this relationship of prescription to ascription that allows ethical statements to achieve the objectivity that West seeks. In spite of her affirmation of the creative power of consciousness-raising and her sensitivity to the danger of accusing any woman of the disjuncture between her own sexuality and the "true" nature of Woman, she cannot avoid—at least as long as she wants to embrace naturalism—telling us of the proper place for Woman.

To summarize, the deconstructive project resists the reinstatement of a theory of female nature or essence as a philosophically misguided bolstering of rigid gender identity which cannot survive the recognition of the performative role of language, and more specifically of metaphor. Thus deconstruction also demonstrates that there is no essence of Woman that can be effectively abstracted from the linguistic representations of Woman. The referent Woman is dependent upon the systems of representation in which she is given meaning.

Moreover—and as we have seen, they are not the same—essentialist or naturalist theories of the feminine have been ethically and politically condemned for providing a new justification for the old stereotypes, even if those stereotypes are now supposedly being used to *affirm* the feminine. The price we pay for the affirmation of the feminine, so the argument goes, even if it could be philosophically defended, is too high. This view that the price is too high is the basis for the sophisticated version of liberal feminism which insists that the only way for women to achieve legal recognition of their equal status to men is, at the very least, to deny the legal relevance of their difference to the degree that it exists. Women are individuals, and as individuals they should be recognized as legal persons and not reduced to their specific gender identity. There is, in other words, no shared female identity. There are only individuals who happen to be women.

But, of course, the feminist response is that this strategy joins forces with the dominant discourses so as to again deny us legal redress. Worse yet, to the degree that what has come to be called liberal feminism accepts masculine norms, it undermines the possibility of recognition of the unnoticed suffering of women as wrong. West seems to have a powerful argument that, without an account that affirms the unique experience of women as *women*, we participate in our silencing. For West, we are not just individuals, we are women, and we cannot escape our destiny as genderized human beings by maintaining the illusion that women and men are just "people."

Moreover, as we have seen, West's challenge to "individualism" is not made just in the name of protecting the reality of a shared female experience, although this is obviously a central goal. Woman's difference should be valued, not just because it is "there," but because it indicates a better way to live. For West, a crucial aspect of feminist theory is to affirm the feminine.

Note, however, that I use the words *affirm* the feminine, for, as already indicated, it is not just a claim of women's suffering as existing that is being made, at least not in West. The claim, as we have seen, is also that there is "value" in this experience and that major social institutions, like law, should not deny this value by privileging the "masculine" as the norm. For West, in order "to prize" the feminine, we must have a phenomenological account that shows us why this way of being in the world is better, and how this experience is rooted in a female nature or essence. We can understand West's project as itself motivated by the attempt to challenge *derelection*. For her, this challenge can only be effective if she develops an essentialist or naturalist account of women's difference so that what women are can be known and thus represented. This is exactly the position that states that, in order for *derelection* to be overcome, there must be a way to know Woman in her essence or nature, otherwise she will again be erased because she cannot be adequately, or more strongly put, authentically represented as who she truly "is," beyond masculine fantasy.

If, however, as I have argued, we must reject West's explicit return to naturalist or essentialist theories of woman's difference because they fail to note the full power of language, the question remains whether we can still *affirm* the feminine. Even if they are not the same, both kinds of theorists rely on the postulation of the core of woman that we can know as her truth. It is precisely this idea that we can discover the truth of women "in reality" or "in nature" that I am challenging, both methodologically and ethically. And yet, if we refuse the affirmation of the feminine inherent in feminist essentialist and naturalist theories of woman, how can we answer the accusation that we are indeed participating in the traditional repression and the disparagement of the feminine at the same time that we also undercut the basis for a "phenomenological" account of female experience upon which West and other radical feminists rely as their basis for a critical take on what is, and for a reconstructed jurisprudence that recognizes women's difference?

One response to this problem is to focus on how the feminine, as a psychoanalytic category, is produced within the masculine signifying order so that it also serves as disruptive force of the very gender system in which it is given meaning. The "feminine" is not celebrated just because it is the feminine, but because it stands in for the heterogeneity that undermines the logic of identity purportedly established by phallogocentrism.

This position has appeal because it does not claim to show what women's nature or essence actually "is." Instead all that is demonstrated is how the feminine is produced within a particular system of gender representation so as to be disruptive of gender identity and hierarchy. The "feminine" is understood as a critical heuristic device within the dichotomous system of gender identity in which the masculine is privileged as the norm. Yet this position carries within the risk that the "not yet" of a new choreography of sexual difference is presented as an actual "reality" now, rather than as a promise that remains to be fulfilled.[17] Even as we want to recognize that the play of sexual difference is not captured by the stereotypes of any gender hierarchy, we also do not want to deny the tragedy of women's suffering, including in its form as *derelection*. The explosive power of feminine jurisprudence can only too easily be cut off by the reality of a legal system that denies the feminine in the name of the masculine; however, it can also be cut off by undermining the actual experience of suffering that exists now in the name of a possibility that "exists," but as a dream, not an actuality. It is important to note, and we will return to why this is the case, that Derrida, in his "Choreographies,"[18] is very careful to make this distinction between the dream of a new choreography of sexual difference that has not been and cannot be erased in spite of the oppressiveness of our current system of gender representation, and the reality of the oppression of women. Derrida's "utopianism" in this interview is often interpreted to mean that he is not a "feminist." But this is a seriously mistaken reading. Of course, Derrida is for legal reforms that *would* alleviate the most aggravated abuses against women, but these reforms cannot ultimately touch the deeper underlying problem of sexual difference as it has become expressed in rigid gender identities. Feminism, if it is conceived as a struggle of women for political power—and this definition is of course only one definition of feminism— cannot reach the "underlying" problem of why sexual difference has taken the limited—and oppressive, because limited—form it has. Put simply, feminism, on this definition, replicates the dichotomous structure of gender hierarchy, even if it also seeks to put women on top. Therefore, there must be a "beyond" to feminism *so conceived* if we are to realize the dream of a new choreography of sexual difference. (We will return to Derrida's own dream of a new choreography of sexual difference.)

Even if we recognize the need to move beyond a conception of feminism that identifies it solely as a power-seeking ideology, we still need to ask: is it just the critical heuristic force of difference that is valued and figured in the feminine, or is there something "valuable" in the feminine that cannot be reduced to the affirmation, in general, of heterogeneity? If, on the other hand, we affirm the feminine for its own sake, how can we do so without returning to essentialist or naturalist conceptions of women? In order to even begin to answer these questions, we must continue to think differently about the insights of what is frequently labelled "postmodern" philosophy, as these insights demand that we rethink the philosophical underpinnings of feminism. We begin this exploration within the analysis of Julia Kristeva, which opens up to the possibility of a non-naturalist view of the specificity of feminine difference from within the framework of Jacques Lacan.

Julia Kristeva's Exploration of Feminine Difference

To adequately understand Kristeva and the developments in her thinking of the relationship of women to the symbolic, we must put her account of mothering, and the irreducibility of feminine difference, into the context of Jacques Lacan's psychoanalytic theory. Lacan's central insight provides a corrective to the biologistic readings of Freud's account of gender differentiation through the castration complex, and corrects the American object relations theorists' stress on the mother/child relation, rather than on the Oedipal complex. According to Lacan, the genesis of linguistic consciousness occurs when the infant recognizes itself as having an identity separate from the mother, because the mother is other to himself. It is only in fantasy that he can always call her back and have her satisfy his desires. The famous *fort/da* (gone/here) game invented by Freud's grandson, Ernst, and described by Freud is the acting out of this fantasy projection.[19] The primordial moment of separation is experienced by the infant both as loss, and as the gaining of identity. The pain of this loss results in a primary repression that simultaneously buries the memory of the relationship to the mother in the unconscious, and catapults the infant into the symbolic realm to seek to fulfill its desire for the Other. Simply put, we speak out of unfulfilled desire. Once projected into language, this primary identification with the Mother is expressed only through the disruptive force of the unconscious. For Lacan, we speak from a primordial loss which, because it is signified as the signifier of the phallus, blocks expression of what has been lost.

> All these propositions merely veil over the fact that the phallus can only play its role as veiled, that is, as in itself the sign of the latency with which everything signifiable is struck as soon as it is raised (*aufgehoben*) to the function of signifier.
>
> The phallus is the signifier of this *Aufhebung* itself which it inaugurates (initiates) by its own disappearance. This is why the demon of Αἰδώς [*Scham*, shame] in the ancient mysteries rises up at exactly the moment when the phallus is unveiled (cf. the famous painting of the Villa of Pompei).
>
> It then becomes the bar which, at the hands of this demon, strikes the signified, branding it as the bastard offspring of its signifying concatenation.[20]

The subject is divided from the fulfillment of its own desire by this bar. The unrepresentable desire for the phallic mother is only remembered in the fantasy projection that compensates for her absence. It is the phallic mother and what she represents—not the actual mother—and what "she wants" that cannot be spoken in the conventional language of the symbolic. This is why Kristeva emphasizes that we can only reach her through the semiotic, and not through the symbolic. Thus, in her early work, before she became obsessed with her desire for the Law, Kristeva insisted that the feminine, when "identified" as the phallic mother, embodied the dream of an undistorted relation to the Other. This relation lies at the foundation of social life, but cannot be adequately represented within the symbolic through the semiotic. Kristeva's early emphasis on the dynamic between the semiotic and the symbolic demonstrated a profound break with Lacan. For Kristeva, the semiotic remained in alternation with the symbolic. The impossible desire for the phallic mother prompts the writing of recovery, which Kristeva finds in poetry, but this desire for recovery can only be indicated, never spoken directly. The phallic mother is the lost origin, indeed, the lost paradise, that cannot be directly recollected. From this view of the feminine, "[i]t follows that a feminist practice can only be negative, at odds with what already exists so that we may say 'that's not it' and 'that's still not it.' "[21]

So far in this account, it would seem that both sexes are castrated by their exile from the phallic mother. Lacan, however, goes further, and appropriates signification in general to the masculine. Although Lacanians maintain the difference between the penis and the phallus (the phallus represents lack in both sexes), it remains the case that because the penis can visibly represent the lack, the penis can appear to stand in for the would-be neutral phallus.

> The phallus is the privileged signifier of that mark where the share of the logos is wedded to the advent of desire. One might say that this signifier is chosen as what stands out as most easily seized upon in the real of sexual copulation, and also as the most symbolic in the literal (typographical) sense of the term, since it is the equivalent in that relation of the (logical) copula. One might also say that by virtue of its turgidity, it is the image of the vital flow as it is transmitted in generation.[22]

The phallus, as the transcendental signifier, cannot be totally separated from its representation by the penis, even if it is an illusion that the two are identified, and an illusion only maintained by the symbolic. This illusion is the basis of a masculine subjectivity that is rooted in the *fantasy* that to have a penis is to "have" the phallus and, therefore, to be able to satisfy the mother's desire. The masculine child "sees" his mother's lack, which gains significance as her castration. As a result, the fantasy that she is the phallic mother and, therefore, capable of self-fulfillment, is destroyed.

Clinical practice demonstrates that this test of the desire of the Other is not decisive in the sense that the subject learns from it whether or not he has a real phallus, but inasmuch as he learns that the mother does not. This is the moment of experience without which no symptomatic or structural consequence (that is, phobia or *penisneid*) referring to the castration complex can take effect. It is here that the conjunction is signed between desire, in so far as the phallic signifier is its mark, and the threat or nostalgia of lack-in-having.[23]

Sexual difference is based on the significance that this experience of "sighting" comes to have in the symbolic. To have the penis is identified with being potent, able to satisfy the mother's desire. This fantasy identification explains why, for Lacan, the symbolic is never fully separated from the masculine imaginary, in which the masculine subject invests in the illusion that he can regain what he lost, the power to forever call her back. This illusion, as the projected standpoint of the masculine, seems "real." Woman, as a result, is identified only by her lack of the phallus. She is difference *from* the phallus. Again, to quote Lacan:

But simply by keeping to the function of the phallus, we can pinpoint the structures which will govern the relations between the sexes.

Let us say that these relations will revolve around a being and a having which, because they refer to a signifier, the phallus, have the contradictory effect of on the one hand lending reality to the subject in that signifier, and on the other making unreal the relations to be signified.[24]

The man has the illusion of having the phallus, in the sense of the potency to keep her. The woman "is" for him as the phallus, as his projected desire. She signifies for him. It is this significance that woman gives him that mirrors his identity. But the bar, the phallus that splits the man from fulfillment of his desire, is also the basis for the psychical fantasy of Woman.[25] This fantasy is the divide of the Woman of desire into either the "good" or the "bad" phallic mother, and, of course, it lies at the basis of the more conventional split of the wife/mistress. The Woman of desire signifies the lost paradise that at the same time is the threat to masculine identity. The "bad" woman, the seductress, symbolizes the danger of desire itself. But no matter how the Woman is projected—wife/mistress, whore/saint—she "is" only as fantasy. She is presented as the basis of the symbolic, but as fantasy.

As a result, women can know themselves only as this difference, as this lack, the "being" that has no being other than as "their" fantasy. As the lack that gives the illusionary security of the masculine projection, women are given significance for men. As Lacan remarks:

> There is woman only as excluded by the nature of things which is the nature of words, and it has to be said that if there is one thing they themselves are complaining about enough at the moment, it is well and truly that—only they don't know what they are saying, which is all the difference between them and me.[26]

Men speak of Woman. There is no "she" there, other than as she is spoken and written. But it is because Woman "is" only as written, and, indeed, as fantasy, that Lacan's position is technically anti-essentialist. This is the basis for Lacan's infamous assertion that Woman does not exist, which is just another way of saying that the phallic mother and our repressed relationship to her cannot be adequately represented.

> *The* woman can only be written with *The* crossed through. There is no such thing as *The* woman, where the definite article stands for the universal. There is no such thing as *The* woman since of her essence - having already risked the term, why think twice about it? - of her essence, she is not all.[27]

This is also a way of insisting that women cannot tell of the experience of Woman, with a capital "W," because it is exactly this experience as universal which is beyond representation. Lacan, in other words, seems to undermine all attempts on the part of the feminists or anti-feminists to tell us what Woman, with a capital "W," is. At the same time, the Woman or the feminine is "there" in her absence as the lack that marks the ultimate object of desire in all subjects. To say that she is unknowable is not, then, to argue that her lack is not felt. Indeed, Woman as lack is constitutive of genderized subjectivity. Even so, Woman does not exist as a "reality" present to the subject, but as a loss.

As a result, Lacan explains some of the great myths of the quest in which masculine identity seeks to ground itself as quests for her. The feminine becomes the Holy Grail. Within Lacan's framework, the myths of Woman are about this quest to ground masculine subjectivity. Because they tell us about masculine subjectivity, and not about Woman, they cannot serve as clues to unlocking her mystery.

As a result, women are cut off from the myths that could give the feminine meaning and therefore, in Lacan's sense, we are silenced before the mystery of the ground of our own identity, of our origin. The "feminine" is given meaning in the *symbolic order* that belies her very existence, as the Other in their myths and fantasies of that order. Woman "is" imaginary. But it is important to note here that feminine *jouissance*[28] remains as the sexuality that escapes from its place as established by the phallic order. The symbolic is not all, not the whole truth. To quote Lacan:

> It none the less remains that if she is excluded by the nature of things, it is precisely that in being not all, she has, in relation to what the phallic function designates of *jouissance*, a supplementary *jouissance*.[29]

Yet, women cannot knowingly engage the feminine in order to develop a non-phallic orientation to, or contact with, other women, in spite of their lived *jouissance* which might seemingly unite them. Women are instead appropriated by the imaginary feminine as it informs male fantasy. She "is" the phallus, the signifier of his desire. As a result, we are divided from one another, competing for them. Every woman is a threat to every other, as the one who can take away the man by signifying his desire more graphically than the one before. Our definition within the symbolic thus renders solidarity between women nearly impossible.

The "truth" of the feminine is rooted in a primordial desire for the Other that cannot be erased, and thus continues to threaten the order of the symbolic in spite of fantasy compensations. Lacan criticizes the American object relations emphasis on the mother/child relationship, and the corresponding focus on the relationship of psychic disorders to "good" and "bad" mothering, as based on the denial of desire itself. The result is that women are blamed for the lack of satisfaction of desire. If only "Mommy" had been good, I would have been fine. The result is to seek the good mommy who will now secure identity and the fulfillment of desire. Lacan, on the other hand, drives home that it is not "bad" mothering that causes the misery. To think that she is the cause of unhappiness is a projection of the masculine imaginary.

As absence, the feminine remains a subversive force in Lacanian psychoanalysis. More specifically, Lacan recognizes that her desire cannot be contained by the symbolic constructs that purport to define it, precisely because of her otherness as defined by the system of gender identity.

> There is a *jouissance*, since we are dealing with *jouissance*, a *jouissance* of the body which is, if the expression be allowed, *beyond the phallus*. That would be pretty good and it would give a different substance to the WLM [*Mouvement de libération des femmes*]. A *jouissance* beyond the phallus. . . .[30]

Kristeva accepts this basic Lacanian framework, but as we have seen, she attempts to value the lingering fantasy figure of the phallic mother through its expression in the poetry of the semiotic by insisting, at least in her early writings, that the semiotic cannot be simply obliterated by the symbolic. This affirmation of the semiotic helps us to understand the tension within her own Lacanianism that would, at first glance, seem to belie her own attempt to make the maternal a basis for an explanation of feminine difference. Lacan denies that the feminine or the phallic mother is closer to women than to men; even if that cut defines the two sexes as different, and therefore, is given different meaning depending on one's sex. Kristeva, on the other hand, attempts to draw close the connection between Woman and women. Kristeva argues that, first through pregnancy, women experience an Other within themselves: "redoubling up of the body, separation and coexistence of the self and of an other, of nature and consciousness, of physiology and speech."[31] By giving birth, the woman actually experiences the other in herself becoming Other. She also "realizes" the potential of "being" like her mother by becoming her, the mother.

> By giving birth, the woman enters into contact with her mother; she becomes, she is her own mother; they are the same continuity differentiating itself. She thus actualizes the homosexual facet of motherhood, through which a woman is simultaneously closer to her instinctual memory, more open to her own psychosis, and consequently, more negatory of the social, symbolic bond.[32]

For Kristeva, this becoming *the mother* who is primordially attached to the Other, the child, is necessarily undermined by the disruptive force of the symbolic, which turns the child over to the Father. The univocal power of signification is established as the Law of the Father. The Law separates the child from the mother and also suppresses "the maternal drives," drives of the mother as a mother, and the drive of the child for this idyllic dyad of *jouissance*.[33] Kristeva, here, is describing the state of *derelection* in which women cannot represent or express the libidinal relation to the maternal in the symbolic. But the repressed maternal drives remain, echoed in the rhythms, the fractures, the very playing with meaning of poetic language. The "maternal body," however, has no designation in the symbolic except as a fantasized unity in which the mother is one with the child. Therefore, it does not express the experience of the maternal body from the position of the pregnant woman, which is not one of unity, but of non-identity with herself and with her child. It is precisely this experience of non-identity which allows it to be expressed, even if not in the symbolic, which can only express the state as a unity of wholeness and, therefore, as that of which we cannot speak once we have been absolutely separated from it by our own entry into the symbolic.

Thus, the "maternal body" is found only in the ruins of the symbolic, expressed in poetry as a primordial, if dispersed, materiality associated with the sweetest pleasure and, ultimately, with the fragility of the flesh. The semiotic, however, is not *prelinguistic*; instead, the semiotic is the expression of the prelinguistic, the maternal body, in the poetic relation of its influence. The semiotic is also, then, not a second, competing modality of language. Rather, the semiotic should be conceived as the irrepressible Other of conventional language which bursts forth as poetry, and yet is still within language. The multiplication of meaning through the dissolute force of metaphor cannot be safely relegated to the other realm of poetry and the semiotic. But even so, for Kristeva, it is in the rhythms, the very beats of poetry, that we *primarily* find the remnants of the maternal body. (I say primarily because the regression to sound without the insistence on narrative meaning is also an expression of erotic pleasure.) The repressed "maternal drives" are, then, never completely repressed; they overflow the edifice of the symbolic, corroding it all the while.

More specifically, the maternal body is continually remembered, and indeed regenerated, as the drive in actual women to procreate.

> Material compulsion, spasm of a memory belonging to the species that either binds together or splits apart to perpetuate itself, series of markers with no other significance than the eternal return of the life-death biological cycle. How can we verbalize this pre-linguistic, unrepresentable memory? Heraclitus' flux, Epicurus' atoms, the whirling dust of cabalic, Arab, and Indian mystics, and the stippled drawings of psychedelics—all seem better metaphors than the theories of Being, the logos, and its laws.[34]

The maternal, it should be noted, if related to biology, is not simplistically determined by it. It is not, in and of itself, because women can and do mother that they become associated with the repressed maternal body. The maternal body as the repressed of the masculine order, takes on the significance that it does because it is the remnant of a primordial *jouissance* excluded by the dominance of the symbolic. The primordial *jouissance* of the mother/child dyad is suppressed by the Law of the Father, a cultural structure, not a biological reality. Mothering takes on the significance it does only within the patriarchal order that would deny the maternal body and its disruptive force. The maternal body symbolizes the repressed within our current system of gender representation. The maternal, in other words, has significance as the repressed, not just as a fact of biological nature.

> The speaker reaches this limit, this requisite of sociality, only by virtue of a particular, discursive practice called "art." A woman also attains it (and in our society, *especially*) through the strange

form of split symbolization (threshold of language and instinctual drive, of the "symbolic" and the "semiotic") of which the act of giving birth consists.[35]

Yet, according to Kristeva, in spite of its structural, rather than merely biological, significance, mothering gives women in our culture "access" to the split symbolization usually open only to the artist. Thus, women can overcome the destructive dualities created by the separation from the mother by relating as mothers themselves, a relation in which heterogeneity is not lived as opposition, as a threat to the supposed unity of the subject. Women's reproductive capacity carries within it the potential to overcome, at least to some degree, the "effects" of the castration that both genders suffer in their separation from the phallic mother. In this way, women are differentiated from men in their relationship to the feminine. By mothering, women can learn to relate in a non-dominating way that is inaccessible to the masculine subject, at least to the degree that he accepts his castration. However, since Kristeva associates the semiotic with the feminine, and not just with actual empirical women, she always leaves open the possibility that men, too, can reach beyond their own gender identity to reconnect with the repressed mother. Connection, of course, implies separation as well as attachment. In spite of this recognition that the semiotic is not the unique province of women, women are still different from men in their relationship to their castration from Woman, and thus to the semiotic, because they can mother themselves. Mothering, in this way, potentially creates a difference between the genders in their internalization of the separation from the phallic mother.

According to Kristeva, women's capacity to mother, and their differentiated relationship to the repressed maternal, and to the maternal body, even affects women's sense of time. Masculine temporality is chronological because it is projected toward a goal. In the sense that masculine temporality is goal-oriented, it is also oriented toward the future. Masculine time is linear. The "normal" language of the symbolic, since it is masculine, for Kristeva, expresses the view of time as an order and sequence of words oriented toward coherent expression of a message, as in traditional theories of narration. Women's time, on the other hand, at least as it is connected to motherhood, is cyclical time (regeneration) and monumental time:

> As for time, female subjectivity would seem to provide a specific measure that essentially retains *repetition* and *eternity* from among the multiple modalities of time known through the history of civilizations. On the one hand, there are cycles, gestation, the eternal recurrence of a biological rhythm which conforms to that of nature and imposes a temporality whose stereotyping may shock, but whose regularity and unison with what is experienced as extra-

subjective time, cosmic time, occasion vertiginous visions and unnameable *jouissance*. On the other hand, and perhaps as a consequence, there is the massive presence of a monumental temporality,
without cleavage or escape, which has so little to do with linear
time (which passes) that the very word "temporality" hardly fits:
all-encompassing and infinite like imaginary space, this temporality
reminds one of Kronos in Hesiod's mythology, the incestuous son
whose massive presence covered all of Gea in order to separate her
from Ouranos, the father. Or one is reminded of the various myths
of resurrection which, in all religious beliefs, perpetuate the vestige
of an anterior or concomitant maternal cult, right up to its most
recent elaboration, Christianity, in which the body of the Virgin
Mother does not die but moves from one spatiality to another
within the same time via dormition (according to the Orthodox
faith) or via assumption (the Catholic faith).[36]

Feminism itself is regenerative, but feminism re-evolves; it does not simply
repeat itself. This regeneration involves the re-opening of woman's space, a
space for each of us to be a woman, differently. The generations of women
do not simply reduplicate one another.

For Kristeva, the primary demand of the first generation of feminists was
the entrance of women into linear time. It was not a coincidence, then, that
this generation of women rejected motherhood. Kristeva reminds us that
Simone de Beauvoir, in *The Second Sex*,[37] militantly rejected motherhood as
the worst kind of complicity in women's subordination. For de Beauvoir,
the very reality of pregnancy, and indeed, even its presence as a potential in
women's monthly periods, immersed women in the body in such a way as
to undermine women's capacity for the subjectivity that arises above its
material conditions. According to de Beauvoir, woman's freedom as a human
being is constantly undermined by the pull the species has on her. Her
individuation depends on this struggle against her body and the burden of
motherhood. This repugnance toward motherhood reflected a generation's
aspiration to break from the cyclical, regenerative role women had supposedly been forced into precisely because they could reproduce. The second
generation, or regeneration, of feminism refused this denial of the maternal,
and with it, rejected the view of goal-oriented subjectivity associated with
the linear view of time. The return to the acceptance and, indeed, affirmation
of the maternal role has itself been part of the more general affirmation of
the feminine that Kristeva associates with the second wave of feminism.

The desire to be a mother, considered alienating and even reactionary by the preceding generation of feminists, has obviously not
become a standard for the present generation. But we have seen in

the past few years an increasing number of women who not only consider their maternity compatible with their professional life or their feminist involvement (certain improvements in the quality of life are also at the origin of this: an increase in the number of daycare centres and nursery schools, more active participation of men in child care and domestic life, etc.), but also find it indispensable to their discovery, not of the plenitude, but of the complexity of the female experience with all that this complexity comprises in joy and pain. This tendency has its extreme: in the refusal of the paternal function by lesbian and single mothers can be seen one of the most violent forms taken by the rejection of the symbolic outlined above, as well as one of the most fervent divinizations of maternal power—all of which cannot help but trouble an entire legal and moral order without, however, proposing an alternative to it.[38]

As a result, a crucial aspect of the regenerative feminist politics this time around is the translation of these maternal practices into the legal sphere. Here, Kristeva is very close to West in her advocacy that women themselves must elaborate what this different conception of maternal practices must mean for the legal system.

In Kristeva, this continuing desire for motherhood, which indicates, for her, the "existence" of the maternal drives, also carries a challenge to the traditional conception of subjectivity as differentiation through self-assertion. Pregnancy, as a bodily condition, challenges the self-identification of the subject, the illusion that the subject is one against the Other. This challenge not only has implications for society and politics, but for the elaboration of a utopian ethical moment from within woman's actual experience. The arrival of the child culminates in the possibility of a different relation to the Other, inexpressible in terms of traditional notions of love between the sexes or even between human beings of the same sex.

The arrival of the child, on the other hand, leads the mother into the labyrinths of an experience that, without the child, she would only rarely encounter: love for an other. Not for herself, nor for an identical being, and still less for another person with whom "I" fuse (love or sexual passion). But the slow, difficult and delightful apprenticeship in attentiveness, gentleness, forgetting oneself. The ability to succeed in this path without masochism and without annihilating one's affective, intellectual and professional personality—such would seem to be the stakes to be won through guiltless maternity. It then becomes a creation in the strong sense of the term.[39]

This utopian moment is found, in part, in the return to the religious, which itself is associated with the re-acceptance of the cyclical and monumental view of time. However, it also leads to the challenge to the traditional Freudian interpretation of why women want to mother. In Freud, the desire for a child expresses the mature women's resolution of her penis envy. In Kristeva, the desire for the child is affirmed not only as an idealization of the relationship to the phallic mother, in which the pregnant woman can dream of narcissistic completeness in which she contains the Other, but also as an actual, different experience of love beyond the dream of narcissistic perfection, which is only there as fantasy. Indeed, for Kristeva, a mistake of feminism is to completely identify the experience of mothering with the fantasy of a relationship to the phallic mother, as important as this fantasy may be as the mark of the beyond to symbolic order, the semiotic. To make this identification is to reduce women's experience to the fantasy of the masculine imaginary in which he projects unity of mother with child.

> If it is not possible to say of a *woman* what she *is* (without running the risk of abolishing her difference), would it perhaps be different concerning the *mother*, since that is the only function of the "other sex" to which we can definitely attribute existence? And yet, there too, we are caught in a paradox. First, we live in a civilization where the *consecrated* (religious or secular) representation of femininity is absorbed by motherhood. If, however, one looks at it more closely, this motherhood is the *fantasy* that is nurtured by the adult, man or woman, of a lost territory; what is more, it involves less an idealized archaic mother than the idealization of the *relationship* that binds us to her, one that cannot be localized—an idealization of primary narcissism. Now, when feminism demands a new representation of femininity, it seems to identify motherhood with that idealized misconception and, because it rejects the image and its misuse, feminism circumvents the real experience that fantasy overshadows. The result?—A negation or rejection of motherhood by some avant-garde feminist groups. Or else an acceptance—conscious or not—of its traditional representations by the great mass of people, women and men.[40]

Just as West would have us investigate women's hedonic experience to find a different articulation of our pleasure as a disruptive force to the traditional masculine definition of femininity, Kristeva would have us listen to women, not only in their experience of pregnancy and child-rearing, but also in the pain of childbirth itself. West, of course, would agree with this need to listen to women's experience as mothers. For Kristeva, we need to understand just how the traditional, idealized edifice of motherhood represses the experience of women as the reproducers of the species.

Kristeva's "Stabat Mater"—the title refers to the Latin hymn of Mary's agony at the crucifixion—is such an exploration, based on Kristeva's own experience of childbirth and mothering. The style is not a coincidence. Kristeva's poetic evocation of her own pain and suffering, as well as intense joy in childbirth, disrupts her professional personality. On the other side of the page she writes a historical, philosophical analysis of the reabsorption of femininity into maternity within Christianity.

Kristeva writes in remembrance of her pain so as to disorder her own professional text on the Christian views of the mother which cannot adequately express what childbirth and mothering meant to her.

> One does not give birth in pain, one gives birth to pain: the child represents it and henceforth it settles in, it is continuous. Obviously you may close your eyes, cover up your ears, teach courses, run errands, tidy up the house, think about objects, subjects. But a mother is always branded by pain, she yields to it. "And a sword will pierce your own soul too. . . ."[41]

Kristeva ties this reconnection to mothering as an actual experience to woman's rebellion against the structures of traditional narrative language. We cannot say what we go through in their language. When we try to translate, we falsify our experience. The "immeasurable, unconfinable,"[42] pregnant body needs its own language. Poetic evocation, itself associated with woman's time, disrupts a linear narrative. So Kristeva interrupts herself in order to express herself. This need in Kristeva for the disruption of the linear narrative of masculine discourse is part of the reconnection with motherhood. The link between this reconnection with motherhood and the affirmation of the avant-garde writing that disrupts the symbolic through reconnection with the semiotic is embodied in this text.

> The "just the same" of motherly peace of mind, more persistent than philosophical doubt, gnaws, on account of its basic disbelief, at the symbolic's allmightiness. It bypasses perverse negation ("I know, but just the same") and constitutes the basis of the social bond in its generality, in the sense of "resembling others and eventually the species." Such an attitude is frightening when one imagines that it can crush everything the other (the child) has that is specifically irreducible: rooted in that disposition of motherly love, besides, we find the leaden strap it can become, smothering any different individuality. But it is there, too, that the speaking being

> finds a refuge when his/her symbolic shell cracks and a crest emerges where speech causes biology to show through. . . .[43]

For Kristeva, the loss of religion has left women with no beyond to the "here" of the masculine symbolic, no way to reach what is Other. Feminine paranoia, in Kristeva, has in part to do with this lack left by the decline of religion. We have "nowhere" to find a beyond to their world. We are surrounded by "them." Replacement of religion, Kristeva suggests, is perhaps possible only as "herethics," rather than the morality of the masculine symbolic. For Kristeva, the difference between the "herethical" and the moral lies precisely in the willingness of the former rather than the latter to deal with the troublesome questions of sexual difference.

> Nothing, however, suggests that a feminine ethics is possible, and Spinoza excluded women from his (along with children and the insane). Now, if a contemporary ethics is no longer seen as being the same as morality; if ethics amounts to not avoiding the embarrassing and inevitable problematics of the law but giving it flesh, language and *jouissance*—in that case its reformulation demands the contribution of women. Of women who harbour the desire to reproduce (to have stability). Of women who are available so that our speaking species, which knows it is moral, might withstand death. Of mothers. For an heretical ethics separated from morality, an *herethics*, is perhaps no more than that which in life makes bonds, thoughts, and therefore the thought of death bearable: herethics is undeath [*a-mort*], love. . . .[44]

We have seen then, that for Kristeva, the actual experience of women in childbirth and mothering has significant implications for what kind of ethics would evolve beyond the utopian dream of primary narcissism through the idealized relationship to the mother. But it is also important to note her emphasis on a certain kind of woman's participation in "her ethics," "a woman who seeks to reproduce," and who, therefore, seeks stability. There are two points to make here. The mother, as the one who explicitly seeks security, is privileged in the unique feminine quest for herethics. Those who do not mother have been left out of this quest for stability and therefore, as Kristeva has indicated elsewhere, are more easily subject to the absolute negativity of one who is entirely left out of the symbolic. This explains why, for Kristeva, some women are prone to terrorism. "Mothers" cannot risk terrorism. But does that mean that women who do not seek "stability" cannot participate in "herethics"? At least in "Stabat Mater," the answer would seem to be yes. Thus, although Kristeva constantly reminds us that she is aware of the cultural specificity of her own writing as a European woman—and indeed, even suggests that the third generation of feminists which she now sees forming will "break free of its belief in Woman, Her Power, Her Writing, so as to channel this demand for difference into each and every element of the female whole,"[45]—she also continues to locate the universal, in the sense of what women share, in their capacity to mother and in their maternal role.

Even so, it would be incorrect to argue that Kristeva's account of the maternal is either simplistically naturalistic or ontological, because the *significance* of the maternal is given within the gender structures of the Lacanian framework, and not by the very "being" of woman. On one level, then, it would be possible to render consistent Kristeva's insistence that Woman has no given ontological status with her writings on the maternal. Thus, unlike Judith Butler, I would not argue that Kristeva has to posit "female generativity" as "an uncaused cause."[46] Indeed, under Lacanianism, we are caused to take up our definition as Woman. The repressed maternal takes on the meaning it does for Kristeva only within the cultural framework described by Lacan. (I will, however, argue that the later Kristeva is ultimately more reactionary than Lacan in her sentimentalization of maternity, but I will not do so by identifying femaleness as pure generativity.)

To my mind, the most provocative insight in Kristeva's writing on the maternal lies in her explicit challenge to the Freudian conception of why women mother. Yet, in spite of my defense against the charge that she *necessarily* reinstates the very ontological or naturalist account of Woman she otherwise challenges—certainly there are places in her text when she does so—her emphasis on maternity inevitably returns the feminine to a nearly, if not perfect, identification with a biologically given capacity. Even if that capacity is understood to be given significance only within culture, it is still that capacity that provides the sex-specificity of the feminine and renders the feminine irreducible to the role of "being" the phallus established by symbolic order. I will return to my critique of Kristeva shortly. For now I want to return to the difference between Kristeva and West, by contrasting their competing psychological frameworks.

The value of Kristeva's account of the feminine is that it gives us more room to explain why men, too, can care and love. Since West accepts the story of masculine "separation" from the mother as crucial to achievement of male identity in a society in which women are the prime caretakers of children, she cannot give us an explanation of how a man could get beyond this identity. Kristeva's psychoanalytic framework shows us how men can escape entrapment in gender identity because, at least on a theoretical plane, both the masculine and the feminine positions are accessible to both sexes— even if not in exactly the same way, and even though men cannot personally have the experience of a woman who gives birth and mothers.

We have already discussed the philosophical deconstruction of West's essentialism, but if we take West out of her own essentialism and simply read her against the backdrop of implicit acceptance of object relations theory as it has been passed down in American feminism, her vision of gender identity is still inadequate.

The Limits of Object Relations Theory

The American feminist narrative of object relations theory, while it has many rich variations, can be summarized as follows: the very basis of male identity is to differentiate the self from the primary caretaker, who, in the usual case in our society, is a woman. His differentiation involves his recognition that he is not like her. Rather than *identify with* her, he can only become himself through his distinctiveness from her. To be a self is to be separate and unlike her. The process of male differentiation is to *identify against* the Other. Separation, in this sense, also demands opposition.

The little girl, on the other hand, cannot help but identify with the primary caretaker since, at least in the sense that they are of the same sex, they are alike. Differentiation, then, is never complete if by differentiation one means the emphasis on how the self is distinct and separate from the primary caretaker. The little girl inevitably, as a potential and future mother, cannot help but recognize herself in the Other, her mother. Her identity is thus relational at the core, since it involves identifying with, rather than against, the Other. This is the basis, not only for a different structure of identity, but also, for writers like Carol Gilligan,[47] of a different ethic, an ethic of care. Because of the differentiated relation to the mother, men and women are not alike. Feminist object relations theorists stress that this difference is inevitable in a culture in which women do the child-rearing. It is a cultural, not a biological reality.

The only solution to this difference, which frequently expresses itself in "the war between the sexes," is to introduce men into child-rearing so that boy children will also have the experience of *identifying with* as the basis of identity rather than *separation from* and *identification against*. As long as women are the primary caretakers, there will be the two worlds West eloquently describes. And, more importantly, women will continue to identify with their role as mothers to define who they themselves are. The result—and it is this result that has recently been of concern to Nancy Chodorow—is that the social structures that reproduce women as mothers will be reinforced through the acceptance of role differentiation by women and men.[48] Thus change, because it demands that men as well as women mother, would have to involve the challenge to the social structures that identify women with the maternal function. Yet it is difficult to see how this challenge can take place.

Why is this difficulty so hard to overcome in object relations theory? The answer is as follows: psychic structure, in this version of object relations theory, is understood as engendered by social relations. The result is the reduction of psychic structure to social reality. This reduction in turn makes it difficult to explain how there could be a fundamental transformation of current gender identity, because the psyche is identified with a context of gender division already in place at the time of analysis. Unlike the Lacanian psychoanalytic framework, the feminine position is not even theoretically available to males, nor is the masculine position accessible to women.

Thus, even if Nancy Chodorow understands mothering as a social activity completely separable from the biological capacity to reproduce and, therefore, open to men as an activity, her own version of object relations theory cannot explain why men would be motivated to mother. Indeed, given who they are fated by society to become as men, the opposite conclusion would seem to follow, since mothering would be an activity identified with women and the primary caretaker from whom the little boy must separate himself in order to gain his male identity. As a result, the two realities that are created by the theory of differentiation would seem to undermine the political program of challenging the current structure of gender identity which, in turn, reproduces the role of mothering for women, but not for men.

The two "realities" in this version of object relations theory, one male, one female, lie at the basis of West's analysis of the writers in the Conference of Critical Legal Studies. For West, the male subject may well live out the fundamental contradiction as it has been elaborated in critical legal studies precisely because men don't connect to others in the primordial way that women do—because of our reproductive capacities and our assumption of the maternal role. West summarizes the "fundamental contradiction" as it has been expressed in the work of Duncan Kennedy as an accurate expression of masculine subjectivity.

> According to Kennedy, we value *both* autonomy and connection, and fear *both* annihilation by the other and alienation from him, and all for good reason. The other is both necessary to our continued existence and a threat to that continued existence. While it is true that the dominant liberal story of autonomy and annihilation serves to perpetuate the status quo, it does not follow from that fact that the subjective desires for freedom and security which those liberal values reify are entirely *false*. Rather, Kennedy argues, collectivity is both essential to our identity and an obstacle to it. We have contradictory desires and values because our essential human condition—physical separation from the collectivity which is necessary to our identity—is itself contradictory.[49]

But this reality is not the same for women, according to West, although she recognizes that women, too, may fear intimacy as an invasion against their personhood. Even so, West believes that men, more than women, internalize their separation from, and opposition to, others as the very basis for their identity. The reason that women fear intimacy is because their unique bodily structure makes them so easily subject to invasion. Thus, the fear of intimacy is not the same in men and women. This mistake of identifying what can seem like a similar experience, but is indeed differentiated once we understand what it "actually" expresses, is a tendency West associates with "liberal" male theorists who would deny the significance of sexual difference. In prosaic terms, it is the mistake of asserting that women are also afraid of intimacy, that men also have broken hearts, etc. Yes, this may be the case, but for West, this experience, even if it is categorized as the "same" in popular language, does not reach the specificity of women's experience which makes it different and uniquely female. It is this experience that we must seek to reveal through consciousness-raising.

The fundamental theoretical problem with the American feminist version of object relations theory, including as it is implicit in West, is that it collapses psychic structure into social relations. As we have seen, the result is that two separate realities, one male and one female, are inevitably established. Because West accepts the story of masculine separation from the mother as the foundation for male identity, she cannot provide an explanation of why men could get beyond this identity. Moreover, there would be no reason they would want to. As I have already argued, the opposite would be the case since this form of differentiation from what is identified as female is experienced as the very basis of male identity. If a change in child-rearing is the only way to challenge this structure of gender identity, what would motivate men to embrace the change? Women may understandably want to end the "war between the sexes" because of their gender specific desire for love, but men would not want or seek change. The problem is not only that object relations theory reinstates two realities, it does so in such a way as to nearly foreclose the possibility of change stemming from the internal motivation of the subjects themselves.

The Lacanian Account of Masculine Subjectivity and the Basis For Female Solidarity As Loss of the Mother

The Lacanian account, on the other hand, turns the object relations story on its head and gives us at least one way to develop an account of how and why men suffer under the Law of the Father, and therefore might seek its fall. Although both genders are cut off from the repressed mother and, theoretically at least, have access to the position of the Other, it is men, to the degree they become traditional, heterosexual men, who are fundamentally "connected" to one another in the order of the symbolic. Without this connection, there would be no ground, illusory though it may be, for masculine identity.

At first glance, this may seem a strange argument because of the association of connection with a particular normative practice of intimacy. But I am using connection here in a special sense. Masculine identity is not about separation from, but subordination to, the reign of the symbolic which is the foundation of social order. The order of the symbolic, in turn, is what provides the basis for the "boys' club." The myth of the autonomous man protects against the painful recognition that brothers find their masculinity only through their subordination to the Law of the Father and that it is this shared reality of the Law that maintains their sense of belonging, their identities as men.[50] Women are the Other to this club. That is what marks its boundaries and defines its membership. The Lacanian account of gender difference helps us to explain why men are fundamentally "wimps," even if brutal to women. Sexual difference engenders a shared, social, masculine "reality." This social "reality," however, is not as West sees it through the window of object relations. Instead, the legal norms described by West represent a fantasy projection that men have achieved autonomy; they do not reflect the actual social "reality" created by sexual difference. That "reality" is one of subordination to the Law of the Father, based on the fear of castration by the father.[51] With the illusion that one has the phallus, comes the fear that one can lose it. Such representations of autonomy, etc., are understood as the fantasies of the man subordinated to the masculine order and more generally in his relations to other men. There is no "real" masculine superiority in Lacan. Male privilege is based on a fantasy identification that to have the penis is to have the phallus. Anatomy figures, but ultimately as a sham. Thus for Lacan, "what might be called a man, the male speaking being, strictly disappears as an effect of discourse, . . . by being inscribed within it solely as castration."[52]

The male sex, in other words, is subjected by gender structures. The fantasy of the autonomous, macho man is compensation for acceptance of the man's castration. But as fantasy, it carefully protects against the tension with reality of castration that continually threatens to break in.

Fantasy, in other words, may not be enough compensation for the acceptance of castration. Thus, the Lacanian framework can potentially explain masculine rebellion against the very order that would seem to be in their name, even if traditional Lacanians rarely follow through on the political implications of the position that masculine superiority is a pretense paid for by castration. It can also explain why such rebellion through a positioning *vis à vis* the feminine is possible for men.

Under this framework—if not developed by Lacan himself because for him the problem of woman's position is "insolvable"—there is also a basis for the solidarity of women through gender specificity. Solidarity grows from the shared experience of exile and, more profoundly, of mourning for the feminine that is shut out of the realm of the symbolic except as represented in male fantasy. This interpretation gives a different meaning to the Lacanian insight that women cannot easily find themselves in the representations of the feminine that do appear in masculine fantasy, because these fantasies represent the male loss of the mother. These are not our fantasies, but theirs, of a projected Other who could secure their identity.

Perhaps the most elegant expression of the community of mourning that "unites" women, because it is "universal" in patriarchy, is to be found in the novels of Marguerite Duras. Marie Stretter weeps continually.

> She looks . . . imprisoned in a kind of suffering. But . . . a very old suffering . . . too old to make her sad anymore. . . . *Pause* —And yet she cries . . . .[53]

But her tears are not hers alone. There is no love that can fill in this lack. The mourning is not for the man who does not come, but for the feminine that is shut out.

In the opening pages of *The Vice-Consul*,[54] and in the dramatization of the novel, *India Song*, a young Laotian peasant woman is sent away by her mother because there is no place for her at home, now that she is pregnant. She can neither save herself, nor her child, in a world in which the feminine has no place. In her dreams, she is returned to the mother. But her dreams cannot be realized. Her only escape from incessant longing is madness. She embraces the lack that is her only identity: "She's always been trying to lose herself, really, ever since her life began."[55]

Instead of seeking to establish female identity through identification with the imaginary father—a theoretical move we will return to in my discussion of Kristeva's recent writings—Duras turns us to mourning and to the subversive power of the "holes" in discourse that point us beyond the order of the symbolic. In order to write of Woman, we need:

> [A] hole-word, whose center would have been hollowed out into a hole, the kind of hole in which all other words would have been buried. It would have been impossible to utter it, but it would have been made to reverberate. Enormous, endless, an empty gong, it would have held back anyone who had wanted to leave, it would have convinced them of the impossible, it would have made them deaf to any other word save that one, in one fell swoop it would have defined the future and the moment themselves. By its absence, this word ruins all the others, it contaminates them, it is also the dead dog on the beach at high noon, this hole of flesh.[56]

We mourn for the phallic mother that never has been, and yet reminds us of the "not yet" in which the feminine would not be reduced to male fantasy, including the fantasy that the female lover is merely this Mother replacement that secures his identity. The woman in Duras' *Malady of Death* grows impatient with the man's identification of her with the lost mother who cannot be brought back again, or with any of the other projections of the psychical fantasy of Woman. She only plays the whore knowing herself to be playful. She takes on the position he puts her in without ever embracing it since, it being his fantasy, only he can possess it. The woman who is figured as the feminine in *Malady of Death* is absent in her slumbering, and eternally fleeing the full presence that would allow her to be possessed as his fantasy.

> Perhaps you'd look for her outside your room, on the beaches, outside cafes, in the streets. But you wouldn't be able to find her, because in the light of day you can't recognize anyone. You wouldn't recognize her. All you know of her is her sleeping body beneath her shut or half shut eyes.[57]

In Duras' *Blue Eyes, Black Hair*,[58] the Lacanian notion that "the sexual relation founders in non-sense"[59] is given body. The disruption of the "old dream of symmetry" in which we desire only what is complementary to "their" desire means that the sexes forever "miss" one another. We are banned from meeting by the phallus that signifies desire, but can never be given as a reality to the Other. As Lacan explains the tragedy inherent in his own analysis of gender, "[l]ove rarely comes true, as each of us knows, and it only lasts for a time. For what is love other than banging one's head against a wall, since there is no sexual relation?"[60] In Duras' allegory, it is the lack of connection that characterizes the involvement of the lovers. "The life they live—better off dead. She stops again in front of him, looks at him, weeps, says again, 'Because of this love which has taken everything and is impossible.' "[61] It is only in the male fantasy of the third, the imagined other man, that the two sexes come "together" in the same space. But the two lovers never meet. They are with one another only through the absent third who marks their separation and gives desire only as the guarantee of unfulfillment. The third stands in as the phallus, as the bar to the fulfillment of desire that also gives expression to desire. The utopia of fulfillment is only there as lack, as absence. Yet even so, the unavowable community[62] refuses the reality in which it must remain unavowable.

Thus, unlike in the feminist interpretation of object relations theory, the solidarity of women through their defined specificity does not develop out of, but against what is. Ironically, the condemnation of the silencing of women takes the form of living out, and therefore exposing, the silence. The lack of reality associated with being the phallus is what makes identification between women possible. It is not the woman as mother, but the lack of the phallic mother that identifies woman as Woman. At the same time, in *The Vice-Consul*, the conditions of actual mothering for third-world and poor women are unveiled. It is not that there is nothing in the feminine to be affirmed, but rather that the nothing that is the feminine, as the "being" of the phallus, is recognized as lack, not as the illusion of seductive presence, and as lack lived as the resistance of passivity.

The problem with object relations theory, then, is threefold. First, it argues that social relations determine psychic structure, thereby reinstating a rigid gender divide with West's two realities, one male and one female. Second, by collapsing psychic structure into social relations, object relations theory also identifies the masculine and the feminine with actual men and women. Yet as we have seen, Freud and Lacan teach us that there are no such things as men and women in any theoretically pure sense. As split subjects we are all defined as both masculine and feminine and, theoretically, have access to position ourselves as the Other.

Without in any way denying how deeply imprinted our gender identity is within our social context, it is still possible to overflow the boundaries of identity and, more specifically, for men to desire change. This leads to my third objection. Object relations, as interpreted by the American feminists, cannot provide an internal basis for why men might seek to undermine the Law of the Father, because of the tendency expressed in West to take the fantasy of masculinity as reality. We at least should be able to "see" that having the penis is not having the phallus.

Despite the problems with object relations theory, it does provide us with both an account of female specificity, and a story of why this specificity would be valued as a more nurturing and loving way of being in the world. The feminist appropriation of object relations, in other words, gives us hope now, and a standard by which to assess "male" behavior. It should be noted that the male way of being in the world is not necessarily condemned in the literature, but it is always understood as incomplete, as female relational patterns are also insufficient for the adult personality. Men are overdifferentiated; women, too dependent. In the most romantic version of this tale, a tale with strong Hegelian overtones, by striving to overcome this incompleteness, we find each other in mutual recognition. In contrast to Duras' allegories, we can find hope in what is.

It is undoubtedly difficult, although not impossible, to engage the feminine as a political practice from within Duras' allegory of the feminine. This undoubtedly explains why both West and Kristeva, in spite of their divergent frameworks, have turned to mothering and women's reproductive capacity as the basis for a feminine practice of writing—and in West's case for a feminist politics and reconstructive jurisprudence—rooted in the way women are, or at the very least potentially can be. As we will also see shortly in

Kristeva, specifically in her more recent writings, the emphasis on actual maternity is connected to the need for women to seek stabilization. Duras' women, who live through their lack, are close to the madness that Kristeva fears tracks women down in a masculine-dominated society. Mourning becomes an all encompassing despair or grief because there can be no location of feminine identity. Our refusal of the loss of the Mother becomes the uncomfortable yearning for an impossible fulfillment. Maternity, for Kristeva, provides at least one opportunity for achieving a feminine identity, and yet achieving it differently. Even though Kristeva clearly shows us that this emphasis on female generativity need not rely on object relations theory, and therefore fall prey to its weaknesses, there are still inherent difficulties in her own analysis. West and Kristeva, in spite of their divergent frameworks, both locate feminine specificity, and what is to be valued in that specificity, in women's reproductive life.

As we have seen, however, the maternal, in the early Kristeva, is not just the actual experience of pregnancy and reproductive capacity, but the possibility of reconnection of women with the repressed maternal—which can be more easily achieved by women than men because of the potential for mothering. At least the early Kristeva, with Hélène Cixous, fantasizes the disruptive possibility associated with the maternal. The "not yet" is already "here" in this potential for resurrection of the repressed maternal. The repressed maternal indicates the "place" of the feminine imaginary which, of course, can never be located "in reality." But in the early Kristeva, women can move closer to the lost Mother as they mother themselves. This conception of the maternal and the maternal body gives us a different relationship to the Other that involves the non-identity of the subject, and thus belies the oppositional structure of separation associated with masculine subjectivity.

The Critique of West and Kristeva

It is obvious, of course, that not all women mother and, therefore, some would not have this experience of difference, particularly as it stands in for an ideal of the self, in and through heterogeneity. But more importantly, maternity identifies the feminine with the mother. It is precisely the separation of the feminine from its identification with the mother that Duras' allegories underscore.

Michéle Montrelay's analysis of the young girl's primordial relation to her own body, even once this relation is represented in the symbolic—despite its weakness—is more helpful because it roots feminine specificity in our "sex" and not in mothering.[63] Mothering is a capacity that may or may not be exercised by women, and more importantly, that feminists have insisted all women need not choose in order to become "real" women. If it is the actual experience of mothering that provides the "ideal" of a different way of relating to the Other, some women would inevitably be excluded. Feminism, then, would not rely on the experience of women, but on that of mothers.

Although it is clearly meant to unite, the "privileging" of the actual experience of mothering and childbirth can also separate. In Kristeva, mothers have a unique contribution to make to "herethics." The reason for this differentiation among women is because women who mother also seek the stability that is crucial to ethics.[64] But there is also at least the suggestion that it is mothers who are closer to the feminine. The danger here is in the perpetuation of the idea that women who do not mother are not only not "full" women, they also carry within them the constant danger of instability and social disruption.

In other words, Kristeva ultimately fails to understand the implications of Lacan's insight, that the reduction of the feminine to the maternal functions within "the psychical fantasy of Woman." The idealization of the mother, including the properties associated with that function—nurturing, infinite compassion, security, never-questioned Love—is grasped as part of that fantasy. Unlike Freud, Lacan does not see the assumption of the maternal function as a resolution of the Woman's penis envy. The reduction of the feminine to the maternal, in other words, is part of the subjection of women. That women who do not mother are somehow evil, unstable, etc., is a component of the "psychical fantasy of Woman" Lacan brilliantly describes. To buy into it in the way that Kristeva does, even in her early writing, clearly bolsters the illusion that this fantasy is truth. It also, as we will see shortly, helps us to explain the connection between Kristeva's later rejection of the writing of the fantasy of the maternal as one metaphorization of utopian possibility, and her own earlier writing. From the beginning there is a tendency in Kristeva to idealize the maternal function as against the disruptive power of the imaginary "tie" to the phallic mother, never completely cut off by the symbolic.

The maternal, then, is not *just* metaphor or a projected fantasy for a different relation to the Other. In Kristeva, the pregnant mother actually does give us a different representation of the self. Kristeva suggests that this is an *actual experience* that pregnant women have, which then culminates, and indeed, transcends itself, in mothering. In part, one's attitude toward the other within oneself will turn on whether it is welcome or not. If unwelcome, the experience can be of invasion, precisely because the fetus is other. As we have seen, for West, it is the vulnerability before this possibility of invasion that should be protected against in the right to abortion. The evocation of the maternal body as another relation to self and other must be done carefully in order to sensitively recognize the experience of an unwanted pregnancy. It is interesting to note that Kristeva has little to say about the right to abortion. I would suggest that this may not be a coincidence, but results from her idealization of the maternal function.[65] A central criticism, of course, is that the maternal love Kristeva beautifully evokes as possibly the only true love is sentimentalized if it is thought to be universal. The burden of class, racial and national oppression all too frequently undermines her postulation of this ideal love as real. Perhaps this is an ideal, at least in the way Kristeva defines it, only open to middle-class women who have the time and the freedom to focus on their maternity. Toni Morrison, in *Beloved*,[66] hauntingly reminds us that "[u]nless carefree, mother love is a killer."[67] I am not arguing that some women do not achieve the ideal Kristeva beautifully evokes. Rather, I am insisting that the ideal does not necessarily or inevitably flow from the actual experience of mothering. The danger here is in rooting the feminine in a specificity dependent on certain social conditions that some women will never achieve, whether or not they mother!

But even if we recognize that the maternal and the maternal body is being used as a metaphor for the feminine as the repressed, not the actual, experience of mothering, we would still have the problem of the perpetuation of the identification of Woman as mother. It is clearer in Cixous than it is in Kristeva that the repressed maternal is a metaphor for the disruptive power of the feminine. In Cixous, the maternal metaphorizes the lost paradise of intimacy, if not unity, not only with the phallic mother, but more generally with the world around us.[68] As in some of Kristeva's early writings, the maternal is the idealized relationship that is sought in the mother and lingers in our longing for her. But even so, the maternal is but one metaphor in which the feminine can be presented. It is not that the maternal, as a metaphor for the repressed feminine and as experience, is not significant, but it is important that the feminine not be *reduced* to the metaphor of the maternal. I do not want to suggest that we should not continue Kristeva's research into the experience of mothering. Rather, as in my criticism of West, I am suggesting that we must change the status of the investigation into the experience of women.

The next problem with relying on the experience of women in mothering and, more specifically, in their potential for reproduction, as the basis of feminist theory, is that women themselves disagree as to what that experience "is," let alone as to what it ultimately means for a female identity. This debate, as already suggested, is crucial for the question of women's right to abortion.

Not only do we potentially entrap ourselves in a contaminated ideal of the maternal function, because it is part of the psychical/psychological fantasy of Woman, we also have the further problem of determining exactly what the actual experience of women is as an empirical matter, and as a subjectively felt "reality," when there is no consensus among us. Without consensus, we are confronted with the dilemma of how we uncover shared experience.

West herself recognizes that in a fragmented society like our own, there will be a problem with any attempt to root feminine experience in women's consensus of their subjectively expressed understanding of their reality. This is why she turns to an essentialist or naturalist theory of women. Citing Adrienne Rich, West explains:

> [O]ne of women's most disabling problems is that women *lie*. For a multitude of reasons, we lie to ourselves and to others. And, one thing women lie about more than any other, perhaps, is the quality and content of our own hedonic lives. . . . This lying has hurt us. We lie so often we don't know when we are doing it. . . . We lie so often that we lack a self who lies.[69]

I suggest that we place West's concern about the female propensity to lie into a different problematic, the problematic offered by Lyotard's writing on the *differend*.[70] The *differend* is precisely that which has been shut out of the traditional legal discourse and the social conventions of meaning. But it also expresses the reality of *derelection*, in which we have to search for ourselves in masculine fantasies. The silencing of women, because of *derelection*, can be understood as the *differend*. The resultant harm to women either disappears, because it cannot be represented as a harm within the law, or it is translated in a way so as to be inadequate to our experience. It is not so much, then, that we are lying, as that we cannot discover the "truth" of our experience in the current system of gender representation. The "truth" of our own experience awaits the discourse in which it can be expressed, which is what West sees clearly in the example of reproductive rights. We are, in a very profound sense, creating our experience as we write differently.

Within law, this attempt to give expression to the *differend* is necessary if we are to avoid the danger of analogizing women's experience to that of men in order to find redress within the legal system. We cannot give expression to the *differend* simply by turning Woman into "a litigant," if such transformation demands that the suffering of women be translated into the prevailing norms of the system in which that suffering cannot be adequately signified, if it can be signified at all.

Think again of the right to abortion and the rhetoric in which in the debate over whether such a right exists has taken place. This rhetoric more often than not erases the uniqueness of pregnancy as a condition in order to guarantee the right. Feminist jurisprudence thus demands a new idiom in which Woman can be heard without translating her suffering into a harm already recognized as such within the prevailing system. West attempts this in her discussion of abortion. Our "reality" disappears within the legal system if it cannot be signified. As Lyotard explains:

In the *differend*, something "asks" to be put into phrases, and suffers from the wrong of not being able to be put into phrases right away. This is when the human beings who thought they could use language as an instrument of communication learn through the feeling of pain which accompanies silence (and of pleasure which accompanies the invention of a new idiom) that they are summoned by language, not to augment to their profit the quantity of information communicable through existing idioms, but to recognize that what remains to be phrased exceeds what they can presently phrase, and that they must be allowed to institute idioms which do not yet exist.[71]

But do we need to root this "reality" in a biologically constituted, sex specific capacity if we are to avoid the problem of social fragmentation I pointed to earlier? West, at least, would seem to think so. Indeed, West would seem to suggest that without this designation of feminine specificity in universally shared capacity, her "phenomenology" would not be possible. Before answering this question, it is important to remember what is at stake.

In law, a shift in the representation of feminine "reality" can have important political and legal implications, because such shifts allow us to see modes of behavior as "harms" to women that were formerly thought to be outside the parameters of the legal system. We expand the scope of litigation to transform women from silenced victims who cannot express, let alone seek legal redress for, the harm they have endured, into plaintiffs who now "find" the words in which to speak.

The plaintiff lodges his or her complaint before the tribunal, the accused argues in such a way as to show the inanity of the accusation. Litigation takes place. I would like to call a *differend* (*differend*) the case where the plaintiff is divested of the means to argue and becomes for that reason a victim.[72]

For example, the debate over what kind of male behavior constitutes sexual harassment inevitably turns on how the legal system "sees" women, or more precisely, allows them to be seen. If women are seen as "asking for it" when they dress in a way to enhance their attractiveness, then it would make sense to allow evidence of the woman's dress in a sexual harassment case. After all, how would the poor man know that she did not want his advances? Evidentiary standards and procedures, of course, define what is relevant. But I am suggesting that what is relevant will turn not just on the interpretation of those procedures and standards, but on how one "sees" women and sexual relations. As a result, an aspect of the redefinition of the legal wrong, as well as the harm to women, will involve the process of changing the representation of feminine desire.

The criticisms of West that I have enumerated thus far do not necessarily undermine her "phenomenology," at least in a weak sense. West wants to bring into view harms to women that have remained invisible within our current legal system. West is also concerned to show that women have been harmed, in spite of what they might say about it, particularly in areas like wife-battery and sexual harassment. In order to do that, she believes we are forced to rely on some account of the "objective" reality of all women, irreducible to women's subjective perceptions. This objective "reality" is rooted in her account of female nature; it does not rest on consensus between women as to what that "reality" is, which is why West's phenomenology can be thought to solve the problem of lack of consensus. We can meet her aspirations, however, by trying to show that the very system of gender representation harms women by defining and enforcing "reality" in such a way as to make legal redress difficult if not impossible. We do not, in other words, need to point to an "objective" reality rooted in the nature of all women in order to overcome the dilemma created by lack of consensus, but only to the production of a particular view of woman within a particular system of legal definition.

And what tool or literary device do we use to bring women's "reality" into view if we cannot simply "unveil" it as inherent in maternity or women's reproductive capacity more generally? I want to suggest that the tool is primarily—and only primarily, because it is a mistake to think we can completely separate metonomy from metaphor—metonomy. Metonomy, as Jakobson suggests, is frequently employed in "realistic" narratives.[73] The narratives of women's difference, and of their shared "experience" as potential or actual reproducers, offered to us by Kristeva and West, frequently proceed through metonomy. For Jakobson, metonomy has the connection with "realistic" narratives precisely because it involves the contiguity that is dependent upon contexture. But, at the same time, because metonomy moves along the axis of contiguity, the "reality" of women's difference is never consolidated. Contiguity disorder allows for the exploitation of the contextual aspect of language. The combination and recombination of words along the axis of contiguity is crucial to the practice of consciousness-raising.

West cannot simply rely on "observation," description, or a theory of female nature that ultimately returns to biology. Indeed, she understands that this is the case in her essay on women's hedonic experience, in which she emphasizes the centrality of consciousness-raising as the "feminist method" in which we transform our pleasure through its "redefinition" in consciousness-raising. West also rejects the normative condemnation of some women by others because of a particular practice, which is not to say that she denies any normative aspects to sexuality altogether. We instead have to "discover" together what we experience as normatively unaccept-able. This process, as I have suggested, demands that we move along the axis of contiguity seeking the recombination of elements that may let us know our "experience" differently. In law, contiguity disorder allows for the combination of concepts it previously made no sense to think of in combination or in proximity. We can proceed by metonymy, or even by oxymoron. The classic example is "date rape." To relocate in proximity what had not been thought to be in a relation, and what by definition could not have been thought to be in relation—"date" and "rape"—allows us to bring the feminine *differend* into view. "Date rape" gives us a new "reality," one in which it is possible for a woman to both be on a date and to be raped. To understand an "experience" as a date rape, is very different from knowing it as an example of "boys just being boys," or worse yet, of just believing that the woman "wanted it."[74] It is possible, then, to separate West's jurispru-dential project from her own naturalist account of female specificity.

The need to protect the possibility of a new choreography of sexual difference is the fourth objection to West's and Kristeva's account of moth-ering as the basis for what is different in the feminine. The first way of stating the objection is the following: Freud and Lacan teach us that there are no such "things" as men and women in any theoretically pure sense. As split subjects we all are potentially defined as both masculine and feminine, because there can be no pure referent outside the system of gender representa-tion that designates our sex. The Lacanian story reveals the feminine inherent in the very constitution of masculine desire in and through the imaginary relation to the Mother, as it also demonstrates that women, as well as men, are masculine insofar as they enter the symbolic. Genderized subjectivity, as it is produced as a system, is produced imperfectly. Gender identity is only ever bounded by historically contingent circumstances, so that such con-straint can never, in a theoretical sense, be total. As a result, there cannot be the sharply divided, because totally genderized, "realities" West describes. I do not want to entirely reject West's account of the differences between men and women in their experiences of acquiring an identity through the internalization of a genderized social reality. Far from it. But I do want to argue that this experience is not and cannot be the whole story, precisely because of the disjunction between social reality and psychic life.

Kristeva uses both metaphor and metonymy in her discussions of mater-nity and pregnancy. But there is a dimension to the maternal in Kristeva that is lacking in West. At least in the early Kristeva, the maternal or, more precisely, the metaphorized relation to the phallic mother, expresses the undistorted or non-violent relation to the Other, which lies at the base of social life, but can never be adequately expressed in it. Kristeva rejects that this relation is reducible to the unity of mother and child projected by the masculine imaginary. Yet, at the same time, Kristeva does not consistently understand the status of her own appeal to the repressed maternal as fantasy or an ethical embodiment of the relation to the Other that indicates the feminine imaginary. If she had, she might have been able to come up with a solution to women's depression other than accommodation to the symbolic. It is important to distinguish the explicit appeal to fantasy because it helps us understand the role of fantasy, and of the feminine imaginary, in feminist theory more generally. Kristeva's desire for the law ultimately leads her to forsake the fantasy in the name of accommodation to the symbolic. We will return to Kristeva's accommodation shortly.

Hélène Cixous' Fantasy of the Maternal

I want to stress here that I use the word "fantasy" deliberately because it is precisely the recognition of the relation with the phallic mother as fantasy that is often lost in the Anglo-American critiques of Kristeva, and particularly of Hélène Cixous. The attempt in Cixous is not to find a universal capacity by which we can identify women as a designatable group. Her writing instead gives body to the utopian language of the imaginary relationship to the phallic mother. Fantasy is a literary device. Affirmed by women, this fantasy is rewritten, not just appropriated.

> So! Now she's her sea, he'll say to me (as he holds out to me his basin full of water from the little phallic mother he doesn't succeed in separating himself from). Seas and mothers.
> But that's it—our seas are what we make them, fishy or not, impenetrable or muddled, red or black, high and rough or flat and smooth, narrow straits or shoreless, and we ourselves are sea, sands, corals, seaweeds, beaches, tides, swimmers, children, waves . . . seas and mothers.[75]

Indeed, for Cixous, the rewriting of the fantasy is necessary if we are to engage the feminine differently and to move beyond the repudiation of the mother inevitable under the Law of the Father.

> In woman there is always, more or less, something of "the mother" repairing and feeding, resisting separation, a force that does not let itself be cut off but that runs codes ragged. The relationship to childhood (the child she was, she is, she acts and makes and starts anew, and unties at the place where, as a same she even others herself), is no more cut off than is the relationship to the "mother," *as it consists of* delights and violences. Text, my body: traversed by lilting flows; listen to me, it is not a captivating, clinging "mother"; it is the equivoice that, touching you, affects you, pushes

you away from your breast to come to language, that summons
your strength; it is the rhyth-me that laughs you; the one intimately
addressed who makes all metaphors, all body(?)—bodies(?)—possible and desirable, who is no more describable than god, soul, or
the Other; the part of you that puts space between yourself and
pushes you to inscribe your woman's style in language. Voice: milk
that could go on forever. Found again. The lost mother/bitter-lost.
Eternity: is voice mixed with milk.[76]

The quotation marks indicate the recognition of the fantasy, and that it
cannot be completely erased by the symbolic. We are not completely barred
from the mother by the phallus. The Voice of her remains within Woman
and is heard with the resurrection of what has been repudiated.

The Voice sings from a time before law, before the Symbolic took
one's breath away and reappropriated it into language under its
authority of separation. The deepest, the oldest, the loveliest Visita-
tion. Within each woman the first, nameless love is singing.[77]

But the her that remains is, of course, not the actual mother, but the
mother as metaphorized within the fantasy of utopian possibility. This is
not our actual social role or function, but the embodiment of what might
be, the not yet, in which the repressed returns and makes itself heard as the
voice of her longing and *jouissance*.

How come this privileged relationship with Voice? Because no
woman piles up as many defenses against instinctual drives as a
man does. You don't prop things up, you don't brick things up the
way he does, you don't withdraw from pleasure so "prudently."
Even if phallic mystification has contaminated good relations in
general, woman is never far from the "mother" (I do not mean the
role but the "mother" as no-name and as source of goods). There
is always at least a little good mother milk left in her. She writes
with white ink.[78]

The fantasy is used both to give body to the utopian dream of an undistorted relation to the Other, and to envision a feminine self that would seek
to change society so as to realize that dream. But, of course, the fantasy
metaphorization of the mother is also used to specify the feminine as the
embodiment of the dream of Other love. The mother, so fantasized, who
carries the Other within herself and, therefore, is not one, presents the
relation to the Other not rooted in the fear of the traditional dichotomy,
subject versus object. The vision of the tie to the maternal does not differ

considerably from the early Kristeva. But Cixous is explicit in her appeal to the feminine as the metaphorization of Other love as it indicates the feminine imaginary.

> But I am speaking here of femininity as keeping alive the other that is confided to her, that visits her, that she can love as other. The loving to be other, another, without its necessarily going the route of abasing what is same, herself.[79]

This is not a description of the way women necessarily are. Cixous carefully distinguishes the feminine, and feminine writing, from a description of Woman or of women. The fantasy embodies what the feminine is as this fantasy projection of the feminine imaginary, not as an actual reality that is expressed in the lives of all women as they survive under the patriarchal order.

But the fantasy also plays a role in the internalization of a gender and sex identification not based on the repudiation of the feminine. Gender identity, as Roy Schafer,[80] amongst others, has argued, is never simply copying through identification. Any theory of *stable* gender relations and identities mistakenly understands the assumptions of identity as simply copying. The role of fantasy is not properly understood. Yet, as Schafer argues, identification involves not only copying, but more importantly, the projection of an idealized Other. Identification in this sense involves wish, and seeks fulfillment in a fantasy. Thus, identification not only involves interpretation (this is the mother I would have liked to have), but also the fantasy projection (this *is* my relationship to the idealized Other). These fantasies are introjected as the basis of a genderized self; but this genderized self cannot be protected against the fantasy element on which gender identification is built. Cixous should be understood to deliberately play with the interpretation of the fantasy identification so to break the bonds which have tied women to their role within the phallogocentric order, as other to them. By this move, Cixous seeks to open up the space for identification with the feminine that is not confined to the conventional pronouncements of what women's difference actually "is."

> If woman has always functioned "within" man's discourse, a signifier referring always to the opposing signifier that annihilates its particular energy, puts down or stifles its very different sounds, now it is time for her to displace this "within," explode it, overturn it, grab it, make it hers, take it in, take it into her women's mouth, bite its tongue with her woman's teeth, make up her own tongue to get inside of it. And you will see how easily she will well up,

from this "within" where she was hidden and dormant, to the lips where her foams will overflow.[81]

The fantasy of the mother, of the feminine as Other-Love,[82] is the attempt to keep the "elsewhere" to masculine reality alive by breathing form into it. The fantasy, in other words, is not the projection of anatomical difference, but of the Other-Love promised in the disruptive force of feminine *jouissance*, itself presented as allegory.

> But *sexual difference* is not determined simply by the fantasized relation to anatomy, which depends to a great extent on catching *sight* of something, thus on the strange importance that is accorded to exteriority and to that which is specular in sexuality's development. A voyeur's theory, of course.
> No, the difference, in my opinion, becomes most clearly perceived on the level of *jouissance*, inasmuch as a woman's instinctual economy cannot be identified by a man or referred to the masculine economy.[83]

Cixous then, unlike Kristeva, explicitly develops the repressed maternal as a fantasy that can give expression to the operation of a feminine imaginary. There is no attempt to stabilize the fantasy through the connection of the fantasy to the actual experience of mothering. Her writing is the explicit use of literary language to evoke the feminine through the projected significance of the return of the repressed, including the repressed specificity of feminine desire. It is the fantasy as fantasy that continues to be important as *one* way of evoking the connection between the feminine and utopian possibility. We will explore in the next chapter whether or not such an explicit use of fantasy can survive deconstruction. For now, I want to focus on the difficulties for feminine writing created by Kristeva's later rejection of the fantasy as one metaphorization of the feminine as an irrepressible utopian possibility.

Kristeva's Turn From the Mother

In Kristeva's later writing, the "utopian" dream of the idealized relation to the phallic mother as the fantasy or imaginary Other love that lies at the foundation of social life, but cannot be adequately represented, is almost entirely rejected. As we have seen, even in her early writings, Kristeva was wary of the disruptive force of such a fantasy. The longing for the stability of an idealized maternal function was always there, pitted against her own writings on the semiotic. In her later writing this tension is gone. Kristeva focuses almost exclusively on the establishment of individual identity rather than on the possibility of shaking up the tyranny of the symbolic through the semiotic.

Within the Lacanian framework, Kristeva questions the inevitability of the phallus as the transcendental signifier which protects the production of meaning at the same time that it designates Woman as the imaginary, the unreachable. As Cynthia Chase has argued, at least in one interpretation of Lacan, the production of individual identity and meaning is inevitable, because the projection of the phallus as the unity of signifier and signified, even if only as the fantasy of the One, allows for the establishment of the symbolic order.[84] The law may only be self-reinforcing, but it is that. This unity of signifier and signified rests on a metaphor, but within the Lacanian framework, it is a metaphor that stands in as the "reality" of the law, and as such, relegates the process on which it became law to the "prehistory" of the imaginary. The later Kristeva, like Lacan, insists that the very condition for the *arising* of the subject is identification with the phallus. This identification results not from the desire *for* the mother, but the reading of the desire *of* the mother which the child interprets as the mother's desire for the phallus. Kristeva is concerned with the desire of the Other, the desire of desire, as it ultimately implies identification with the phallus precisely because it may not take place if it is rooted in a reading of the mother's desire and is not simply an expression of an inevitable desire *for* her. The danger here is that the phallus may not be given its significative status and, therefore, the very assent to identity in the symbolic may be blocked.

In the later Kristeva, identification with the imaginary father is necessary if the child is to correctly read the mother's desire as the desire for the phallus. This identification is in turn the abjection of the phallic mother. Without this abjection of the phallic mother, the child is left with the primary narcissistic rejection, the ultimate *negative* answer to the question, "What does mother want?—Not me." If the child *figures out* and affirms the mother's desire as more than rejection of the child, because it is *for* the phallus, then a stable identity through identification with the imaginary father is *possible*. But for Kristeva, this demands a primordial identification with the imaginary father/abjection of the phallic mother in the *pre-Oedipal stage*. A correct "reading" of the desire of the mother and the corresponding identification with the phallus that yields the production of meaning, and is the precondition for the subject, is thus always at risk. Since the identification with the phallus demands a reading and is not just given, our condition as subjects is precarious.

Her suspicion of her own earlier "utopian" dream of the phallic mother stems in part from her concern with female melancholia in which a woman who does not achieve this *pre-Oedipal* identification with the imaginary father will fail to achieve the "status" of subject. In the later Kristeva, it is clear that the mother cannot "signify."[85] As Kristeva explains, "[t]he denial of the signifier is shored up by a denial of the father's function, which is precisely to guarantee the establishment of the signifier."[86] Kristeva is now concerned with how women can achieve the *paternal* function and have an identity at all, not with the break-up of the structures of identification in the symbolic through the dream of the return of the re-metaphorized maternal.

Thus, it should also be noted that in Kristeva, *the abjection of the mother* is necessary for the rise of subjectivity. The imaginary father is the projection of the realization that the mother has not achieved the fantasy of narcissistic perfection, complete in herself. She wants something other, she is not whole, but has a hole. To identify with the imaginary father is to read her desire, but it is also to take up the position of the masculine, if the masculine is defined as precisely this identification with the phallus. In this sense, the later Kristeva's "subject in process" has as its precondition the affirmation of the masculine (and of the paradigm of heterosexuality). Ironically, there is less room in the later Kristeva for the break-up of the symbolic through the subversive power of the feminine than there is in Lacan, precisely because identification with the imaginary father is pushed back to the pre-Oedipal phase. This ultimately means that there can be no place for the feminine imaginary "in" and "through" which the woman writes. The woman artist or writer, to the degree that she maintains her sanity, writes from the position of the paternal. This archaic identification of the woman with Woman must be broken if the individual woman is to save herself from the abnegation of the symbolic which will not only silence her, but also put her at risk of depression, melancholia and suicide. The depressed person stays outside the door, refusing to pay the price for entering the Law which demands the abjection of the Thing or the phallic mother in the moment of identification with the imaginary father. For Kristeva, it is only through identification with the imaginary father that this loss of the Thing can be borne.

> The "primary identification" with the "father in individual prehistory" would be the means, the link that might enable one to become reconciled with the loss of the Thing. Primary identification initiates a compensation for the Thing and at the same time secures the subject to another dimension, that of imaginary adherence, reminding one of the bond of faith, which is just what disintegrates in the depressed person.[87]

To refuse what Kristeva calls "negation" is to lose sense, and ultimately to lose language. Thus, the refusal of the abjection of the mother leads to silence. Without the abjection of the mother, the subject cannot write.

> The spectacular collapse of meaning with depressive persons—and, at the limit, the meaning of life—allows us to assume that they

experience difficulty integrating the universal signifying sequence, that is, language. In the best of cases, speaking beings and their language are like one: is not speech our "second nature"? In contrast, the speech of the depressed is to them like an alien skin; melancholy persons are foreigners in their maternal tongue. They have lost the meaning—the value—of their mother tongue for want of losing the mother.[88]

And what is negation, and its significance in this context for Kristeva? Negation in the later Kristeva is—and here she refers to Freud—a "process that inserts an aspect of desire and unconscious idea into consciousness."[89] For Kristeva, the outcome of this is that we accept the repression, and I would argue more specifically the repression of the mother, even if she remains as a sign, as nonreal. But, of course, this sign, which can only be found in the realm of the symbolic if it "maintains" what is essential of the repressed for the subject, only does so as acceptance of the repression of the fantasized mother. It is this acceptance of repression that allows mourning for the phallic mother to be "fulfilled" and, therefore, no longer be mourning. We "fulfill" our mourning for the lost mother by identifying with the imaginary father.

The depressive woman is the one who cannot let go of the "lost mother." For her, object loss is not tolerable and she remains faithful to her loss through her depression. To end her depression, the woman must let go of her fantasized relationship with the mother, which is the denial of loss through imagined attachment. Kristeva is deadly serious—and I would argue that her seriousness is, indeed, deadly for women—when she writes that *matricide* is necessary for subjectivity to exist.

For man and for woman the loss of the mother is a biological and psychic necessity, the first step on the way to becoming autonomous. Matricide is our vital necessity, the *sine qua non* condition of our individuation, provided that it takes place under optimal circumstances and can be eroticized—whether the lost object is recovered as erotic object (as is the case for male heterosexuality or female homosexuality), or it is transposed by means of an unbelievable symbolic effort, the advent of which one can only admire, which eroticizes the *Other* (the other sex, in the case of the heterosexual woman) or transforms cultural constructs into a "sublime" erotic object (one thinks of the cathexes, by men and women, in social bonds, intellectual and aesthetic productions, etc.). The lesser or greater violence of matricidal drive, depending on individuals and the milieu's tolerance, entails, when it is hindered, its inversion on the self; the maternal object having been introjected, the depressive or melancholic putting to death of the self is what follows, instead of matricide.[90]

The either/or Kristeva offers is stark. We kill the mother to find ourselves. But, in spite of what she argues, matricide is not mourning. Matricide should instead be understood as the repression of mourning. Is this the "essential repression" that identification with the imaginary father demands? We will return later in my discussion of deconstruction to the masculine subject who mourns for the mother, recognizing her inevitable loss, but at the same time refusing to kill her. For now, I want only to note that in the later Kristeva, mourning is fulfilled only in rejection. But what Kristeva fails to note is that the very ideal of "fulfilled" mourning is contradictory. If it is truly mourning for the Other, the object of mourning remains, as the Other. The lost mother remains as loss of a primordial tie that still indicates the mark of a "previous" attachment. In mourning, we live the loss. If mourning were to be "fulfilled," or at least displaced through identification with the imaginary father, it would no longer be mourning. Yet, according to Kristeva, this is the transference to the phallic position that allows the child to *read* the mother's desire.

But for women it is also the denial of the woman's imaginary, which would allow us to engage in feminine writing by resurrecting the mother in the imaginary. She is lost as real. And yet she remains. We dream of her. Kristeva shuts her out, and with her, the mourning that preserves utopian longing even as loss. In Kristeva, literature restores what is "real." When a woman writes she finds herself in the symbolic. By doing so, she establishes her identity in "reality." The feminine imaginary is forsaken as the mother is killed. Our only "reality" becomes what they have given us. But it is within this reality that we can work.

> Literary creation is that adventure of the body and signs that bears witness to the affect—to sadness as imprint of separation and beginning of the symbol's sway; to joy as imprint of the triumph that settles me in the universe of artifice and symbol, which I try to harmonize in the best possible way with my experience of reality.[91]

When we write, we write through our identification with the imaginary father. Kristeva believes that if we deny abjection of the phallic mother, which is identification with the father, we sign ourselves off. And yet Duras writes. And writes. And writes. Through her mourning which is never fulfilled, only written. The stakes for women are high in Kristeva's analysis. I want to insist that she puts us at the stake precisely because of her analysis. Accept the phallus and the phallic order, or you will not survive as a speaking subject.

But of what would "we" speak, of what would "we" write, we who are women, if "we" can only write from the position of the masculine, as the Woman who has assumed her place in the symbolic? Would we not but write through our very silencing of Woman? Would not our pleasure, our love, our selves, be lost in the very gesture that was to give them meaning? Isn't this where we are left, with their reality, when we forsake our imaginary and the fantasy of Other-Love?

Kristeva worries about the sanity of women who forsake Daddy. But they wrote, and as we read them, they live. For Kristeva, the haunting line to Daddy, "you do not do, you do not do,"[92] leaves us only with suicide. Kristeva, unfortunately, would have us survive at the cost of forsaking our dream of who "we" might be, differently, if the mother was not rejected, even as we realized that she was lost, only because she was herself, living. Is Kristeva's *Black Sun* not itself the symbol of the eclipsed mother? The eclipse of the mother, far from being mourning for her, is her denial. Perhaps the greatest challenge for feminine identification is to mourn Woman while simultaneously resurrecting her as imaginary so that "there" can be a place for the feminine imaginary which allows us to write, but as women who do not deny Woman. My suggestion here is that the later Kristeva can only save women by forsaking Woman. Salvation, thus, once again takes the form of the repudiation of the feminine. What Kristeva at times affirmed in her earlier writing, the feminine and, more specifically, the utopian potential inherent in the fantasized relationship to Woman, is lost. Lost too is the hope that we are not cemented in the symbolic that has engraved gender identity in stone.

I take the time to remark on Kristeva's later text not only to indicate that she has become suspicious of her own earlier utopianism—and perhaps this explains why she has not returned to her own suggested investigation into the actual experience of mothering—but also to contrast her own positioning *vis à vis* the repressed maternal to that of Cixous and Irigaray. Both Cixous and Irigaray are concerned with how the feminine lives on, and how we as women can move within the feminine to ultimately escape our confinement within femininity as it has been defined, as merely opposition or difference from them within the masculine order of the symbolic. The emphasis, then, is not on the achievement of identity within the masculine order through the assumption of the paternal function, but of the possibility left open because such identification is almost entirely foreclosed to women except at the cost of abjection of the mother.

> So ask yourselves just what "nature" is speaking along their theo-
> retical or practical lines. And if you find yourselves attracted by
> something other than what *their* laws, rules, and rituals prescribe,
> realize that—perhaps—you have come across your "*nature*" . . . .

Don't force yourselves to repeat, don't congeal your dreams or desires in unique and definitive representations. You have so many continents to explore that if you set up borders for yourselves you won't be able to "enjoy" all of your own "nature."[93]

The cost, then, for the repudiation of the feminine through the rejection of the mother is that fate is reinscribed in the repetition of the same old story, the establishment of the father as ego-ideal and as norm. But if we are to counter this fate through an appeal to a different destiny, how do we do so without reverting to essentialist or naturalist claims we have so far rejected? Does a different *destiny* necessarily imply a pregiven destination, a *telos*, located in our biological specificity as females, or at the very least, the established conventions of a system of gender representation? If not, then we must once again think through the account of the specificity of feminine difference in evoking the fantasy of the mother against the backdrop of postmodern critiques, not only of essentialism or naturalism, but of gender identity structures more generally. But we must do so now with the explicit focus on the relationship of the feminine to fantasy and, more specifically, as the projection of a threshold to the beyond of a new choreography of sexual difference.

Derelection and Its Attempted Solution

It is only once we keep in mind the utopian moment in "feminine" writing that we can both challenge *derelection* and respond to Kristeva while not reinforcing the omnipresence of the symbolic. Kristeva clearly leaves us in a state of *derelection*. One aspect of *derelection* is precisely the matricide that Kristeva endorses. Within both the Lacanian and the Freudian framework, the little girl can neither represent her relationship to her mother, nor can she metaphorize her own desire, her "sex," to herself. If a woman presents herself in relation to her mother, she does so only as a phallic positioning, as an expression of her longing to satisfy her mother's desire. In Freud, lesbianism is an expression of exactly this phallic positioning and thus a denial of femininity. Kristeva ultimately comes very close to Freud in her view of lesbianism. As a result, for both Freud and Kristeva, the suppression of the libidinal relationship to the mother is thus part of the "ascent" to "normal" femininity and to "normal" heterosexuality. But without the ability to represent this libidinal relationship as other than phallic, the little girl is cut off from another specifically feminine contact for identification. This cut from the mother is her castration. As Irigaray explains:

This "castration" that Freud accounts for in terms of "nature," "anatomy," could equally well be interpreted as the prohibition that enjoins woman—at least in this history—from ever imagining, fancying, re-presenting, symbolizing, etc. (and none of these words is adequate, as all are borrowed from a discourse which aids and abets that prohibition) her own relationship to beginning. The "fact of castration" has to be understood as a definitive prohibition against establishing one's own economy of the desire for origin. Hence, the hole, the lack, the fault, the "castration" that greets the little girl as she enters as a subject into representative systems. This is the indispensable assumption governing her appearance upon the scene of "presence," where neither her libido nor her sex/organs have any right to any "truth" except the truth that casts her as "less than," other side, backside, of the representation thereby perpetuated.[94]

Matricide, and the repudiation of the feminine more generally, is thus motivated in women by their shame of coming from a castrated Other. Their beginning is necessarily devalorized. A woman is "cast out of a *primary metaphorization* of her desire and she becomes inscribed into the phallic metaphors of the small male."[95] To be cast out is to live in this abandonment, which then is taken on as the repudiation of the feminine. As outcast, woman is in a state of *derelection*. As we have seen, this state of *derelection* is brilliantly portrayed in Duras' allegories.

But how can we challenge *derelection*? One solution which has been offered is the development of a feminine symbolic in which the mother/daughter relationship could be represented. This solution has been eloquently advocated by Margaret Whitford, and indeed, attributed to Irigaray.[96] I completely agree with Whitford's reading of Irigaray that argues that she is not an essentialist, in the sense that she seeks the truth of Woman in femaleness, nor pre-Lacanian, in that she locates the feminine in a pregiven, prelinguistic libido. I will return to why later on. For now, I want to focus on Whitford's thoughtful reading of how Irigaray understands the significance of a solution to women's inability to achieve a primary metaphorization of their desire within the masculine symbolic order. For Whitford, Irigaray is close to object relations theory in her understanding of the psychic cost to women of a fusional relation to the mother from which the little girl is never properly differentiated. As a result, *derelection* is expressed in part as this failure of individuation.[97] Thus, Whitford's own reading of Irigaray's poetic writings of "her sex," and of her book, *This Sex Which Is Not One*, de-emphasizes the feminine as a celebration of a different relation to the Other, and "her-self" as Other, beyond castration and the masculine subject's illusion of being one with itself. Instead, Whitford argues that in *This Sex* Irigaray describes a symptom of *derelection*. "*The sex that is neither one, nor two*"[98] becomes a warning to women of their own state of *derelection* in which adequate separation from the mother does not take place. The only solution to this fusion with the mother is to symbolize the relationship of the mother and daughter so that it can be understood as a *relationship*, and not lived as a reduplication in which a woman's only identity is to become her mother.[99]

I disagree with Whitford's reading for several reasons. First, she identifies Irigaray's solution too closely with object relations theory, and with the implicit solution of strengthening the individual ego, as the answer to "unhealthy" over-dependent relations. Irigaray militantly battles over the insolubility of the positioning of Woman with Lacan and in the name of the feminine that cannot speak.

> The statement is clear enough. Women are in a position of exclusion. And they may complain about it. . . . But it is man's discourse, inasmuch as it sets forth the law—"that's the whole difference between them and me"?—which can know what there is to know about that exclusion. And which furthermore perpetuates it. Without much hope of escape, for women. Their exclusion is *internal* to an order from which nothing escapes: the order of (man's) discourse.[100]

The politics of identification signify Woman and let her "speak." But this battle takes place only within the shared framework based on a rejection of ego psychology.

I want to be very specific in my criticism of Whitford, for obviously she recognizes Irigaray's theoretical rejection of object relations theory. Whitford is arguing that what Irigaray shares with object relations theory is only the common understanding of an unhealthy fusion with the mother as a symptom of disorder. My objection is that Irigaray does not accept object relations conceptions of over-identification with the mother as a *symptom* of personality disorder. Instead, as we shall see, she affirms the path of struggle to reinterpret this so-called *over-identification* as a way of achieving identification fusion between women that would allow for the affirmation of our "sex" and therefore our solidarity foreclosed by Lacan, in which the mother is devalorized and fusion with her can only be understood as life threatening.

Second, and most important, I disagree with her reading of Irigaray's *This Sex*, which would portray this text as expressing a warning about a symptom of *derelection*, rather than as a celebration of "uncapturable" feminine *jouissance*. Irigaray is not rejecting the feminine imaginary, as Whitford at times seems to suggest. In the masculine imaginary the mother is reduced to the maternal role. It is precisely this reduction that Irigaray militantly rejects. But more specifically for Irigaray, it is in the masculine imaginary that the maternal is further reduced to the representation of a safe enclosure. What is recalled in the mother is this idealized image, not the remains of the Woman. "And there almost nothing happens except the (re)production of the child. . . . And even in the mother, it is the cohesion of a 'body' (subject) that he seeks, solid ground, firm foundation. Not those things that recall the woman—the flowing things."[101]

For Irigaray, there is not one specified form which is Woman, including the form of the mother. Again to quote Irigaray,

> But the woman and the mother are not mirrored in the same fashion. A double specularization in and between her/them is already in place. And more. For the sex of woman is not one. And, as *jouissance* bursts out in each of these/her "parts" so all of them can mirror her in dazzling multifaceted difference.[102]

The very expression "dazzling multifaceted difference" belies Whitford's reading of Irigaray's concern with the symptom of fusion, with the mother associated with *derelection*. Yet, this being said, I agree with Whitford that Irigaray is concerned with the reduplication associated with the reduction of the feminine to the maternal function.

> Of the two of us, who was the one, who the other? What shadow or what light grew inside you while you carried me? And did you not grow radiant with light while I lived, a thing held in the horizon of your body? And, did you not grow dim when I took root in your soil? A flower left to its own growth. To contemplate itself without necessarily seeking to see itself. A blossoming not subject to any mold. An efflorescence obeying no already known contours. A design that changed itself endlessly according to the hour of the day. Open to the flux of its own becoming.[103]

In the above quote, the daughter recognizes the cost to the mother/daughter relationship of the feminine being reduced to the maternal function. The mother sees the daughter through the lens of her thwarted desire. The daughter, in other words, is *her* younger self, who can live the possibilities that have been foreclosed to her. The reduction of the daughter to a projection of the mother's longing cannot be separated from life in a patriarchal society in which the mother is denied a life of her own precisely because of the idealization of Woman as mother. The daughter recognizes the basis for the so-called "controlling" mother. But she also recognizes the potential inherent in the intimacy of the mother/daughter relationship for a more egalitarian understanding of one another through identification with their "sex."

Haven't you let yourself be touched by me? Haven't I held your face between my hands? Haven't I learned your body? Living its fullness. Feeling the place of its passage—and of the passage between you and me. Making from your gaze an airy substance to inhabit me and shelter me from our resemblance. From your/my mouth, an unending horizon. In you/me and out of you/me, clothed or not, because of our sex. In proportion to our skin. Neither too large nor too small. Neither wide open nor sutured. Not rent, but slightly parted.[104]

It is this closeness which can only be understood as a dangerous fusion within the order of the symbolic. But Irigaray rejects this interpretation of the mother/daughter relationship, while at the same time understanding how competition between women arises because of our imposed reduplication. If I am just like every other woman, then any other woman can take my place. As a result, every other woman is a potential threat to my place. The problem is less a fusional relationship between women, particularly mothers and daughters, as much as it is the imaginary projection of Woman which does not allow women to fashion their own lives. We need to reinterpret and, more importantly, to *reaffirm* the feminine as other than their projection. This reaffirmation includes the reinterpretation of the "fusional" mother/daughter relation through Irigaray's politics of identification. It also includes the affirmation of the feminine imaginary. As a result, Irigaray is also not concerned with the cohesion of the masculine symbolic that supposedly can make sense of the scattered feminine imaginary.

The (male) subject collects up and stitches together the scattered pieces of female merchandise (scattered in silence, in inconsequential chatter, or in madness) and turns them into coins that have an established value in the marketplace. What needs to be done instead, of course, if she is to begin to speak and be understood, and understand and express herself, is to suspend and melt down all systems of credit. In every sense.[105]

And, I would add here, "systems of credit" to be melted down must include the credit and debt to the symbolic mother, if it is conceived as credit or debt, as it has been by some writers in the Italian feminist movement.[106]

Thus, Whitford's reading of Irigaray neglects the utopian moment in which the feminine is written as other to the differentiation of the masculine subject, which entails his castration. Her *jouissance* spills out of the container in which it is supposedly held fast and defined. But how can this *jouissance* be written at all unless we have a female symbolic in which she can achieve a primary metaphorization of her desire? This is Whitford's question. But for Irigaray, on the contrary, this *primary metaphorization* would itself be undesirable as another form of containment.

> Woman is neither open, nor closed. She is indefinite, in-finite, *form is never complete in her*. She is not infinite but neither is she *a* unit(y), such as letter, number, figure in a series, proper noun, unique object (in a) world of the senses, simple ideality in an intelligible whole, entity of a foundation, etc. This incompleteness in her form, her morphology, allows her continually to become something else, although this is not to say that she is ever univocally nothing. No metaphor completes her. Never is she this, then that, this and that. . . .[107]

The metaphor of the mother does not complete her.[108] Rather than a call for a female symbolic to counter the operation of the masculine imaginary, I would argue that we need to challenge the rigid divide between the imaginary and the symbolic. It is this divide that makes the feminine imaginary, by definition, completely inexpressible. The political danger of advocating a female symbolic lies in its conservatism. *Derelection*, in other words, cannot be solved by accommodation; and the symbolic, as defined, can only give us accommodation to phallic imagery of the feminine, including the image of the mother. I in no way want to deny the importance of metaphorizing the maternal, or the mother/daughter relationship. But I am suggesting that this endless re-metaphorization should not be identified as a *primary metaphorization* of feminine desire that gives us one coherent account of the mother/daughter relationship. The origin that is lost is resurrected as fantasy, not as an actual account of the origin. When we remember the origin, we remember the future of a feminine irreducible to the castrated other of the masculine imaginary.

Irigaray herself does not speak to the status of her writing of the feminine in terms of the symbolic and the imaginary. The result is that she can be interpreted as calling for a female symbolic, for how else could women not only write, but write without denying feminine specificity? But ultimately, this interpretation denies the power of the feminine as the beyond to supposedly omnipresent symbolic. To understand the challenge to the rigid divide between the symbolic and the feminine imaginary which would exclude feminine writing except as translated into the pre-established order, we will now turn to the feminist alliance with deconstruction.

2

The Feminist Alliance
with Deconstruction

The Deconstructive Allegory of Woman

The second approach to the revolutionary power of the feminine also returns us the Lacanian framework, or more precisely, to Derrida's deconstructive reading of Lacan. Derrida shows us how, at least in one reading, Lacan cuts off the revolutionary implications of his own statement "woman does not exist." I emphasize that Derrida engages with one reading of Lacan, because there are clearly moments in Lacan's text where the rigidity of his analysis of the structure of gender identity seems to give way before the significance of his own understanding that the order of the symbolic that establishes sexual difference inevitably fails to secure itself precisely because such security can only come from the Other. Yet this being said, it is difficult, if not impossible, to deny the pessimism of Lacan's account of woman's position, which he understands as subjection; he also sees it as insoluble. In a very special sense, Derrida's intervention is against the conclusion that the problem of the position of woman is "insoluble," which is not at all to say that Derrida attempts to resolve the riddle of femininity. Indeed, his concern that the attempt to resolve this dilemma would once again "pass out sexual identity cards"[1] has made him hesitate before the re-metaphorization of the feminine that I advance. But I will return to our difference later. For now, I want to emphasize his specific intervention into Lacanianism. In Glas,[2] The Post Card,[3] Spurs,[4] and "Choreographies," Derrida exposes the lie of the symbolic identification of the "feminine" as the truth of castration, as the "hole" that can only be filled in, never understood or represented, and certainly not by women themselves. Woman disrupts the very notion of a proper place, even the symbolic "designation" of her as lack of the phallus. The fallacy of the phallus is that it attempts to erect itself as its own truth.

But Derrida gives new significance to the "truth" that Lacan describes. To quote Derrida:

> By determining the place of the lack, the topos of that which is lacking from its place, and in constituting it as a fixed center, Lacan is indeed proposing, at the same time as a truth-discourse, a discourse on the truth of the purloined letter as the truth of *The Purloined Letter*. . . . The link of Femininity and Truth is the ultimate signified of this deciphering. . . . Femininity is the Truth (of) castration, is the best figure of castration, because in the logic of the signifier it has always already been castrated; and Femininity "leaves" something in circulation (here the letter), something detached from itself in order to have it brought back to itself, because she has "never had it: whence truth comes out of the well, but only half-way."[5]

Derrida shows us that within Lacan's own analysis of the subjection of the feminine in the masculine symbolic, the feminine remains the Other. In spite of Lacan's analysis, or perhaps more precisely because he desires to analyze, Lacan validates the unshakeability of the structures of gender identity, even while understanding them as an imposed Law and not a pregiven nature. But this would imply that the symbolic is the whole of what can be represented as "reality." If one takes Lacan at his word, however, there can be no definitive locale for Woman, precisely because she is not all, the *pas tout* which denies the symbolic as totality. Woman cannot, as a result, be contained by any system of gender identification, including the one established by the symbolic in which she is defined as the castrated Other.

Lacan, in other words, indulges in "essentializing fetishes" in spite of his own insight. According to Derrida, he does so because of his conviction that he has grasped the truth of Woman, at least as represented by the masculine symbolic. In the symbolic, her significance is only as the lack of the phallus. This significance in Lacan is not real, as we have seen, in any ontological or biological sense, but nevertheless the structures of gender identity exclude women's difference as expressible, because her difference is identified within what can be represented and thus known. Derrida's first move is to deconstruct Lacan's insistent separation of the established truth of Woman as castration in the symbolic from the fictions that surround and inhabit her. Lacan is determined to show us "that truth inhabits fiction." As Derrida explains, for Lacan:

> "Truth inhabits fiction" cannot be understood in the somewhat perverse sense of a fiction more powerful than the truth which inhabits it, the truth that fiction inscribes within itself. In truth, the

truth inhabits fiction as the master of the house, as the law of the house, as the economy of fiction.[6]

Derrida, on the other hand, reverses the order of the Lacanian relationship of "truth" to fiction, particularly as Lacan's more general statements about the relationship of truth and fiction inform his proclamation of the "truth" of "Woman" as established by the symbolic. Lacan recognizes the "fiction" of sexual difference, but emphasizes the *truth of the economy* that allows this difference to *appear* both inevitable and true, true in the sense of adequate to the reality of the split into two sexes (when, indeed, it is neither inevitable, pregiven in nature, nor true, adequate to the gender divide as we know it). As a result, his own account is one-sided, stressing the ordering of sexual difference in the symbolic and underemphasizing the failure of the fiction ever fully to make itself real except as masculine myth and fantasy.

Derrida, on the other hand, emphasizes the very limit on the symbolic by sexuality which fails to mean what *it is supposed* to within phallogocentrism. Thus, on the reading I will be offering, Derrida shows us the *ethical* significance of the limit on the imposed meaning of sexuality and sexual difference as understood by Lacan. Lacan, of course, understands sexuality as the limit to meaning. But he neglects the ethical and political implication of his own understanding. Derrida corrects this "oversight." In other words, the economy of fiction, which enforces sexual difference, makes itself true precisely through its enforcement.

But Derrida's own emphasis on the limit of the imposed meaning of sexuality and sexual identity does not deny that reference to women, or even to woman as Woman, is embodied in any given social context. In other words, if one were to read Irigaray's "Cosi Fan Tutti"[7] as not only a critique of Lacan, but also of Derrida, she would be identifying them too closely, focussing only on Derrida's first intervention into Lacan. Irigaray writes, "[t]o the objection that this discourse is perhaps not all there is, the response will be that it is women who are 'not-all.' "[8] In other words, Derrida does not simply show the rules of phallogocentrism that would attempt to define woman as the "not-all," even if, as we will see, he does hesitate before the project of refiguration and re-metaphorization inherent in feminine writing. Despite the symbolic reduction of every woman to Woman, the singular, the woman, remains. As we have seen earlier, the deconstruction of the rigid divide between *Sinn* and *Bedeutung*, which also emphasizes the inevitable figurative or metaphorical casting of the real itself, is not meant to deny reference. But since this misreading of deconstruction is common amongst its political foes, I return to it again. To quote Derrida:

To say for example, "deconstruction suspends reference," that deconstruction is a way of enclosing oneself in the sign, in the "signifier," is an enormous naivety stated in that form. . . . Not only is there reference for a text, but never was it proposed that we erase effects of reference or referents. Merely that we rethink these effects of reference. I would indeed say that the referent is textual. The referent is in the text. Yet that does not exempt us from having to describe very rigorously the necessity of those referents.[9]

Translated into the sphere of feminist politics, Derrida recognizes the need to "describe" the referent Woman as it has been played with on the historical stage and as it has trapped, oppressed, and subordinated actual women. Within the context of the last chapter, Derrida understands the need for metonymic strategies to make the sexual *differend* "appear." Derrida, in other words, completely understands the importance of bringing the dance of the maverick feminist in line with the "revolution" that seeks to end the practical "reality" of women's subordination:

The most serious part of the difficulty is the necessity to bring the dance and its tempo into tune with the "revolution." The lack of place for [*l'atopie*] or the madness of the dance—this bit of luck can also compromise the political chances of feminism and serve as an alibi for deserting organized, patient, laborious "feminist" struggles when brought into contact with all the forms of resistance that a dance movement cannot dispel, even though the dance is not synonymous with either powerlessness or fragility. I will not insist on this point, but you can surely see the kind of impossible and necessary compromise that I am alluding to: an incessant, daily negotiation—individual or not—sometimes microscopic, sometimes punctuated by a poker-like gamble; always deprived of insurance, whether it be in private life or within institutions. Each man and each woman must commit his or her own singularity, the untranslatable factor of his or her life and death.[10]

But he is also writing that such "descriptions" are never pure explanations, as if Woman could be separated from the texts in which she has been told. Our oppression is not a fiction, nor is it all of reality, a site, indeed, a prison from which escape is impossible. If escape were impossible, it would also be impossible to avoid replicating the very structure of rigid gender identity which has imprisoned women, and made the dance of the maverick feminist so difficult to keep up. Yet this being said, these fictions as representations are still "there" for us. Indeed, as I will argue, it is only through these metaphors, representations and fictions that we attempt to reach Woman.

But to reach for Woman is not to have her. To think that man has grasped Woman, once and for all is the illusion of possessing the phallus. Thus, there is another way to understand the significance of the inability to separate the "truth" of Woman from the fictions in which she is represented and through which she portrays herself. She remains veiled. Therefore, we cannot know once and for all who or what she is, because the fictions in which we confront her always carry within them the possibility of multiple interpretations. There is no ultimate outside referent in which this process of interpretation comes to an end, such as nature or biology or even conventional gender structures. As a result, we cannot "discover" the ground of *feminine identity*. But, at the same time, Woman is not just reduced to lack, to the *pas tout*, because the metaphors of her produce an always-shifting "reality." If there is a danger in Duras' extraordinary allegories of the feminine,[11] it is in the seeming implicit acceptance of the truth of the feminine as lack of the phallus. Thus, the *only* "basis" for female solidarity is the unavowable community of mourning.

Derrida, on the other hand, wants to affirm the power to dance differently. He bows to the maverick feminist, determined to escape the confines of the given stereotypes of the feminine. Correctly understood, the feminine also opens the space in which the performative power of the metaphors of the feminine can operate to enhance and expand our "reality." We are not fated to simply repeat the same old dance, we can *be* out of step precisely because our place cannot be exactly established by the order of the symbolic. The feminine is not engraved in stone. To quote Derrida:

> Perhaps woman does not have a history, not so much because of any notion of the "Eternal Feminine" but because all alone she can resist and step back from a certain history [precisely in order to dance] in which revolution, or at least the "concept" of revolution, is generally inscribed. That history is one of continuous progress, despite the revolutionary break—oriented in the case of the women's movement towards the reappropriation of woman's own essence, her own specific difference, oriented in short towards a notion of woman's "truth." Your "maverick feminist" showed herself ready to break with the most authorized, the most dogmatic form of consensus, one that claims (and this is the most serious aspect of it) to speak out in the name of revolution and history. Perhaps she was thinking of a completely other history: a history of paradoxical laws and non-dialectical discontinuities, a history of absolutely heterogeneous pockets, irreducible particularities, of unheard of and incalculable sexual differences; a history of women who have—centuries ago—"gone further" by stepping back with their lone dance, or who are today inventing sexual idioms at a distance from the main forum of feminist activity with a kind of reserve that does not necessarily prevent them from subscribing to

the movement and even, occasionally, from becoming a militant for it.[12]

Derrida's emphasis on the possibility of breaking beyond the identification of the feminine as the opposition of the castrated Other is inherently ethical and political.

As Derrida reminds us, there is always more to the story of Woman than meets the eye, including Lacan's eye, and his identification of Woman with castration. To quote Derrida:

> The feminine distance abstracts truth from itself in a *suspension* of the relation with castration. This relation is suspended much as one might tauten or stretch a canvas, or a relation, which nevertheless remains—suspended—in indecision. . . . It is with castration that this relation is suspended, not with the truth of castration—in which woman does not believe anyway—and not with the truth inasmuch as it might be castration. Nor is it the relation with truth-castration that is suspended, for that is precisely a man's affair. That is the masculine *concern*, the *concern* of the male who has never come of age, who is never sufficiently skeptical or dissimulating. In such an affair the male, in his credulousness and naivety (which is always sexual, pretending even at times to masterful expertise), castrates himself and from the secretion of his act fashions the snare of truth-castration.[13]

In other words, the reinstatement of rigid gender identity in the symbolic is replicated in Lacan's own account of Woman. In this sense, he, and other men who think they know Woman, participate in their own castration by imprisoning themselves in a system of gender representation that cuts off their own desire for her and replaces it with the illusion that they have grasped her in their fantasies. What they know is only the content of those fantasies, not Woman. Yet even as the absent phallic mother (*mere*), she is more (*mehr*). Lacan cannot hold her down in his own description of the economy of sexual difference. His truth is already an assertion. As Derrida reminds us:

> Woman (truth) will not be pinned down. In truth woman, truth will not be pinned down. That which will not be pinned down by truth is, in truth—*feminine*. This should not, however, be hastily mistaken for a woman's femininity, for female sexuality, or for any other of those essentializing fetishes which might still tantalize the dogmatic philosopher, the impotent artist or the inexperienced seducer who has not yet escaped his foolish hopes of capture.[14]

Spurs, then, is mistakenly read as just another attempt to identify Woman with truth, or more precisely, with the absence of truth. Gayatri Spivak, for example has read *Spurs* in this way. To quote Spivak:

> "Woman", then, is a name that is the non-truth of truth in Derrida reading Nietzsche. To emphasize the status of a *name* in thinkers of this type, I quote a celebrated passage by Foucault on power. "[Power] is the *name* that one attributes to a complex strategical situation in a particular society." This particular species of nominalism, an obsession with names that are necessarily misnames, names that are necessarily catachreses, "writing", "*différance*", "power"—"woman" in this case—names that have no adequate literal referent, characterize poststructuralism in general, in spite of local differences.[15]

We have, however, already seen that the deconstruction of a strong sense of reference, in which representation finally yields to the real, does not at all deny reference, but only argues for the way in which reference "takes place" once the relationship between *Sinn* and *Bedeutung* is correctly understood. Technically, then, it would be a mistake to confuse Derrida's position with nominalism. "Reality" is not just a name we give it. Put in his own language, the historical burden of our "situatedness," which Derrida calls palleonomy, would forbid Spivak's "poststructuralist" nominalism.

But, for my purposes here, I want to refocus on the text of *Spurs*. Spivak confuses Derrida's reading of Nietzsche with an acceptance of his position, which is that Woman, stereotypically understood, can evoke the non-truth of truth which can never be told in a strong philosophical sense but only indicated. To state the non-truth of truth, would, of course, reinstate truth. Spivak realizes that Nietzsche uses a name such as Woman, precisely because he is caught in the snare of the masculine stereotypes of Woman. But so does Derrida. In his engagement with Nietzsche's text, Derrida shows us how the affirmation of the stereotypes creates a spillage beyond what they have been taken to mean, including by Nietzsche. Thus, Derrida recognizes that in Nietzsche, "Woman is but one name for that untruth of truth,"[16] but this is not the end of the story which is constantly taken up in its own performative re-stylization. We are not to take Nietzsche or Heidegger at their word. Derrida offers an alternative: "Instead, let us attempt to decipher this *inscription of the woman*. Surely its necessity is not one of a concept-less metaphorical or allegorical illustration. Nor could it be that of a pure concept bare of any fantastic designs."[17]

These "fantastic designs" operate in Nietzsche's text, to create a heterogeneity of meaning that undermines Nietzsche's own misogyny. In other words, Derrida shows us that given the play of style, when an author tries to use

Woman for his purposes, he will find himself being used by the very terms he means to control. "If Nietzsche had indeed meant to say something, might it not be just that limit to the will to mean, which, much as a necessarily differential will to power, is forever divided; folded and manifolded."[18]

In *Spurs*, which is why I speak of this text in the context of the deconstruction of Lacan, the engagement is not just concerned with the non-truth of truth, the limit of appropriation, but with the limit to the truth of castration. On the level of ontology, sexual difference does not take place. But just as Nietzsche's language escapes him, so does the linguistic designation of Woman in the symbolic fail to contain Woman. It is not that Woman is or names indeterminacy in Derrida's text, it is instead that Woman cannot be contained by any definition, including Nietzsche's name for her as the non-truth of truth. Yet this being said, we still have to understand the power of ontology and its replacement by the symbolic, to perform as totality, and thus to hide the undecidability which belies the truth of castration and the truth of Woman as the castrated Other. Again to quote Derrida: "Although there is no truth in itself of the sexual difference in itself, all of ontology nonetheless, with its inspection, appropriation, identification and verification of identity, has resulted in concealing, even as it presupposes it, this undecidability."[19]

Derrida, then, understands that because he writes within the problematic of gender opposition that has been established, he cannot simply dislocate himself from it. He moves within the myths and allegories of the feminine to expose the traditional role they are given within phallogocentrism:

> The truth value (that is, Woman as the major allegory of truth in Western discourse) and its correlative, Femininity (the essence or truth of Woman), are there to assuage such hermeneutic anxiety. These are the places that one should acknowledge, at least that is if one is interested in doing so; they are the foundations or anchorings of Western rationality (of what I have called "phallogocentrism" [as the complicity of Western metaphysics with a notion of male firstness]). Such recognition should not make of either the truth value or femininity an object of knowledge (at stake are the norms of knowledge and knowledge as norm); still less should it make of them a place to inhabit, a home. It should rather permit the invention of an other inscription, one very old and very new, a displacement of bodies and places that is quite different.[20]

Yet Derrida's desire for the new choreography of sexual difference also makes him wary of any attempt to introduce a new concept or representation of Woman, even if through the retelling of myth, to replace the phallogocentric structures we have in place now, because this change would again turn her into an object of knowledge. Woman would again be normalized, her proper place established. Thus, in response to Christie MacDonald's question as to whether and how we can change the representation of Woman through the "'second' and more radical phase of deconstruction,"[21] in which the dichotomous hierarchy of the masculine and the feminine is reversed, Derrida responds:

> No, I do not believe that we have one, [a new concept of Woman] if indeed it is possible to *have* such a thing or if such a thing could exist or show promise of existing. Personally, I am not sure that I feel the lack of it. Before having one that is new, are we certain of having had an old one? It is the word "concept" or "conception" that I would in turn question in its relationship to any essence which is rigorously or properly identifiable.[22]

Derrida, in other words, does not want feminism to be another excuse for passing out "sexual identity cards."[23] There is no ultimate feminine "identity" that can be established as authentic once and for all. But this suspicion of re-identification also prevents Derrida from proclaiming the truth of Woman as absence or, more specifically, as the absence of truth. This is Lacan's concept of what the symbolic has effectively imposed. Derrida instead celebrates the potential in the feminine to refuse castration, and by so doing, the ability of actual women to dance differently.

The misinterpretation of Derrida insists that he, in spite of himself, evokes Woman as the absence signified by the lack of the phallus. This misreading stems from the failure to note the full implications of Derrida's deconstruction of the Lacanian relationship of truth and fiction as it relates to Woman, implications that I will argue later Derrida himself does not take to their full conclusions. Again, this does not mean the relationship of truth and fiction is *just* reversed, because it is precisely Lacan's point, in one sense, that the Woman is a fiction. Derrida is simply exposing that the so-called truth of Woman that establishes her lack as a *fact* of sexual difference itself takes place in the textuality of effects we know as the referent, "Woman." As a result, "there is" no erection of sexual difference that can absolutely guarantee the replication of the current gender divide. The phallus is "itself" a metaphor that stands in for sexual difference. But, as the stand-in for sexual difference, the phallus can never be fully erected as the sexual barrier that divides into two and effectively, once and for all, blocks the chance of a new choreography of sexual difference.

Thus, if Lacan recognizes the status of the phallus as metaphor, he nevertheless fails to take into account the full significance of his own analysis for "overcoming" the current designation of the feminine as lack. Derrida, on the other hand, fully exposes the metaphorical transference that hides itself as the *literal* assumption that "there is" inescapable castration and that, therefore, we cannot escape the fate imposed by the Law of the Father.

Stated within the technical language of Lacan's own analysis, the real itself cannot be completely severed from the linguistic code of the symbolic. Lacan himself realizes that there cannot be this completed severance because both the real and the imaginary are inevitably "mixed up" with the One of the signifier.

> As for the imaginary and the real which are here mixed up with the One of the signifier, what can be said about them? What can be said about their quality, what Charles Sanders Peirce calls *firstness*, about what it is that divides them up into different qualities? How, in this instance, can we separate out something like life and death? Who knows where to situate them?—since the One of the signifier comes down as a cause on both sides. It would, therefore, be a mistake to think that it is the imaginary which is mortal and the real which is the living.[24]

But if the divide is caused by the transcendental signifier, even if it is ontologically arbitrary, it still establishes and is established by a discourse in and through which the divide is erected. Yet a linguistic code cannot be frozen, because of the slippage of meaning inherent in the metaphoricity of language. The metaphoricity of the phallus, in other words, makes its erection less guaranteed to continue to stand up. If this possibility of the fall of the phallus frightens the later Kristeva, it pleases Derrida.

The Subject of Mourning

Lacan, in other words, at least at times belies the force of his own insight into the linguistic formation of the unconscious. Lacan, as we have seen, recognizes the relation between the symbolic and the masculine imaginary. There is no pure beyond to the symbolic, but there is also not a complete cut from either the feminine imaginary, and the idealized mother, or the real, because they only "are" in language. The three realms Lacan differentiates are intermingled, and thus the Law of the Father is marked and contaminated by what it needs to shut out to achieve the imaginary self-presence of phallic authority. Derrida reminds us of the significance of this intermingling:

> That does not mean (to say) that there is no castration, but that this *there is* does not take place. There is that one cannot cut through to a decision between the two contrary and recognized functions of the fetish, any more than between the thing itself and its supplement. Any more than between the sexes.[25]

The erection of the *Ca*—Lacan's own term for the erection of sexual difference in the unconscious—is just that, an erection and, as all erections, is fated to fall: The Law of the Father "is" only against what it represses, the idealized symbiotic relationship of the infant to the mother. But this moment of repression marks the Law of the Father itself, indeed, makes it what *it is*. The Law of the Father is authoritative because it is *phallic* (and, therefore, *not* feminine). Lacan's assertions of the secure place of the Father, established by the replication of the Law itself in and through discourse, is exposed as a mechanism of denial to protect against the "return" of the feminine. The illusion of self-presence of the male authority figure who pronounces the law "is" exposed as precisely that illusion. The Law rests on the repressed underside of the feminine which, even when held down, continues to disrupt the purported unity of the Law. The feminine "operator" can intensify the effect of her disruption. Derrida's *Spurs* is a hymn to her power of disruption.

> The question of the woman suspends the decidable opposition of true and non-true and inaugurates the epochal regime of quotation marks which is to be enforced for every concept belonging to the system of philosophical decidability. . . . Truth in the guise of production, the unveiling/dissimulation of the present product, is dismantled. The veil no more raised than it is lowered. Its suspension is delimited—the epoch. To de-limit, to undo, to come undone, when it is a matter of the veil, is that not once again tantamount to unveiling? even to the destruction of a fetish? This question, *inasmuch as it is a question*, remains—interminably.[26]

Woman remains "interminably," in spite of the denial of the mark she has left on the priest of phallic Law. The mother remains. Declarations to the contrary do not erase her. "Remain(s)—the Mother."[27] Derrida's tribute to woman is to remember her, she who came first and gave him birth, knowing all the while that she is irreducible to an object of his memory. She is never reducible to his introjection, yet, when he calls himself, recalls himself as a subject, pulls himself together, he does so through her. "I call myself my mother who calls herself (in) me."[28] A subject marked by the mother cannot unify himself, but can only recall himself through her. This recall at the "basis" of subjectivity itself disrupts the presence of the symbolic and, of course, the identity of the masculine subject. Derrida's performance, in *Glas*, is done as the masculine subject who refuses his castration:

> I am (following) the mother. The text. The mother is *behind*—all that I follow, am, do, seem—the mother follows. As she follows absolutely, she always survives—a future that will never have been

presentable—what she will have engendered, attending, impassive, fascinating and provoking. . . .[29]

She remains in the words that inadequately seek to embody her, and even in the analysis that would ultimately seek to reduce her and thus identify her as the "term of regression," as, for example, Kristeva does.

> The mother would present for analysis the term of a regression, a signified of the last instance, only if you knew what the mother names or means (to say), that with which she is pregnant. Now you would be able to know it only after you had exhausted all the remain(s), all the objects, all the names the text puts in her place (galley, gallery, executioner, flowers of every species are only *examples* of her). To the extent you will not have thoroughly spelled out each of these words and each of these things, there will remain something of the mother.[30]

We can contrast Derrida's remembrance of the mother, and more specifically his responsibility to remember that he follows her, with Kristeva's insistence that matricide is *necessary* for the achievement of subjectivity. For Derrida, matricide is never completed once and for all. We only think we have killed her. Her trace, however, remains and marks the subject, even after he enters the realm of the symbolic. This mark or, perhaps more graphically, this scar, cannot simply be wiped out and/or successfully displaced through fulfilled mourning. Mourning fulfilled is denial in itself of the otherness of the Other, here, of the repressed as mother. The "subject" of *Glas* mourns for himself as he mourns for the one who has made him what he is. The "subject" is only there for himself in and through the dialogue with the Other, who is never fully present and yet who calls him to mourning by her very absence. To take on the name of the Other, to recall the trace of the mother in one's self, is to refuse castration imposed by the symbolic. For Derrida, the denial of the mother does not kill her, since her repression can never be complete, even at the moment that it is asserted that she is finished. In this sense, Derrida challenges the complete eclipse of the pre-Oedipal period by the Oedipal. This challenge follows from Derrida's problematization of the divide between the symbolic and the imaginary. Culture, and the subject's very identity within language, is no longer understood through a necessary identification with the father. Instead, the writer writes through the mourning that recognizes the tie to the mother. We can now see the challenge to Kristeva. Derrida gives us another account that potentially revolutionizes the subject's relationship to language because one's entry into language would no longer be based on the acceptance of paternal authority. Following the mother, recalling her, is not a holding on, but a letting go, that also does not cannibalize the mother. Derrida does not simply reproject the imaginary unity of mother and child. Nor does Derrida, writing from the position of the masculine, resurrect her as Cixous does directly in her fantasy of Other-Love.[31] Cixous' fantasy uses introjection as the basis of projection, connection to otherness. In Derrida, the incompleteness of introjection, because of the limits of memory and of recall, does not yield an embodied fantasy developed as fable—a step that I agree with Cixous feminine writing must take—but it does belie the inevitability and, indeed, the possibility of completed matricide. The symbolic is after the mother. The refusal of the logic of the father is the subject of denunciation echoed by the writer who witnesses to the failure of the repression of the mother in himself. From the side of the masculine, Derrida echoes the denunciation, Daddy, "you do not do, you do not do,"[32] but by recalling his mother's name:

> Subject of denunciation: I call myself my mother who calls herself (in) me. To give, to accuse. Dative, accusative. I bear my mother's name, I am (following) my mother's name, I call my mother to myself, I call my mother for myself, I call my mother in myself, recall myself to my mother. I decline the same subjugation in all cases.[33]

For Kristeva, on the other hand, this refusal of the separation from the mother protects against loss of the Thing only at the cost of identity. In Kristeva's own language, Derrida's denial of what she calls the *negation* essential to achieving entry into the symbolic rests on his refusal to repudiate the feminine. Through this refusal Derrida plays with the "reality" of "splitting," the result for Kristeva of negation and the necessary condition for identity. By playing with himself, he refuses the very castration that Kristeva argues we must assume if we are to avoid crippling depression and the silence it brings us to.

> If I write two texts at once, you will not be able to castrate me. If I delinearize, I erect. But at the same time I divide my act and my desire. I—mark(s) the division, and always escaping you, I simulate unceasingly and take my pleasure nowhere. I castrate myself—I remain(s) myself thus—and I "play at coming" [*je "joue a jouir"*]? Finally almost.[34]

Derrida's allegorical reading of the feminine, then, is itself utopian in that it refuses the so-called realism of castration. The feminine is not the symbol of the reality of castration, but of the undeniability of the "uncastratable." To quote Derrida:

The undeniable is the uncastratable.

That does not mean (to say) that there is no castration, but that this *there is* does not take place. There is that one cannot cut through to a decision between the two contrary and recognized functions of the fetish, any more than between the thing itself and its supplement. Any more than between the sexes.[35]

Woman is the very figure in Derrida's *Glas* of the constitutive power of the not yet. The mother "is" the Other, the "beyond" to the symbolic: "If one fell on the mother's first name, perhaps one would see that she shines, she, and keeps watch in the depths of the night, illuminates the galley that she leads on in full sail."[36] But as the Other she is not only caused to be outside, she also affects the definition of what is. The effort to separate absolutely from the mother is exposed as the pretense the masculine subject is compelled to play out to assuage his longing for the mother and his fear of her, and not as the necessary basis for identity.

Feminine Restylization

When Derrida writes of the masculine positioning he specifically appeals to Lacan:

> In such an affair the male, in his credulousness and naivety (which is always sexual, pretending even at times to masterful expertise), castrates himself and from the secretion of his act fashions the snare of truth-castration. (Perhaps at this point one ought to interrogate—and "unboss"—the metaphorical full-blown sail of truth's declamation, of the castration and phallocentrism, for example, in Lacan's discourse).[37]

Woman continually plays with her truth, taking up through performance the position to which she has supposedly been placed. But in Derrida's staging of this performance she knows that she is "playing."

> Unable to seduce or to give vent to desire without it, "woman" is in need of castration's effect. But evidently she does not believe in it. She who, unbelieving, still plays with castration, she is "woman." She takes aim and amuses herself (*en joue*) with it as she would with a new concept or structure of belief, but even as she plays she is gleefully anticipating her laughter, her mockery of man. With a knowledge that would out-measure the most self-respecting dogmatic or credulous philosopher, woman knows that castration *does not take place*.[38]

The "truth" of feminine "reality," once we understand its inevitable meta-phorical dimension, does not and cannot lie in properties of the object Woman or in the rigid gender divide of the *Ca*, but is grounded in the systems of representation that have become so stabilized that they appear unshakable. The language of the feminine, however, is how we actually operate to displace the stereotypes associated with gender difference under-stood as the opposition established by the Law of the Father.

Derrida's engagement with the language at least traditionally associated with the feminine body, then, is not a coincidence. Derrida frequently posi-tions himself through the feminine—all the while knowing that what he does is not the same as when a woman does it—so as to split his writing.

Thus, his very style of writing in a chorus of "polysexual" voices also expresses his desire for the disruption of the prescriptive order of gender identity associated with the reification of either male or female identities. For Derrida, an "answer" to the question, "Who are we sexually?"—if indeed it should even be risked—cannot be approached if the standpoint of either male or female is reified so that the author speaks and writes from a unified, genderized position. As Derrida explains:

> At the approach of this shadowy area it has always seemed to me that the voice itself had to be divided in order to say that which is given to thought or speech. No monological discourse—and by that I mean here mono-sexual discourse—can dominate with a single voice, a single tone, the space of this half-light, even if the "proffered discourse" is then signed by a sexually marked patronymic. Thus, to limit myself to one account, and not to pro-pose an example, I have felt the necessity for a chorus, for a choreographic text with polysexual signatures.[39]

The attempt to achieve a "choreographic text with polysexual signatures" should obviously not be confused with an attempt to reinstate a sexually neutral position from which to write. Derrida consistently argues that such a position within our system of gender identity is impossible, which is why the choreographic text still involves designatable masculine and feminine voices, at the same that it tries to blur the traits and lines of thought traditionally associated with the gender opposition. Derrida deliberately resexualizes the supposedly neutral language of philosophy by using words which carry associations with the feminine body—hymen and invagination, for example. However, he also hesitates before the danger that such a use of language, while recognizing the repressed feminine, will do so in such a way as to again reinforce rigid gender identity. Derrida recognizes that one can never know for sure whether any attempt to shift the boundaries of meaning and representation through a rewriting of language is complicit or breaks with existing ideology. The use of words associated with the feminine body could only too easily reinstate phallocentric discourse by perpetuating myths of what that body is from the masculine view point. Derrida believes he has chosen his words carefully to disrupt traditional associations that would, as we will see, seem to be determinate of the feminine. In this way, his feminization of language is different from the writing of the feminine "sex" in Cixous and Irigaray. His purpose is not directly to affirm through re-metaphorization her "sex," but it is still to challenge the gender hierarchy reflected in the masculinization of language. The introduction of such language carries a performative aspect that can never be totally assessed, but which unmasks the pretense of neutrality and questions the current line of cleavage between the sexes that would rigidly designate: this is masculine, this is feminine. The hymen "is" between male and female, but as what gives way "in love."

> One could say quite accurately that the hymen *does not exist.* Anything constituting the value of existence is foreign to the "hymen." And if there were hymen—I am not saying if the hymen existed—property value would be no more appropriate to it for reasons that I have stressed in the texts to which you refer. How can one then attribute the *existence* of the hymen *properly* to woman? Not that it is any more the distinguishing feature of man or, for that matter, of the human creature. I would say the same for the term "invagination" which has, moreover, always been reinscribed in a chiasmus, one doubly folded, redoubled and inversed, etc.[40]

The link between the Other, Woman, as the more (*mère/mehr*) of a given state of affairs is the threshold. We are constantly invited to cross through the fetishization of essentialist conceptions of sexual difference, which in turn creates the opening for new interpretations. This link, evoked as the hymen, is both the invitation to cross over and yet also a barrier to full accessibility.

But Derrida also knows only too well what is at risk in this refusal of the gender-neutral position, symbolized by his feminine resexualization of language. The gender-neutral position would inevitably, if unconsciously, erase feminine difference and again privilege the masculine, in the guise of a neutered being. Yet, traditionally, ethics has been conceived as involving a universal position attainable for all subjects, and thus independent of their sexual markings. Ethics seems, then, to involve the ability, at least for the purposes of morality, to speak of humanity in general and in a language that reflects that generality.

Thus the possibility of ethics could be saved, if one takes ethics to mean that relationship to the other which accounts for no other determination or sexual characteristic in particular. What kind of an ethics would there be if belonging to one sex or another became its law or privilege? What if the universality of moral laws were modelled on or limited according to the sexes? What if their universality were not unconditional, without sexual condition in particular?[41]

So, how do we resolve this dilemma?

If we do not accept the possibility of achieving a neutral position, then by definition morality itself will be sexually marked. More importantly, ethics and morality will seemingly be marked by the privileging of the masculine, if we understand the sexual opposition not only as a dichotomy but as a hierarchy in which the feminine, as more than the Other of opposition to them, is erased. The hierarchy establishes us as their counterpart, which is what Luce Irigaray has called the "old dream of symmetry."[42] As Derrida explains:

One could, I think, demonstrate this: when sexual difference is determined by *opposition* in the dialectical sense [according to the Hegelian movement of speculative dialectics which remains so powerful even beyond Hegel's text], one appears to set off "the war between the sexes"; but one precipitates the end with victory going to the masculine sex. The determination of sexual difference in opposition is destined, designed, in truth, for truth; it is so in order to erase sexual difference. The dialectical opposition neutralizes or supersedes . . . the difference. However, according to a surreptitious operation that must be flushed out, one insures phallocentric mastery under the cover of neutralization every time. These are now well-known paradoxes.[43]

The only way out of this paradox is to work within the hierarchy to reverse the order of repression. This is why Derrida positions himself through the feminization of language. Because rebellion against metaphysical oppositions cannot amount simply to a denial of their existence or an attempt to rise above them in already established "neutral" discourse, there must be a "phase" of overturning. This phase is necessary for the intervention into the hierarchical structure of opposition. But it is not a phase that one simply surpasses, because the oppositions continually reassert themselves. The phase, then, is structural, not temporal. We never just get "over it." We cannot settle down once and for all. In that sense deconstruction is interminable. There can be no clear line between "phase one" and "phase two." As Derrida explains:

> I am not sure that "phase two" marks a split with "phase one," a split whose form would be cut along an indivisible line. The relationship between these two phases doubtless has another structure. I spoke of two distinct phases for the sake of clarity, but the relationship of one phase to another is marked less by conceptual determinations (that is, where a new concept follows an archaic one) than by a transformation or general deformation of logic . . . .[44]

It is the reformation of the logic of sexual difference as opposition, and the corresponding repression of the feminine upon which it rests, that deconstruction seeks to disrupt. This operation demands a double gesture not easily practiced without either erasing the feminine or essentializing woman's difference. Therefore, in spite of his recognition that the phase of overturning is necessary, Derrida does not seek a new concept or representation of Woman. Even his resexualization of language is potentially worrisome to Derrida if it again fetishizes feminine sexual difference. There is a tension, then, between Derrida's insistence on the phase of overturning and his uneasiness with attempts to give body to the feminine, attempts which need not necessarily involve the imposition of a new concept. The danger is that Derrida jumps too quickly to the new "choreography of sexual difference," in spite of his great care to recognize the phallocentric nature of traditional metaphysics. To resolve this tension, we will need to return to an interpretation of the Derridean "double gesture" as it is relevant to the kind of "double writing" I will suggest is crucial to feminism. But I do want to remark here that this hesitancy is what ultimately separates Derrida's own position from the feminine writing of her "sex," a writing that I will argue later demands not that we reconceptualize woman, but that we at least affirm the continuous process of re-metaphorization and re-symbolization.

Thus, If I do not agree with Irigaray's criticism—if it indeed is a criticism of Derrida—that Derrida only shows us how the Lacanian schema is not all, he does hesitate before the feminine writing that celebrates her "sex" and allows for identification between women based on this affirmation. Ultimately, however, I will argue that once we understand female writing as I interpret, we can understand this hesitation as not necessary to Derrida's own vision of a new choreography of sexual difference. And, we can understand the relationship of a dream of a new choreography of sexual difference with feminine writing and the political and ethical celebration of women. I will return to this discussion of how we should understand double writing in the last chapter. Let me just stress for now why I advocate the alliance of deconstruction with feminism, rather than stating that the deconstruction of phallogocentrism is feminism.[45]

For the moment I want to emphasize an ambivalence, in spite of his acute awareness of the phallocentric bias of so-called strategies of neutralization, in Derrida's relationship to both Heidegger's and Levinas' attempts—as different as the two are—to think difference without sexual markings. As Derrida explains, in Levinas' extraordinary interpretation of Genesis, the man Isch would still come first.[46] Secondariness, however, would no longer be the woman. It would instead be the divide between the masculine and the feminine. Thus, as Derrida remarks, "[i]t is not feminine sexuality that would be second but only the relationship to sexual difference."[47] Derrida notes that this attempt to think what is prior and/or superior to all sexual markings is motivated in part by the desire to save a traditional conception of ethics. The danger, as Derrida well recognizes, is that the identification of the masculine as prior, even if as "spirit," still puts masculinity in command. If the divide between man and woman is the fall into sexual markings, sexual difference can only be interpreted as a "loss." (It would be too simple to argue that this is clearly Levinas' position because, in his way, he values the feminine.) In his recent essay on Levinas, Derrida, through the voice of the feminine interlocutor, questions the secondariness of sexual difference, as the desire for the erasure of *feminine* sexual difference in the supposed neutrality of the "*il*." As with Derrida's questioning of the separation of the symbolic and the feminine imaginary, the interlocutor exposes the way feminine sexual difference marks the so-called neutral "*il:*"

> The other as feminine (me), far from being derived or secondary, would become the other of the Saying of the wholly other, of this one in any case; . . . then the Work, apparently signed by the Pro- noun He, would be dictated, aspired and inspired by the desire to make She secondary, therefore *by* She [*Elle*].[48]

The motivation in Heidegger is different, of course, because the concern is not to protect the traditional concept of ethics. Heidegger seeks to express an analytic of *Dasein* that is neither an anthropology, nor an ethics, nor a metaphysics. For Heidegger, sexual markings are determinations that occur "after" the analytic of *Dasein*, and must ground their study in anthropology. In this sense, *Dasein* is neuter and must be neuter, as between the two sexes. Derrida rightly points out that *Dasein*'s a-sexuality, *vis à vis* the sexual markings of either sex, does not imply the absence of sexuality, but only the absence of the determination by sex or gender. *Dasein*, in other words, is not inherently scarred by the opposition between the sexes so that there could be no analytic other than through that reality of the genderized subject. Yet in his text, "Ontological Difference/Sexual Difference," Derrida still worries that Heidegger, with Levinas, risks the erasure of feminine sexual difference. Likewise in *Spurs*, he explicitly recognizes the connection between the definition of propriation and of sexual difference as he defends Nietzsche against Heidegger's reading of him.

> As a result, the question, "what *is* proper-ty (*propre*), what *is* appropriation, expropriation, mastery, servitude, etc.", is no longer possible. Not only is propriation a sexual operation, but *before* it there was no sexuality. And because it is finally undecidable, propriation is more powerful than the question *ti esti*, more powerful than the veil of truth or the meaning of being.[49]

In his recognition of propriation as a sexual operation, Derrida is clearly not seeking to erase sexual difference in *différance*, the supposedly ultimate name for the non-truth of truth.[50] To do so would be again to try to mistakenly separate the question of propriation or even the question of Being from sexual difference. And therefore another angle is one of Derrida's central contributions to feminism, for he explicitly argues that fundamental philosophical questions cannot be separated from the thinking of sexual difference. Yet, this being said, Derrida also tries to remind us of exactly what this neutrality amounts to within the analytic of *Dasein*, so that we can assess whether this risk *should* be taken.

> Not that the *Dasein* does not ontically or in fact belong to a sex; not that it is deprived of sexuality; but the *Dasein* as *Dasein* does not carry with it the mark of this opposition (or alternative) between the two sexes. Insofar as these marks are opposable and binary, they are not existential structures. Nor do they allude in this respect to any primitive or subsequent bi-sexuality. .... This gives an idea of what stakes were involved in a neutralization that fell back this side of both sexual difference and its binary marking, if not this side of sexuality itself. This would be the title of the enormous problem that in this context I must limit myself to merely naming: ontological difference and sexual difference.[51]

I use the word "scarred" deliberately. I have suggested that Derrida's resistance to Lacan is inherently ethical and political, done in the name of saving the dream of a new choreography of sexual difference. As Derrida explicitly states, the very divide of the sexes can itself be seen as a scar, not just as a fall from a prior wholeness, but rather, as a limit on the proliferation of sexual voices, each with its own unique notes.

From within Derrida's own ethical positioning *vis à vis* Lacan, the appeal of Heidegger's analytic of *Dasein* is as follows: Heidegger does not think of

Dasein as fundamentally scarred by the opposition between the sexes. Taking the leap which I think Derrida makes, if this scar is psychological or anthropological and not ontological, then there may be a passage out, a *sortie*, for our current gender hierarchy with its rigid gender identification.[52] Sexual difference, in other words, is not fundamental, at least not in the sense of the rigid divide into two genders. There may be a passage that would be more than the dead end of the replication of the anthropological determination we associate with male and female. As Derrida remarks, however, "it is a passage that may no longer be thought, punctuated or opened up according to those polarities to which we have been referring for some time (originary/derivative, ontological/ontic, ontology/anthropology, the thought of being/metaphysics or ethics, etc.)."[53] If ontological, it is inevitable that humanity will always in this way be divided in two. Derrida desires to resist this merciless closure, which he also argues marks the homosexual/heterosexual opposition.

Derrida is certainly not defending the dominant matrix of heterosexuality when he insists that homosexuality and heterosexuality are the "same" under the current gender divide. Instead, he is indicating that the patriarchal order can only define homosexuality as opposition, as the other to heterosexuality within the divide of the two sexes or genders. It is only within the structure of a dominant heterosexuality, in which homosexuality is forbidden, and specifically between women as regression, that homosexuality is rigidly designated as *homo-sexuality*. It is the sexual/gender divide itself that gives a limited reading to lived sexuality. How does one even indicate the passage that cannot be thought? One *way* to do so is to evoke difference and, indeed, the gift as "before" sexual difference, although not in any strict temporal sense, because this would once again reinstate the originary/derivative divide. Thus, Derrida wonders:

> [W]hether sexual difference, femininity for example—however irreducible it may be—does not remain derived from and subordinated to either the question of destination or the thought of the gift (I say "thought" because one cannot say philosophy, theory, logic, structure, scene or anything else; when one can no longer use any word of this sort, when one can say almost nothing else, one says "thought," but one could show that this too is excessive). I do not know. Must one think "difference" "before" sexual difference or taking off "from" it? Has this question, if not a meaning (we are at the origin of meaning here, and the origin cannot "have meaning") at least something of a chance of opening up anything at all, however im-pertinent it may appear?[54]

It would be a mistake to suggest that Derrida pretends to know the answer to his last question; just as it is a mistake to think he simplistically erases sexual difference by privileging *différance* as the ultimate name for the non-truth of truth. Clearly, he has not settled on one approach to the dream of a new choreography of sexual difference. But he is tempted by thinking difference or the gift "before" sexual difference because of the ethical desire to break open our closure into two sexes. As attractive and as necessary as I think it is to keep dreaming the dream of a new choreography of sexual difference, I also want to argue that we should, indeed must, in the sense of ethical obligation, take off from within sexual difference. This may be my central disagreement with him although I understand he does not pretend to answer his own question. But for me, the answer is clear. Only by taking off from within sexual difference can we "affirm" the feminine. This affirmation is a necessary phase in the effort to "overturn" the hierarchy of sexual difference as it is thought and lived as opposition. This also means that we must risk metaphoric transference, even as we recognize our claims for the feminine within a continual process of reinterpretation, that does not entail a primary re-metaphorization of feminine desire as the basis for the process itself.

I understand Derrida's concern about the reconceptualization of woman as just one more way of reinterpreting rigid gender identity. But I would argue that metaphoric transference cannot be simplistically identified with creating a new stabilized "representation" or concept of Woman which just defines what she is, because metaphoric transference implies like and yet the not like that is the *transference*. The like and the not like, to which we will return, is the possibility within metaphoric transference of the slippage or the "spill over" of meaning which lies in the contradiction of metaphor itself—the assertion of identification through transference. I do not want to deny that metaphoric transference risks the erasure of the moment of transference and, therefore, of the not like, at the very moment it seemingly reinstates identification ("Woman as . . ."). But I do want to contrast metaphoric transference as necessary to figure Woman—ironically, even as allegory—with traditional claims set forth by explicit essentialist or naturalist theories of women, such as the one offered by West,[55] that state what women are. To the degree that representation is understood as a "descriptive" statement (even if with normative implications) of an accurate and thus authentic, because not distorted, reflection of what women are, this presentation erases the performative aspect of language. The metaphors of Woman, in and through which she is performed, are enacted signifiers which, as such, act on us as genderized subjects. But this performance keeps us from "getting to the Other" of the prediscursive "reality" of gender or of sex. Metaphoric transference, in other words, recognizes the constitutive powers of metaphor, but only as metaphor.

Without the metaphors that evoke the feminine we cannot give body to the figure of the feminine. We would, therefore, again be in danger of replicating the repudiation of the feminine, and thus remaining in a state of *derelection*. The affirmation of the irreducibility of the feminine, at least within our Western culture or context, cannot be done without some mode of expression in which feminine desire is written.

Derrida's "suspicion" of metaphor is related to the entanglement of metaphoric transference with the re-institutionalization of the proper I discussed earlier. Metaphoric transference, for Derrida, again locates the proper place of women. We have seen a similar suspicion of the re-institutionalization of rigid gender identity in Derrida's questioning of the need for a "new" concept or representation of Woman as part of the "second" phase of deconstruction. It should be stressed that the "suspicion" is both ethically and politically motivated by the dream of a new choreography of sexual difference which would disrupt the accepted patterns of so-called masculine and feminine behavior. For Derrida, it is precisely the prescriptive order of gender identity "that a problematics of woman and a problematics of difference, as sexual difference, should disrupt along the way."[56] In this I agree with him, but the question remains how the disruption is to be carried out, and more specifically what exactly is the role of feminine sexual difference in that disruption. My argument is that this disruption must include the transformation that affirms feminine writing of her "sex," such as developed in the writing of Irigaray and Cixous.

I am only too well aware that my interpretation of Derrida's allegory of the feminine seems to belie the metalinguistic stance associated with deconstruction, which would condemn any attempt to write the feminine as inherently suspect because it returns us to the language of "full presence" in which the feminine could at last be known. I will return later to why I reject the interpretation that reduces deconstruction to a "point" about metalinguistics and to why I believe that this interpretation misunderstands the complexity of the "double writing" Derrida calls us to. For now, it is enough to see that Derrida's "reminder" of the danger of metaphoric transference, particularly as it might operate within the thinking of the feminine, is itself ethical. In spite of our difference over his hesitancy at the affirmation of the feminine, it would be a serious error to interpret deconstruction as out of hand discarding "feminine writing" as inevitably essentialist. Metaphor does imply metaphysics. But Derrida has never argued that we can simply be beyond metaphysics. More importantly, as he well knows, it would not be his place, let alone a position that he would want to defend, to assert that the feminine should once again be discarded, because of the specter of metaphysics. The question of style remains, and is indicated by what Derrida "means" by the irreducibility of the feminine. We will return to what Derrida means by the irreducibility of the feminine in a moment.

It is important to note first just how fundamentally misunderstood Derrida has been by his feminist critics. Derrida has been accused of advocating women's non-identity within patriarchal society. But was that not what patriarchy always rested on, women's non-identity? Deconstruction, in this reading, is just a disguise of the worst aspects of patriarchy. Who wants to fight for the non-identity we have had imposed upon us? Feminists, on the other hand, assert *our* identity, at last.

As we have seen, Derrida does not postulate Woman's "essential" identity. Rather, he argues that "sex" and gender are not *identical*. He does so in the name of a new choreography of sexual difference in which lived sexuality would be free from the presence of gender hierarchy in which the sexual relation is "non-sense." But he also does so in the name of the irreducible feminine within gender hierarchy, even if he at times waffles about how one would write of this irreducible feminine. The philosophical question is, "How does one write of Woman, particularly as woman?" Derrida does not pretend to know what Woman *is*. But he does give Woman center stage and lets her play. Of course, this playing involves the explicit recognition of Woman as myth and allegory. But this reminder is also of the revolutionary power of the feminine to be Other than the limits imposed on her in projected fantasy. The undeniability of uncastratability keeps open possibility.

Freud speculated that women's sexual repression affected their intelligence. Derrida reverses this insight. The "maverick feminist" *knows* her uncastratability. She has nothing to lose, and so she dances. The politics of her difference are the politics of the possibility to dance. She may dance differently, but that dance demands that Derrida recognize the Other, and sexual difference. He would not recognize the feminine as difference if he reduced feminine sexual difference to non-being. This so-called non-being, as he understands it, could only be grasped as the Other to being and therefore as not different at all. Derrida is serious when he writes of the irreducibility of the feminine to description by a given system of ideality. The misreading of Derrida which argues that his deconstruction of gender identity necessarily entails reducing women to the nothing, or the *pas tout* they have been defined to be, mistakenly conflates Derrida's position with the very position he deconstructs. This is why I disagree with Irigaray's reading of him in "Cosi Fan Tutti."[57]

But how can Derrida justify his indication that the "feminine" or more specifically, femininity, may be irreducible when he seems to hesitate before the re-metaphorization of the feminine? What does he mean by irreducible, if he does not mean to indicate that the feminine has a unique substance or being that can be identified as different? Irreducible, in other words, to what? Here again we are returned to the Lacanian framework. On the one hand, Derrida's recognition of the irreducibility of femininity indicates that masculine and feminine are not simply free-floating categories that are interchangeable, because so little is marked or determined by gender that they can stand in for one another. Sexual difference takes shape because the Law of phallogocentrism *does* have the power to perform gender difference, even if it does not have the power to enact itself as a coherent whole that inevitably gives the last word. The masculine and the feminine in this sense are irreducible to one another because there is a differential relation to the phallus. The man "has" the penis, the woman *is* the phallus. In Lacan, the phallus *is* only as lack, as the signifier of the desire of the Other. Therefore, on one interpretation, to be the "phallus" is to not *be* at all. The challenge to Lacan is that the erection of the phallus can be played with, divide itself, split and split again. But this challenge is not a challenge at all if it merely erases the feminine.

For many interpreters of Lacan the feminine is *reducible* to her position as the phallus. Yet Lacan also states that this positioning demands the rejection of "an essential part of her femininity."

> Paradoxical as this formulation might seem, I would say that it is in order to be the phallus, that is to say, the signifier of the desire of the Other, that the woman will reject an essential part of her femininity, notably all its attributes through masquerade. It is for what she is not that she expects to be desired as well as loved.[58]

Is "her essential femininity" the "irreducibility" of feminine desire to which Derrida refers, in which the feminine would be "more" than just the positioning as the phallus in order to signify the man's desire? And if so what is this more? Perhaps her own style? Here, again we are returned to the significance for Lacan of the unnameability of the feminine within the realm of the symbolic. In one sense, then, there is no prediscursive *reality* for Lacan, because what is real for us is established by the symbolic. But the very act of castration that marks the child's entry into the symbolic also indicates the "beyond," of the imaginary and the real. We *are cut* off, that is, by the reality imposed by the symbolic. But to be castrated, cut off, is to be cut off from something—the real, on the one hand, and the imaginary and the feminine on the other. The Law of the Father makes itself there as reality, but its power is only in its performance. Can this performance secure itself against reinterpretation? If not, can the feminine be reducible, as a standard interpretation of Lacan would have "it"? This possibility of re-interpretation, as we have seen, is exactly what frightens Kristeva. For Derrida, however, it is precisely the possibility of reinterpretation that gives the hope that we are not to be forever imprisoned in our current gender roles. We can perform our roles differently. "Finally almost."[59]

Derrida demonstrates the contamination of the Law of the Father from within, by how it would repress the feminine. Therefore, as the repressed Other, the feminine is irreducible to what it supposedly is designated to be, the lack that signifies within the symbolic, because this designation is a defense. The irreducibility of the feminine also results from what Derrida calls the logic of parergonality,[60] by which Derrida means to indicate that the very frame by which we denote our context, our reality, also implies "more," precisely because our reality is enframed. Yes, we are always within a scene, and in terms of the performance of sexual difference, within the hierarchy of the masculine and feminine and the roles it cuts out for us within the symbolic. But it is also the very placement within a scene which disrupts the very dichotomies upon which this placement seems to rest, including the inside/outside dichotomy. This irreducibility of the feminine to its designation within the symbolic does not necessarily imply the appeal to a prediscursive reality—as has sometimes been suggested by critics of the possibility of a feminine writing—"outside" of the phallogocentric order. Thus writers, like Irigaray and Cixous, need not appeal to a prediscursive libido in order to write and rewrite the feminine. The feminine can only be completely silenced, beyond expression, if the symbolic is understood as absolutely cut off from the feminine imaginary. But as I have argued, this absolute cut belies the very constitutive power of language, of reality, and in turn the force of language to perform and thus shift that reality. There may be no feminine but within writing, but that does not mean that the feminine can be reduced to what has already been written.[61] Time is relevant here, because the reduction of the feminine to what has already been written turns us toward the past. The feminine within language performs and, therefore, disrupts the "reality" of phallogocentrism with its purportedly established propositions of what the feminine is.

> Three types of such a statement are to be found. Furthermore, these three fundamental propositions represent three positions of value which themselves derive from three different situations. And according to a particular sort of investigation (which can be more than indicated here) these positions of value might in fact be read in the terms (for example) of the psychoanalytic meaning of the word "position". In the first of these propositions the woman, taken as a figure or potentate of falsehood, finds herself censured, debased and despised. . . . Similarly, in the second proposition, the woman is censured, debased and despised, only in this case it is as the figure or potentate of truth. . . . Whichever, woman, through her guile and naivety (and her guile is always contaminated by naivety), remains nonetheless within the economy of truth's system. . . . The woman, up to this point then, is twice castration: once as truth and once as nontruth.[62]

But there is a fourth positioning, that in Derrida's reading of Nietzsche's engagement with different propositions of Woman is allowed and then affirmed as the woman with style. The woman with style plays with her own sex in and through the effects of castration:

> In the instance of the third proposition, however, beyond the double negation of the first two, woman is recognized and affirmed as an affirmative power, a dissimulatress, an artist, a Dionysiac. And no longer is it man who affirms her. She affirms herself, in and of herself, in man. Castration, here again, does not take place. And anti-feminism, which condemned woman only so long as she was, so long as she answered to man from the two reactive positions, is in its turn overthrown.[63]

For the Dionysiac woman, her style is her own. She may be nothing but her style, but at the same time she is that, her *style*. She is not simply the signifier of the Other's desire, which would, on the contrary, demand that she reduce herself continually for the man's pleasure. On one reading of Lacan, the truth of the feminine necessarily *reduces* femininity and womanliness to a masquerade in which the masks she puts on are only those demanded of her by the current lover. Strip her down and she will just have on another mask. In other words, her "essence" is that she has no "essence." In order to be nothing so she can "be" the phallus, she must repudiate the feminine as her own "style." Femininity is only the masquerade that is demanded of her in order to dignify man's desire. As a result, Joan Riviere can write in her own analysis of femininity: "The reader may now ask how I define womanliness or where I draw the line between genuine womanliness and the 'masquerade'. My suggestion is not, however, that there is any such difference; whether radical or superficial, they are the same thing."[64]

According to Riviere we, women, take on the masquerade out of fear of the consequences of appearing as masculine, as subjects of language, rather than as a signifier in their discourse. For Riviere it is not loss of love we have to fear, but retribution for the wrong if we reject our position as the signifier of their desire. By definition, it would seem to follow that the "brave" woman refuses the masquerade in the name of her desire to become a potent subject herself. This assertion of potency would be anti-castration.

In Derrida's reading of Nietzsche, however, castration is not refused, as if "it" could simply be refused. Castration, instead, is played with through appropriating the style of the feminine and yet performing it differently. It is not that there is some essential feminine that is prediscursive, revealed when the real is ultimately stripped away, "fetishes which might still tantalize the dogmatic philosopher, the impotent artist or the inexperienced seducer who has not yet escaped his foolish hopes of capture."[65] Instead, there is "the eternal burst [*éclat*] of laughter of the unconscious—or of the woman, the exclamation that indefinitely harasses, questions, ridicules, mocks the essence, the truth (of man)."[66]

Riviere's mistake is precisely to conflate "the truth" that the feminine cannot be pinned down, with the truth of femininity as masquerade and of feminine sexuality as only the play for them. Style, unlike the masquerade, is affirmative. The question of style in woman is akin for Derrida to the question of style in writing:

> Here, in a manner like to that of writing, surely and safely, she forces the proxy's argument to bend before a sort of *kettle logic.* . . . She plays at dissimulation, at ornamentation, deceit, artifice, at an artist's philosophy. Hers is an affirmative power.[67]

She plays, and as she plays she is "more" than just the role she performs. What exactly the role *is* for Derrida is ultimately undecidable, because "it" is only there as performance. I do not want to completely deny the validity of the feminist critique of one reading of *Spurs* that argues that the celebration of the woman of style can "stand in" for the feminine writing of sexual difference and the struggle against our separation. It can seem too facile a glance at the face of the suffering of women within patriarchy,[68] and the need for solidarity between women in order to fight against their subjugation. Restylization can, at least on one interpretation, appear as too individualistic a solution to what is a shared "reality" of subordination that inheres in the gender hierarchy. But that being said, I will want to emphasize the way in which Derrida shows us that the choice is not between castration and anti-castration, repudiation of femininity or its embrace as masquerade out of fear. Cast we may be, but we can still play and restyle. On one interpretation, feminine "writing" is this process of restylization and is therefore "consistent" with Derrida's interpretation of what Nietzsche calls style, simulacrum, woman.

> If the simulacrum is ever going to occur, its writing must be in the interval between several styles. And the insinuation of the woman (of) Nietzsche is that, if there is going to be style, there can only be more than one. The debt falls due. At least two spurs (*éperons*). The anchor is lowered, risked, lost maybe in the abyss between them.[69]

What happens when a woman has balls, spurs? Derrida dares to think about it. Derrida's woman knows that balls are spurs, not a reality of a pregiven sex.

Justice and the Call of the Other

I have so far been conversing on Derrida's own writing on the feminine, femininity and sexual difference, as this body of work gives us a way to approach the feminine as allegory rather than as fact and demonstrates the subversive power of restylization within the dichotomous gender hierarchy. I now want to turn to other aspects of the role deconstruction must play in feminist theory. The first and, perhaps, least understood aspect is the Derridean exposure of what I am going to call the unerasable trace of utopianism in political and ethical thinking. The unerasable trace of utopianism is temporal but in a special sense. This distinction is inadequate; but it is precisely the insistence on inadequation with "reality" that makes deconstruction utopian. This distinction accounts for the difference between the utopianism of the "feminine" as a "redemptive perspective," which does give body to the figure of the feminine through metaphor, and the deconstructive utopianism which breaks up the claim of the social reality, to imprison us in the name of that which cannot be envisioned because it is beyond representation.

I am aware how difficult it is to understand this "unerasable" trace of utopianism. But this is why I refer to this moment—and I use the word reluctantly because it is a structural *moment*—as endlessly "there." It is not a chronological *moment* to be surpassed, which is why I refer to it as unerasable utopianism. Nor is it a projection of utopia: "this is what is would be like," our dream world. This trace of utopianism, that cannot be wiped out can be summarized as follows. The "subject" is never just the hostage of its surroundings, because these surroundings cannot be consolidated into an unshakable reality that defines us and by so doing necessarily limits possibility to the evolution of what already "is."

To imprison us in this way is to spatialize context such that the border, the de-limitization of context, does not "appear" either as the limit or as the indicator of the beyond. There is only the "inside," the presence of a present context. As such it denies the force of temporalization. As we have seen, in *Glas*, the logic of paragonality challenges this limitation on possibility as Woman. "The motif of the limit, of the frontier, of the parting line will furrow the whole sequence. From one mother to the other."[70] The further mistake challenged by the logic of paragonality is that the inside then becomes "identical" with psychic structure. As we have seen, this reduction is the mistake of object relations theory. To quote Levinas against the position that absolutizes context:

> The thesis is exposed imprudently to the reproach of utopianism in an opinion where modern man takes himself as a being among beings, whereas his modernity breaks up as an impossibility to

remain at home. This book escapes the reproach of utopianism—
if utopianism is a reproach, if any thought escapes utopianism—
by recalling that what took place humanly has never been able to
remain closed up in its site.[71]

I will return shortly to the significance for feminist theory of the uneraseable trace of utopianism in deconstruction. First, however, I want to
emphasize that the uneraseable trace of utopianism inheres in Derrida's
understanding of *différance*. It is not a political aside to the otherwise
ethically neutral mechanism of deconstruction. We must look more closely
at the play of *différance* as it relates to temporalization and to Derrida's
unique conception of the future as the not yet of the never has been. *Différance* can be understood as the "truth" that "being" is presented in time
and, therefore, there can be no all encompassing ontology of the "here" and
"now." Any reality, including the Law of the Father, established in and
through the symbolic, is always already divided against itself as soon as it is
presented. The disruption of temporalizing turns us toward the past—if only
in a very specific sense—because this past can just as well be conceived as
the future. The past itself never has been as a fully present and, therefore,
can never be a totally recollectable reality.

Time, or more precisely temporalization, disrupts the very pretense of full
presence of both the present and the past at the very moment that it makes
presentation and representation possible. In like manner, temporalization
disrupts the idea of an origin which we can just discover. The origin never
has been simply present, because we have always already begun once there
is a "reality" that has been "presented." As we have seen, this is the case of
the recalled mother, as Derrida writes of and to her. She is the "before" and
the "after," the "past" and the "future" that disrupts the enclosure of
symbolic. The origin, even as the recalled mother, is related to the trace of
the future of the not yet. The trace always postpones the return to an origin,
as it also disrupts the claim of the present to be all that is.

As we have also seen, deconstruction challenges the rigid divide between
the literal, the real and textuality. What is "real" and what it means to be
"realistic," to pay attention to the real, is always given to us in a text. "Text"
here is meant to refer not only to a literary text, but also to an established
context of meaning through which we read ourselves. The Derridean understanding of the force of temporalization as inherently disruptive of the
"presence" of "reality" adds another dimension to the challenge to the literal
as governing ethical possibility, including the possibility of Cixous' fantasy
of Other-Love.[72] The "real," as either the literal or as the psychologically
plausible, does not completely govern possibility. *Différance* subverts the
claim that "This is all there is!" The trace of Otherness remains. As a result,
différance also undermines the legitimacy of the attempt to *establish* any

particular *context*, including the masculine symbolic, as a kingdom which absolutely rules over us. Establishment is associated with force and with politics. The shutting in of context, the denial of new possibilities yet to be imagined, is exposed as political, not as inevitable and, more importantly, as unethical and, ultimately unjust.

> First consequence: *différance* is not. It is not a present being, however excellent, unique, principaled, or transcendent. It governs nothing, reigns over nothing, and nowhere exercises any authority. It is not announced by any capital letter. Not only is there no kingdom of *différance*, but *différance* instigates the subversion of every kingdom. Which makes it obviously threatening and infallibly dreaded by everything within us that desires a kingdom, the past or future presence of a kingdom. And it is always in the name of a kingdom that one may reproach *différance* with wishing to reign, believing that one sees it aggrandize itself with a capital letter.[73]

Lyotard also reminds us that the tyranny of the real, and with it the appeal to "reality" as the basis of all political action, denies possibilities that have yet to be articulated.[74] The attempt to positively establish the nature of justice is rejected as incomplete because descriptive justification still stands in for prescriptive justice. Prescriptive justice, for Lyotard, demands the end of the erasure of those whose claims do not fit the system. If we say this is what justice is through descriptive justification, no matter how sophisticated the argument, a litigant's claims must be translated into that system. If a victim's claim still cannot be adequately translated, her harm goes unnoticed. If she lies completely outside the current representation of justice, her harm, and indeed her very self disappear. As we have seen in my discussion of West, her argument should be interpreted to emphasize the way in which women are turned into victims precisely because the standard conceptions of justice, including those of an "overlapping consensus,"[75] do not allow for their claims to be pressed because their actual harm cannot be seen within the structure of argument offered. Thus, for West, we must redefine and continually transform such basic legal and normative concepts as freedom and equality.

For both Derrida and Lyotard, even the project of redefinition and evolution would reinstate notions of adequation to pregiven standards. The importance of Lyotard and Derrida, particularly when read in conjunction with the deconstruction of the rigid divide between the real and the literal, emphasizes not only that justice demands its own transformation as prior victims insist on the recognition of the damage and harm they have suffered, but that justice itself remain as unrepresentable as a full description of principle, either as system or theory.

Lyotard, for example, offers a definition of injustice rather than a positive representation of what justice is. Injustice is "damage [*dommage*] accompanied by the loss of means to prove the damage."[76] Lyotard condemns the tyranny of the real, in other words—including the attempt to establish the nature of justice—as "confining resistance within itself."

Resistance, in other words, is potentially silenced if we can only make our claims within the structure of justification offered by any specific theory of justice. Feminism, however, has a particular reason to rebel against the attempt to spell out what justice is within a society and culture scarred by gender hierarchy. As we have seen, a theory of justice or of ethics, traditionally conceived, tries to speak from some position independent of gender markings, because it seeks to rise above contamination by particular interests. If such a position were not possible, if it is not only not possible to be "nowhere," but to be other than a being marked by gender, then moral laws would be implicated in the gender divide.

As a result, we must take off from within sexual difference and not simply pretend to be beyond it. The struggle of feminism within law is to give expression to the sexual difference that has been rendered inarticulate within patriarchy. We must, in other words, be obsessed with the attempt to break through the very conventions and values that supposedly would have us identify justice within a society scarred by the gender hierarchy. The future of our "freedom" is *incalculable* within our current "reality," rooted as it is within gender hierarchy. As Hélène Cixous has written:

> It is impossible to predict what will become of sexual difference—in another time (in two or three hundred years?). But we must make no mistake: men and women are caught up in a web of age-old cultural determinations that are almost unanalyzable in their complexity. One can no more speak of "woman" than of "man" without being trapped within an ideological theater where the proliferation of representations, images, reflections, myths, identifications, transform, deform, constantly change everyone's imaginary and invalidate in advance any conceptualization.[77]

The alliance of feminism with the so-called "avant garde" in literature has precisely to do with this need to speak the unspeakable, to give voice to the imaginary. This is also why "tradition constituted inquiry" does not solve our problems of how we know what justice is. Alasdair MacIntyre, for example, criticizes Derrida for turning social pathology into a philosophy:

> This self-defined success becomes in different versions the freedom from bad faith of the Sartrian individual who rejects determinate social roles, the homelessness of Deleuze's nomadic thinker, and the

presupposition of Derrida's choice between remaining "within," although a stranger to, the already constructed social and intellectual edifice, but only in order to deconstruct it from within, or brutally placing oneself outside in a condition of rupture and discontinuity.[78]

The social pathology of "being outside in a condition of rupture and discontinuity" is what allows women to affirm the feminine, differently, as other than our mere opposition to the masculine. Whose justice? What rationality? Different as the traditions MacIntyre discusses are, they are the traditions of white men. Is MacIntyre's choice of characters an accident? Put somewhat differently, what, for a feminist, is the central problem of relying on the "conversation of mankind" to give us standards of justice? Precisely that it has been the conversation of mankind. Just "joining in" is not enough, since it is their *conversation*, their language. When we, in other words, have a tradition not scarred by the repression of the feminine, the creation of a new idiom may take us further toward the riddance of injustice than it does now. That tradition, however, is not ours.

The deconstruction of the full presence of the social reality and the rigid divide between the literal and the fictional show us why our context, in spite of its undoubted hold on our imagination, cannot pin us down once and for all. Undoubtedly, the deconstruction of the presumption that prescription can be reduced to the language of descriptive justification of tradition-constituted inquiry is important for feminism with its inevitable concern with opening up new idioms so women can be litigants. As Derrida explains:

> The structure I am describing here is a structure in which law (*droit*) is essentially deconstructible, whether because it is founded, constructed on interpretable and transformable textual strata (and that is the history of law (*droit*), its possible and necessary transformation, sometimes its amelioration), or because its ultimate foundation is by definition unfounded. The fact that law is deconstructible is not bad news. We may even see in this a stroke of luck for politics, for all historical progress.[79]

Within feminine jurisprudence, we can and should understand the deconstructibility of law to open up the space for the reinterpretation and reinvocation that allows feminist inroads into the law. And yet, these inroads should not be confused with justice. Deconstruction points us beyond legal reform to justice:

> [I]t is th[e] deconstructible structure of law (*droit*), or if you prefer of justice as *droit*, that also insures the possibility of deconstruction.

Justice in itself, if such a thing exists, outside or beyond law, is not deconstructible. No more than deconstruction itself, if such a thing exists. Deconstruction is justice.[80]

To be just to justice, we must not conflate justice with any given context, even the context that ended a particular injustice for women and the silence surrounding a claim unspeakable within a particular tradition. To quote Derrida:

One must be *juste* with justice, and the first way to do it justice is to hear, read, interpret it, to try to understand where it comes from, what it wants of us, knowing that it does so through singular idioms (*Diké, Jus, justitia, justice, Gerechtigkeit*, to limit ourselves to European idioms which it may also be necessary to delimit in relation to others: we shall come back to this later) and also knowing that this justice always addresses itself to singularity, to the singularity of the Other, despite or even because it pretends to universality. Consequently, never to yield on this point, constantly to maintain an interrogation of the origin, grounds and limits of our conceptual, theoretical or normative apparatus surrounding justice is on deconstruction's part anything but a neutralization of interest in justice, an insensitivity toward injustice. On the contrary, it hyperbolically raises the stakes of exacting justice; it is sensitivity to a sort of essential disproportion that must inscribe excess and inadequation in itself and that strives to denounce not only theoretical limits but also concrete injustices, with the most palpable effects, in the good conscience that dogmatically stops before any inherited determination of justice.[81]

Justice is, in this sense, inherently tied in with the not yet of the never has been:

Justice remains, is yet, to come, *à venir*, it has an, it is *à-venir*, the very dimension of events irreducibly to come. It will always have it, this *à-venir*, and always has. Perhaps it is for this reason that justice, insofar as it is not only a juridical or political concept, opens up for *l'avenir* the transformation, the recasting or refounding of law and politics. "Perhaps," one must always say perhaps for justice. There is an *avenir* for justice and there is no justice except to the degree that some event is possible which, as event, exceeds calculation, rules, programs, anticipations and so forth. Justice as the experience of absolute alterity is unpresentable, but it is the chance of the event and the condition of history. No doubt an unrecognizable history, of course, for those who believe they know what they're talking about when they use this word, whether it's a matter of social, ideological, political, juridical or some other history.[82]

Justice *remains*, as beyond our description, as the call of the Other, which Derrida, quoting Levinas, only dares to evoke as "the equitable honoring of faces."[83] Such honoring would demand the recognition of each one of us in her singularity, not in the commonality we share *as persons as defined by a particular context*, which is precisely why it is beyond our current conception of equality of respect. For Derrida, the most fundamental *aporia* of justice is just that: justice must be singular and yet justice as *law* always implies a general form. This general form can itself be understood as necessary for law if its not to be blatantly unjust, merely the expression of the preference or interest of the judge. Yet the general form still remains in conflict with "the equitable honoring of faces."

> How are we to reconcile the act of justice that must always concern singularity, individuals, irreplaceable groups and lives, the Other or myself *as* Other, in a unique situation, with rule, norm, value or the imperative of justice which necessarily have a general form, even if this generality prescribes a singular application in each case? If I were content to apply a just rule, without a spirit of justice and without in some way inventing the rule and the example for each case, I might be protected by law (*droit*), my action corresponding to objective law, but I would not be just. I would act, Kant would say, *in conformity* with duty, but not *through* duty or *out of respect* for the law.[84]

This *aporia* inheres in the call to justice. As an *aporia*, it cannot be overcome, it must be lived, and lived as a response to the call to justice. In this—and I dare to risk the word to emphasize the distinction—messianic conception of justice (which, technically, is not a conception of justice at all), or what Levinas calls "Jewish humanism," equity is not equality, calculated proportion, equitable distribution or distributive justice, but rather the infinite demand of the call of the Other. We *must* offer sanctity to the Other. Deconstruction, then, serves to expose the presumption of a determinant certitude of a *present* justice precisely through the recognition of the Other as Other, because justice itself operates on the basis of an infinite openness to the Other. "[I]nfinite because it is irreducible, irreducible because owed to the Other, owed to the Other, before any contract, because it has come, the Other's coming as the singularity that is always Other."[85]

It is precisely the reduction of justice to calculated proportion that has made it impossible to think of justice for women other than through our achieving equal measure to men. And yet this attempt to achieve "equal measure" has itself been condemned as unjust. Why is it "just" to take men as the standard, other than that they have always been so and, therefore, the cost is less? The question, of course, remains "To whom?" But, more importantly, from within a messianic conception of justice, the question is itself unjust. Here, we are returned, and profoundly so, to the way in which legal rhetoric all too often compounds justice with law. For example, the debate about the devaluation of women's work is referred to as the debate over *current* justifications for *comparable* worth. To say that we cannot find the basis for evaluating, because we cannot find a way to measure women's worth, and therefore translate the difference between men's and women's worth, is unjust. Moreover, the attack against "comparable worth" as inefficient because it would be too costly to reorganize the evaluation of work is also condemned as unjust. Yet, to demand comparison within the current terms of evaluation is also unjust because those terms inherently reflect the devaluation of women. We can know this injustice, even if we cannot know *justice* once and for all, because it rests on the devaluation of women associated with the repudiation of the feminine within the gender hierarchy. This gender hierarchy is imposed only by its own terms, not by natural necessity. There is no moral justification for perpetuating this hierarchy in the evaluation of work except by an appeal to "what has always been," which is a classic example of the mistake of deriving an "ought" from an "is." The equitable honoring of faces does not allow the confusion of calculable proportion with justice.

Thus, to summarize, the absolute determination of what justice is, is itself unjust. This *injustice* can be evoked through the example of the woman who is forced to translate her harm into the terms of their system. Why should we have to argue that pregnancy is like a hernia or some other disorder correlated with men and therefore recoverable in insurance policies as a disability? It is fundamental, then, that Derrida returns to the relation of justice and translation:

> It is unjust to judge someone who does not understand the language in which the law is inscribed or the judgement pronounced, etc. We could give multiple dramatic examples of violent situations in which a person or group of persons is judged in an idiom they do not understand very well or at all. And however slight or subtle the difference of competence in the mastery of the idiom is here, the violence of injustice has begun when all the members of a community do not share the same idiom throughout. Since in all rigor this ideal situation is never possible, we can perhaps already draw some inferences about what the title of our conference calls, "the possibil-

ity of justice." The violence of this injustice that consists of judging those who don't understand the idiom in which one claims, as one says in French, that "*justice est faite*," ("justice is done," "made") is not just any violence, any injustice. This injustice supposes that the other, the victim of the language's injustice, is capable of a language in general, is man as a speaking animal, in the sense that we, men, give to this word language. Moreover, there was a time, not long ago and not yet over, in which "we, men" meant "we adult white male Europeans, carnivorous and capable of sacrifice".[86]

In this time, "not long ago and not yet over," "man" is called to risk the impossible: to hear and to read the woman's language which is only now being written. To "read" our harms as we interpret them differently. To read the feminine language and its interpretations should be understood as the "man's" obligation before the reconstruction of feminist jurisprudence West describes. If they are to aspire to justice, they must hear our call. Their obligation is to address us, "Address—as direction, as *rectitude*—says something about *droit* (law or right), and what we must not forget when we want justice, when we want to be just, is the *rectitude* of address."[87] Deconstruction uncovers this obligation as an obligation, rather than as a paternalistic response to our failure to speak in *their* discourse. The address emphasizes the singularity of justice. The address is given to the Other. Justice "is" this giving which can never be completed. I address myself to you. But, Derrida insists, that only orients me correctly to the Other:

> This "idea of justice" seems to me to be irreducible in its affirmative character, in its demand of gift without exchange, without circulation, without recognition or gratitude, without economic circularity, without calculation and without rules, without reason and *without rationality*.[88]

Deconstruction gives, rather than represents, so to save the infinite idea of justice as infinite. This is why Derrida can risk the question "For in the end, where will deconstruction find its force, its movement or its motivation if not in this always unsatisfied appeal, beyond the given determinations of what we call, in determined contexts, justice, the possibility of justice?"[89]

In this way, the alliance of deconstruction and feminism is crucial if we are not to endorse a conception of justice that entraps us in what is as the only basis for a positive definition. We are constantly envisioning what cannot be seen or even imagined, a society in which human beings were not crippled by the hierarchical structure of gender identity. To break our silence we are forced to break up the so-called "real." But the *l'avenir* of justice does not mean that we can escape *our responsibility* to engage in political and judicial battles as they are present to us now. The call of the Other is concrete. Justice is beyond calculation, but we must calculate, participate, if we are to meet the obligation to be just. This call to participate, to calculate, to defend, takes on a specific meaning for women lawyers and law professors, for we are the ones, given where we are situated, who are called by other women to give justice, to represent them. We are called by other women to serve justice. We are also called by justice to be just and thus to recognize, to articulate, the injustices of this system of law and of right as it relates to women. But we must also recognize that as we articulate injustices against justice, we do not presume to define justice once and for all. We are called to work within the law but we should not conflate law with justice. As we work within the law we are also called to "remember" the disjuncture between law and justice that deconstruction *always* insists upon.

The call to remembrance is an ethical obligation that results from heeding the Other whose face demands the "equitable honoring of faces." This call to remembrance is also what Derrida calls "[t]he sense of a responsibility without limits, and so necessarily excessive, incalculable, before memory. . . ."[90] This responsibility to remembrance demands that we engage in the genealogy of any established system of justice. It demands that we trace the limits of our current conceptions of justice because they are grounded in conceptions of the legal person that are themselves exclusive.

This responsibility to remember, and to engage in the genealogy of current conceptions of justice called for by our obligation before memory, is crucial to feminism. Catharine MacKinnon's task is best understood to give us a relentless genealogy of our current conceptions of justice so that we will finally see the masculine bias that undermines the claims of our legal system. As important as this genealogy is for feminism, it is not enough. For the deconstruction of the pretense that *law* is justice can only take place against the promise of justice. "Debunking," as the genealogy of justice is often called, demands that we engage justice even if only as the possibility/impossibility of deconstruction, and more specifically of the deconstructibility of law. It is the insistence on justice, or more specifically on the messianic conception of justice, in which gender would no longer govern our rights, that is ultimately necessary for feminism if feminism's appeal to justice is to be other than the power of right reversed, what was once theirs will now be ours. As we will see, in my discussion of MacKinnon,[91] a world in which women become institutional power-players might give us revenge, but it would not heed the call to justice. Crucial, then, to a feminist response to justice, which is other than the replacement of men with women and which, therefore, in spite of its intent, is ultimately reducible to the perpetuation of the same, is this understanding of justice as the possibility/impossibility of deconstruction and, therefore, of the beyond to what "is" law.

Derrida's "unerasable trace of utopianism," in other words, shows us why feminism, as other than the aspiration to achieve the position of the masculine within the world as it is, is possible. However, we cannot simply reach back to an origin universally present for all women to find Woman, because we are always staging our reality from within a cultural context. We have always already begun, which is why temporalization keeps us from recovering the origin. To quote Derrida:

> The structure of delay (*Nach*träglichkeit) in effect forbids that one make of temporalization (temporization) a simple dialectical complication of the living present as an originary and unceasing synthesis—a synthesis constantly directed back on itself, gathered in on itself and gathering—of retentional traces and potential openings. The alterity of the "unconscious" makes us concerned not with horizons of modified—past or future—presents, but with a "past" that has never been present, and which will never be, whose future to come will never be a *production* or a reproduction in the form of presence. Therefore the concept of trace is incompatible with the concept of retention, of the becoming-past of what has been present. One cannot think the trace—and therefore, *différance*—on the basis of the present, or of the presence of the present.[92]

In Kristeva and in West, on the other hand, the basis for the difference between the sexes, which also carries within a "better" way of relating to self and Other, is mothering. The feminine, it should be noted, again takes on an ethical as well as a descriptive meaning. This ethical meaning, however, is rooted in some account of the "*origin*" of how women "are" different.

Deconstruction and the allegorical reading of the feminine it offers helps us to see that "the origin" of the ethical meaning of the feminine is not just here as a description. It is not the origin, but the productive power of poetic signification that *gives* us the ethical significance of the feminine as a redemptive perspective. The ethical meaning of the feminine then gives significance to the "discovery" of feminine specificity. But this specificity is not given once and for all. Thus, deconstruction reverses the relationship between the "is" and the "ought," at least as this relation is frequently presented in Anglo-American feminist theory. Through the elaboration of the "ought to be" associated with an ethical elaboration of the feminine, we can begin to "see" our gender "reality" differently. I want to emphasize, and I will return to this, that to write of the ethical significance of the feminine is not to advocate an *ethics* of the feminine or, indeed, even an *ethics* of sexual difference. As I will suggest later, such an ethics would only reinstate the present order of the same. Of course, as I have argued, given the bipolarity of gender hierarchy, the ethical relation to the Other demands the thinking of sexual difference, not its erasure. But this does not mean that we must develop a *positive* ethics of the feminine. To do so would once again conflate description with prescription. As such, the ethics would be unjust.

One aspect of this attempt to associate sexual difference with the deconstruction of identity logic more generally, is that the question of sexual difference achieves philosophical status. Thus, the thinking of sexual difference cannot be reduced to the political and legal questions of the "rights of women."[93] To think "Woman" as other than opposition is to resist the identity logic replicated in the gender hierarchy.

If, however, we only read Woman allegorically as the figure of the not yet, we would seem to be denying the power of "her-story" as tragedy. Worse yet, we would seem to indicate that the not yet of a new world for women freed from gender hierarchy had arrived, since the disruptive power of *différance* "is," now. But as we have seen, this disruptive power or force that cannot be completely closed off does not need to deny the terrible weight of the institutionalization of conventional gender relations. Derrida always makes the distinction between the dream of a new choreography of sexual difference that has been and cannot be erased, and of the oppressiveness of our current system and the reality of the oppression of women.

More importantly, if what is prized is only the possibility of a new choreography of sexual difference and not the feminine within sexual difference, we will reinstate the gender hierarchy in spite of ourselves. This is why Derrida emphasizes that a moment of reversal of the gender hierarchy is necessary. The question becomes, "How do we give body to the reversal?" Or, indeed should we give body to it? As we have seen, my central difference from Derrida lies in my insistence that we must take off from within sexual difference and more specifically, that we need to affirm the feminine through retelling and re-metaphorization of the myth. If we do not allow for the broad intervention of the power of refiguration through myth, metaphor and, indeed, fantasy and fable, we can potentially participate in the repudiation of the feminine. We must avoid complicity with the mechanisms of a patriarchal society that can only deny the value of the feminine, at the same time that we try to break out of the gender hierarchy that endlessly repeats itself through the reinstatement of rigid gender identity.

It is an illusion however, to think that, when it is convenient to do so, we can just step beyond or strategically relinquish the representations of the feminine, even if they are fictions. These fictions, in the sense that they are representations and not simply the reflection of a ground of feminine identity, still have the power to make themselves "true." We live within a system of gender representation.

3

Feminism Always Modified: The Affirmation of Feminine Difference Rethought

The Critique of MacKinnon

Perhaps the most powerful and compelling account of the "reality" of the female condition within the current system of gender representation has been given to us by Catharine MacKinnon. In MacKinnon's feminist recasting of Marxist materialism, to be female is to be the one who is fucked. "Man fucks woman; subject verb object."[1] This is the ultimate truth of gender in our society. Gender is the result of the objectification of woman's sexuality. Gender identity, in other words, is given by the imposition of male sexuality on women as forced sex. Our sexuality as they know "it" is what we are as women. Sex difference as "their" objectification of us is primary, gender division the result. Woman and/or feminine difference is thus reduced to our sexuality as "it" is seen by them. Our difference becomes the excuse for our subordination. As MacKinnon explains:

> Difference is the velvet glove on the iron fist of domination. The problem then is not that differences are not valued; the problem is that they are defined by power. This is as true when difference is affirmed as when it is denied, when its substance is applauded or disparaged, when women are punished or protected in its name.[2]

Our social world in turn is divided between the "fuckors" and the "fuckees." MacKinnon does not conclude that this fundamental division—fundamental at least to our genderized society and the world it gives us—is necessitated by nature. There is nothing inherent in the female genitalia, or reproductive system more generally, that makes this division inevitable. To quote MacKinnon:

Gender is what gender means. It has no basis in anything other than the social reality its hegemony constructs. The process that gives sexuality its male supremacist meaning is therefore the process through which gender inequality becomes socially real.[3]

But in spite of its socially constructed basis, the reduction of women to their sex is inevitable in our genderized system of the representation of maleness and femaleness, in which femaleness is viewed as an objectified sexuality that is "there" for them. Sexual difference as gender inequality is no less "real" for being socially constructed.

For MacKinnon, the first step in a program of social change is to face the "truth" of this reality. The world could have been different. Sexual identity as gender difference could have another meaning. But it does not have that meaning now.

If, in order to be gendered, something has to be gendered, those of us in the social change business could pack up and go . . . where? We would give up on changing gender, anyway. Of course it could be any way at all. That it could be and isn't, should be and isn't, is what makes it a political problem.[4]

In spite of the possibility for change, femaleness—and I use this word deliberately to separate MacKinnon's conception of femaleness from the understanding of the feminine I am advocating—has the "being" that has been given to it within our social reality. More specifically, femaleness is *literally* what men see it "to be." We are constructed, and completely so, by their gaze. What they see is then given "being" as *social reality*. MacKinnon's epistemology is that the world, in its objectivity, is the world of the male gaze in which women are objectified, reduced to their sexuality, and then subordinated as just that, sexual beings for them.

And why has the world as seen by them become the only world that is "there"? Because the gaze is reinforced and legitimated through male power. What they "see" is taken to be objective. The process of legitimation involves the identification of the male view as other than just one perspective. The male viewpoint is identified as the objective viewpoint uncontaminated by partiality. We are reminded here of Simone de Beauvoir's statement that men are in the right for being men.[5] The identification of their perspective as objective is what gives their vision ethical credibility. It is not one viewpoint on reality amongst others; it becomes the standard of accuracy itself. As MacKinnon explains:

We notice in language as well as in life that the male occupies both the neutral and the male position. This is another way of saying that the neutrality of objectivity and of maleness are coextensive linguistically, whereas women occupy the marked, the gendered, the different, the forever-female position. Another expression of the sex specificity of objectivity socially is that women have been nature. That is, men have been knowers, mind; women have been "to be known," matter, that which is to be controlled and subdued, the acted upon.[6]

For MacKinnon, the state, and more specifically the liberal state, reflects and reinforces the masculine point of view. Law is not neutral *vis à vis* the gender divide; law is male. Law not only reflects, it also reinforces the male viewpoint as legitimate, as law.

> The state is male in the feminist sense: the law sees and treats women the way men see and treat women. The liberal state coercively and authoritatively constitutes the social order in the interest of men as a gender—through its legitimating norms, forms, relation to society, and substantive policies. The state's formal norms recapitulate the male point of view on the level of design.[7]

This design, of course, is not the design that explicitly recognizes the hierarchical stratification between the genders as legitimate in the exercise of state power. Indeed, as MacKinnon recognizes, the liberal state's own claim for legitimacy *must* deny that such stratification continues to exist, at least as it is relevant to the "rule of law" which emphasizes the equality of all as legal persons, and therefore as subjects of right.

> In Anglo-American jurisprudence, morals (value judgements) are deemed separable and separated from politics (power contests), and both from adjudication (interpretation). Neutrality, including judicial decision making that is dispassionate, impersonal, disinterested, and precedential, is considered desirable and descriptive. Courts, forums without predisposition among parties and with no interest of their own, reflect society back to itself resolved. Government of laws, not of men, limits partiality with written constraints and tempers force with reasonable rule-following.[8]

But the so-called breakdown of the hierarchy of gender stratification is exposed as myth once we "see" that the very basis for neutrality rests on a "lie," the "lie" being that with the recognition of all of us as legal persons, the reality of gender inequality is erased. For MacKinnon, it must be remembered, the legal person is itself male-identified. Therefore, the myth that gender inequality has been erased is reinforced by the very language of neutrality. We no longer see the so-called objective perspective as the one legitimated because it is the expression of masculinity. To enforce law, as currently defined, then, is to reinforce the male viewpoint, in spite of law's claim to do the exact opposite. The so-called liberal state is only the rule of men, but now even more dangerous to feminist politics because it is disguised as the rule of law, with its legitimate claim on all of us, because it supposedly offers us "equal respect for persons." Better to recognize the struggle, the politics, that this view of law seems to make invisible. But, according to MacKinnon, this recognition is exactly what male lawmakers seek to prevent, because it would undermine male power. Liberal jurisprudence in this sense is ideology, because it masks the truth of gender stratification. As MacKinnon explains:

> The state is male jurisprudentially, meaning that it adopts the standpoint of male power on the relation between law and society. This stance is especially vivid in constitutional adjudication, thought legitimate to the degree it is neutral on the policy content of legislation. The foundation for its neutrality is the pervasive assumption that conditions that pertain among men on the basis of gender apply to women as well—that is, the assumption that sex inequality does not really exist in society. The Constitution— the constituting document of this state society—with its interpretations assumes that society, absent government intervention, is free and equal; that its laws, in general, reflect that; and that government need and should right only what government has previously wronged. This posture is structural to a constitution of abstinence: for example, "Congress shall make no law abridging the freedom of . . . speech." Those who have freedoms like equality, liberty, privacy, and speech socially keep them legally, free of government intrusion. No one who does not already have them socially is granted them legally.[9]

MacKinnon is repeating a familiar Marxist critique of the liberal state, but with the difference that it is now applied to gender. The Marxist argument in MacKinnon's version goes as follows: social inequality was not wiped out by the liberal state. Far from it. Instead, the liberal state, with its system of rights, serves as the ideology that now justifies the perpetuation of the social inequality it has purportedly overcome. The truth is the continuation of social inequality; the ideology is that such inequality, if it exists at all, is marginal because it has been legally erased. The structure of abstinence, more traditionally called negative liberty, could only be legitimate if it were *true* that the genders were actually equal. The social inequality of women means that the state must "positively" intervene to wipe out the gender hierarchy. But such intervention under the structure of abstinence, identified and justified as the condition of liberty, would appear as "violence." Violence to what? To whom? To the men whose status is protected. What is constitutional and protected is a social order based on hierarchy. As a result, the legitimacy of constitutional order is called into question by MacKinnon's feminism.

In this light, once gender is grasped as a means of social stratification, the status categories basic to medieval law, thought to have been superseded by liberal regimes in aspirational nonhierarchical constructs of abstract personhood, are revealed deeply unchanged. Gender as a status category was simply assumed out of legal existence, suppressed into a presumptively pre-constitutional social order through a constitutional structure designed not to reach it. Speaking descriptively rather than functionally or motivationally, the strategy is first to constitute society unequally prior to law; then to design the constitution, including the law of equality, so that all its guarantees apply only to those values that are taken away by law; then to construct legitimating norms so that the state legitimates itself through noninterference with the status quo. Then, so long as male dominance is so effective in society that it is unnecessary to impose sex inequality through law, such that only the most superficial sex inequalities become *de jure*, not even a legal guarantee of sex inequality will produce social equality.[10]

The First Amendment for MacKinnon is the classic example of the negative state because "[t]he law of the First Amendment secures freedom of speech only from governmental deprivation."[11] But, according to MacKinnon, what happens in "reality" under the rubric of First Amendment jurisprudence is that the rights of men are protected at the expense of the well-being of women. And what is the fundamental right of man so defined? It is not to speak, but to impose his viewpoint and to perpetuate our female difference at the cost of our subordination. For MacKinnon, that is what the debate on pornography is all about, whether or not men have the "right" to continue to subordinate women, and to perpetuate their own status as fuckors. It is not about the right to speak, but about the right to impose viewpoint; and to silence the challengers to that viewpoint. Under MacKinnon's view, it follows that pornography becomes the central culprit of the perpetuation of the very "femaleness" that makes inequality and violence to women inevitable. Pornography is how the male gaze is enforced as reality. The negative state, through its structure as abstinence, then serves to justify this reality as necessary for liberty. The social relation that is enforced is that men get to "fuck" women, and women have no right to resist the reduction of their sexual identity to the man's projected fantasy.

> Pornography, in the feminist view, is a form of forced sex, a practice of sexual politics, an institution of gender inequality. In this perspective, pornography is not harmless fantasy or a corrupt and confused misrepresentation of an otherwise natural and healthy sexuality. Along with the rape and prostitution in which it participates, pornography institutionalizes the sexuality of male supremacy, which fuses the erotization of dominance and submission with the social construction of male and female. Gender is sexual. Pornography constitutes the meaning of that sexuality. Men treat women as who they see women as being. Pornography constructs who that is. Men's power over women means that the way men see women defines who women can be. Pornography is that way.[12]

I want to emphasize the significance of MacKinnon's formulation that men's power over women means that the way men see women defines who women can be. First of all, it makes her own use of the word "perspective" inappropriate. Indeed, MacKinnon herself recognizes the significance of her own claim that a feminine perspective is "impossible." Feminism exists as the critique of male sexuality by showing it as male. Under MacKinnon's view—I use the word deliberately—there can be only one "perspective," the perspective of the male, even if, as MacKinnon says, she uses the word male as an "adjective," not as an unshakable designator of a natural reality.

> By the way, I mean the word male as an adjective. The analysis of sex is social, not biological. This is not to exempt some men or valorize all women; it is to refer to the standpoint from which these acts I have documented are done, that which makes them invisible, glorious, glamorous, and normal. By male, then, I refer to apologists for these data; I refer to the approach that is integral to these acts, to the standard that has normalized these events so that they define masculinity, to the male sex role, and to the way this approach has submerged its gender to become "the" standard. This is what I mean when I speak of the male perspective or male power. . . . A woman can also take the male point of view or exercise male power, although she remains always a woman. Our access to male power is not automatic as men's is; we're not born and raised to it. We can aspire to it.[13]

But an adjective or not, the male perspective is the one that constructs what we as women can be under the given gender hierarchy. Thus, it is not only for MacKinnon that in pornography (as fictional representation) "women substantively desire dispossession and cruelty."[14] So in pornography, so in life.

> Pornography participates in its audience's eroticism because it creates an accessible sexual object, the possession and consumption of which *is* male sexuality, to be consumed and possessed as which *is* female sexuality. In this sense, sex in life is no less mediated than it is in art. Men *have sex* with their *image* of a woman. Escalating explicitness, "exceeding the bounds of candor," is the aesthetic of pornography not because the materials depict objectified sex but because they create the experience of a sexuality that is itself objectified. It is not that life and art imitate each other; in sexuality, they *are* each other.[15]

We can only negate what we *are*, or we affirm our reality as sexualized objects. Therefore, MacKinnon must reject any attempt to affirm the feminine as it is manifested in the lives of actual women as having any normative significance. For MacKinnon, it is profoundly mistaken to emphasize feminine difference as having value. Such affirmations of feminine difference should instead be condemned as complicity in our oppression.

> Gender here is a matter of dominance, not difference. Feminists have noticed that women and men are equally different but not equally powerful. Explaining the subordination of women to men, a political condition, has nothing to do with difference in any fundamental sense. Consequently, it has a *lot* to do with difference, because the ideology of difference has been so central in its enforcement. Another way to say that is, there would be no such thing as what we know as the sex difference—much less would it be the social issue it is or have the social meaning it has—were it not for male dominance. Sometimes people ask me, "Does that mean you think there's no difference between women and men?" The only way I know how to answer that is: of course there is; the difference is that men have power and women do not. I mean simply that men are not socially supreme and women subordinate by nature; the fact that socially they are, constructs the sex difference as we know it. I mean to suggest that the social meaning of difference— in this I include *différance*—is gender-based.[16]

Thus, according to MacKinnon, in spite of their own differences, feminist theorists as divergent in methodology and tradition as Carol Gilligan,[17] Luce Irigaray,[18] and Hélène Cixous[19] make the same, serious mistake in their affirmation of feminine difference. For MacKinnon, the celebration of female difference is part of the *same* old story and therefore, not about difference at all. Women may value relations of care more than men; they may be less oriented to rights rhetoric; they may be more emphatic. But if they are, MacKinnon would insist that they are so as an expression of what men have made them to be. Very simply put, what has been shoved down our throats cannot be valued because this is the way women *are*, which is not to say that MacKinnon does not recognize that there might be a purportedly "independent" ethical argument for these values that are associated with women's reality. But such an argument would have to justify these values independently of empirical claims about what women are. What we *are* is oppressed, our "values," a reflection of that oppression. Values and morals understood only as a reflection of a material position is MacKinnon's application of an interpretation of the Marxist analysis of superstructure in the gender context. The female condition is the condition of subordination, what is manifested within it carries the taint of our violation. The "base" is that we are fucked; the superstructure, the ideology that we like it.

> Women have a history all right, but it is a history both of what was and of what was not allowed to be. So I am critical of affirming what we have been, which necessarily is what we have been permitted, as if it is women's, ours, possessive. As if equality, in spite of everything, already ineluctably exists.[20]

The fight against sexism, in other words, must involve the repudiation of femaleness which, in MacKinnon, is indistinguishable from the feminine. In this sense, MacKinnon also maps the feminine onto femaleness, which is why I have called her an essentialist. For MacKinnon "the damage of sexism is real, and reifying that into differences is an insult to our possibilities."[21]

MacKinnon's program, "Out Now," inevitably follows from her analysis of the gender system. The taint of affirmation of female difference can only be removed once relations between men and women are actually equal. We cannot know what we would be like once relations of equality have been achieved. Only once our domination and subordination have ended would it be possible to develop an affirmative program based on the celebration of what and who women *are*. Until that time we have the fight against domination. An essential aspect of this fight is the battle against the idea that sex, now defined as heterosexual intercourse, is a good thing, in any circumstances, but particularly in circumstances of female subordination. MacKinnon leaves open the possibility that the miracle of a "fuck," irreducible to the woman being fucked, might take place. But such a "fuck" would, indeed, be a miracle within our system of gender identity as it is currently constituted. Sex cannot be separated, in other words, from sexism.

Conceiving the sexual as a realm of the subjective, the final outpost of individual feeling, the touchstone for authentic emotion, is part of the way the sexual works as politics, so that sexual abuse can become what is called sex. Because sexism is basic and has been impervious to basic change, it makes sense that it would live in something socially considered basic, deceptively a part of the given, enshrouded with celebratory myth and ritual. Sex feeling good may mean that one is enjoying one's subordination; it would not be the first time. Or it may mean that one has glimpsed freedom, a rare and valuable and contradictory event.[22]

All sex is not rape, for MacKinnon, but most sex, indeed all heterosexual sex with the exception of "the miracle," is an expression of a system of sex difference which is based on women's oppression. "No More Rape" is the very minimal step that must be taken if we are to move toward the freedom that would make sex, as a rule, rather than as the exception, something other than an expression of our complicity in our violation. MacKinnon also rejects the "let's pretend" utopianism of certain liberal visions as wishful thinking that inevitably incorporates the gender system in spite of its intent. The imagination in MacKinnon is blocked by the all-pervasive reality of sexism. Even when we think we are dreaming of the beyond to sexism, we are, in spite of ourselves, caught up in it. We think, for example, that we have transcended our situation in and through love when we are only once again being fucked. Sexual freedom as an ideal is, for MacKinnon, the classic example of the danger of the pretense of transcendence. As MacKinnon tells us over and over again, no woman ever fucked her way to freedom. The so-called liberal value of sexual freedom, which pretends to be justified by a conception of the "ideal" of an imagined society, is an illusion which leaves women where they have always been: prone, with no purported reason for resisting their position. When we try to resist, we are accused of violating the ideal legitimated in the thought experiment of projected or hypothetical utopia. What, for MacKinnon, is always missing in these projected experiments of the hypothetical imagination is women's contribution. Their ideal, very simply put, is male, and by definition not ours. To quote MacKinnon:

This magical approach to social change, which is methodologically liberal, lives entirely in the head, a head that is more determined by present reality than it is taken seriously, yet it is not sufficiently grounded in that reality to do anything about it. . . . As a strategy for social change (as opposed to a narrative strategy for fiction, for instance), the "let's pretend" strategy is idealist and elitist both. How can its proponents not miss women's voices too much to proceed to imagine *for them* the world they should be part of building?[23]

The beginning of knowledge is to face the sexism and then to try to eradicate it, which is why MacKinnon emphasizes, and exclusively, the narration of our oppression now. Better a negative slogan based on that knowledge, than the pretense that the crippled individuals we are, and will remain in this system of gender identity, can imagine the world where this system of gender identity was not our truth. For MacKinnon, the "negative" reaction to the slogan "No More Rape" or "Out Now" itself signals the way in which the imagination is entrapped by sexism.

Not to mention that to consider "No More Rape" as only a negative, no more than an absence, shows a real failure of imagination. Why does "Out Now" contain a sufficiently positive vision of the future for Vietnam and Nicaragua but not for women? Is it perhaps because Vietnam and Nicaragua exist, can be imagined without incursions, while women are unimaginable without the violation and validation of the male touch?[24]

MacKinnon's militant, programmatic anti-utopianism is the inevitable expression of her argument that there is only one reality for women, and that this reality is the self-enclosed, self-perpetuating reality of male domination. For MacKinnon, women can't escape from the real world; it is not just pretense to think we can, it's the complicity that makes our continued oppression possible. Feminism as politics is a struggle for our power against theirs. For MacKinnon, it is time to face the struggle and join in the battle. According to MacKinnon, feminism must be a power-seeking ideology. She wants to destroy all the pretenses of equal respect which justify further complicity in our oppression.

To summarize, MacKinnon is a "realist" in two senses. First, she is a "realist" in that she argues for a descriptive methodology in which the reality of gender difference, understood as a determinate presence that determines individual identity as sexualized, is traced and brought to consciousness. Thus, she argues against those members of the Conference of Critical Legal Studies who have argued that social and legal reality is indeterminate. From the standpoint of the "reality" of women's subordination, indeterminacy is an illusion.

Indeterminacy, in this light, is a neo-Cartesian mind game that raises acontextualized interpretive possibilities that have no real social meaning or real possibility of any, thus dissolving the ability to criticize the oppressiveness of actual meanings without making space for new ones. The feminist point is simple. Men are women's material conditions. If it happens to women, it happens.[25]

Secondly, and in a related manner, MacKinnon is a "realist" in the colloquial sense in that she insists that women face up to reality. We must confront what male domination has done to us, rather than try to see the world of gender hierarchy through rose-colored glasses. We must, in an unmodified way, condemn our situation as it is now. To quote MacKinnon:

> Feminists say women are not individuals. To retort that we "are" will not make it so; it will obscure the need to *make change so that it can be so.* To retort to the feminist charge that women are not equal, "Oh, you think women aren't equal to men" is to act as though *saying* we "are" will make it so. What it will do instead, what it has done and is doing, is legitimize the vision that we already "are" equal. That *this* life as we live it now is equality for us. It acts as if the purpose of speech is to say what we want reality to be like, as if it already is that way, as if that will help move reality to that place. *This may work in fiction, but it won't work in theory.*[26]

The critique of MacKinnon's realism, then, cannot be separated from her analysis, which, as we can note from her own remarks, involves the separation of an analysis of "reality" from the creative expression of "fiction." Yet the central purpose of this work is to show that the "reality" of woman cannot be separated from the *fictions* in life and in theory for which she is embodied. As we have seen, this does not deny the reality of a constructed world, but only reminds us that reality is constructed through the metaphors in which it is given body. Therefore, there is no rigidly designated reality, even that of gender hierarchy. I accept the validity of MacKinnon's concern that we not justify our current system of gender representation as if the dream of a new choreography of sexual difference had already been realized. We must condemn our oppression, and there is no doubt that MacKinnon's vivid narrations of women's position in patriarchy have made a significant contribution to our "seeing" the world as genderized all the way down. The *power* of MacKinnon's writing lies in the different way of seeing she gives us. Our suffering has either gone unnoticed or been rendered acceptable as the inevitable result of gender difference for too long, far too long. But MacKinnon's theoretical mistake (which reinstates the *absolute* dichotomy between fiction and reality) carries within its own dangers, not the least of which, and in spite of her intent, is privileging the masculine position and reducing femininity and the feminine to a "fact" that can be known. Her understanding of the feminine and femininity replicates, ironically, Lacan's mistake, but without his understanding that male superiority is a "sham."

My critique of MacKinnon emphasizes the contradiction inherent in her own analysis of the all-pervasiveness of the reality of gender identity. That contradiction can be stated simply: without the affirmation of some kind of ideal, even if that ideal be MacKinnon's own implicit conception of freedom, feminism loses its critical edge because it can only reinforce the masculine viewpoint as all of reality. Certainly, MacKinnon's feminism condemns the "is" of women's condition as wrong. Feminism, then, is not merely descriptive, which is why the postulation of a countervailing ideal—even if in a limited critical sense, that under any definition women have not achieved freedom and freedom is important—is necessary. But for MacKinnon, and I agree with her, in our system of gender identity these ideals are themselves tainted by masculine domination. If there is no countervailing feminine "reality" or imaginary, then we are inevitably left with the masculine as the only standard by which we assess the condition of women. This power of imposition cannot be solved by confessing that feminism is "impossible" because there can be no countervailing viewpoint. Nor can it be solved by simply reversing the current order of vision, for example, what they "see" as sex, we "see" as rape. Who are the "we" that "see" and why do we, how can we, see differently so as to be able to reinterpret the meaning of our "sexualized" reality?

Put very simply, MacKinnon's central error is to reduce feminine "reality" to the sexualized object we are for *them* by *identifying* the feminine totally with the "real world" as it is seen and constructed through the male gaze. On one level, MacKinnon explicitly rejects the idea of an objective reality beyond social construction. For MacKinnon, as we have seen, the objective standpoint is the male point of view in disguise. But, for MacKinnon, the exposé is not that the emperor has no clothes. Their disguise is protected; their masquerade gets construed as "real" because it will always be protected by power.

> The *kind* of analysis that such a feminism is, and, specifically, the standard by which it is accepted as valid, is largely a matter of the criteria one adopts for adequacy in a theory. If feminism is a critique of the objective standpoint as male, then we also disavow standard scientific norms as the adequacy criteria for our theory, because the objective standpoint we criticize is the posture of science. In other words, our critique of the objective standpoint as male is a critique of science as a specifically male approach to knowledge. With it, we reject male criteria for verification. We're not seeking truth in its female counterpart either, since that, too, is constructed by male power. We do not vaunt the subjective. We begin by

seeking the truth of and in that which has constructed all this—
that is, in gender.[27]

MacKinnon, in other words, in spite of herself, gives us an unshakable,
objective, unmodified "reality." I am arguing, on the contrary, that this
reality is not as unshakable as it might "look."

"Being" cannot be separated from "seeing," but it cannot be reduced to
it either. We do not see what "is," directly. We see through the world
presented in language. As I have argued, this world is never just presented
as static, because the very language which allows us to "see" also allows us
to see differently, because of the performative power of the metaphors that
constitute reality. To reinterpret is to see differently. Of course, when we
reinterpret, we are seeing what previously had not been seen under the
previous interpretation. But the imagination cannot be effectively blocked
by reality, as MacKinnon believes. Indeed, it is precisely because of the
impossibility of this separation of "being" from "seeing," and then both
from the language in which the world is presented, that what "is" cannot
be reduced to the way one particular group "sees" reality. Other "visions"
are always possible. There is always the possibility of slippage between seeing
and what "is," even if we can only understand the significance of the slippage
from within another "point of view." Through metaphor we can modify the
world, because the world as it "is" appears in the language in which it is
represented. The feminist visionary who sees the world differently and tells
us of her world may be ignored, but "her vision" cannot be taken away from
her.

Ethical feminism "envisions" not only a world in which the viewpoint of
the feminine is appreciated; ethical feminism also "sees" a world "peopled"
by individuals, "sexed" differently, a world beyond castration. Through our
"visions" we affirm the "should be" of a different way of being human. The
"goal" of ethical feminism, which "sees" the "should be" inherent in the
feminine viewpoint, is not *just* power for women, but the redefinition of all
of our fundamental concepts, including power. Feminine power should not,
in other words, be separated from the different, ethical vision of human
"beings" sought after in the feminine, understood as a redemptive perspective. When "Anna Stessa arises," it is not in the form of an erection. (*Anna
Stessa's Rise to Notice* is one of the titles of the mamafesta in *Finnegans
Wake*.)[28] As Cixous explains:

> Her rising: is not erection. But diffusion. Not the shaft. The
> vessel. Let her write! And her text knows in seeking itself that it is
> more than flesh and blood, dough kneading itself, rising, uprising
> openly with resounding, perfumed ingredients, a turbulent com-

pound of flying colors, leafy spaces, and rivers flowing to the sea we feed.[29]

Within the sado-masochistic system of gender representation that MacKinnon describes, on the other hand, in which the masculine is on top and the feminine is on the bottom, the only alternative is reversal of *power*. One is either a slave, or a master. The political goal of empowerment can only be obtained by reversing the hierarchy. But the hierarchy is not dismantled, even if women were to take the upper position. Ethical feminism refuses this alternative as itself just the assumption of the masculine position, and therefore, as no "real" liberation. In MacKinnon's world of "fuckees" and "fuckors," an obviously heterosexual social reality, the only possible alternative to being a "fuckee" is to be a "fuckor." The sado-masochistic system of gender identity is, as a result, confirmed at the same time that it is supposedly being rejected. Without an ethical affirmation of the feminine which involves a different way of envisioning political struggle itself, we cannot slip beyond the replication of hierarchy inherent in the master/slave dialectic.

A very real danger, then, inherent in MacKinnon's transposition of the Marxist paradigm to gender is that it must reject any ethical ideal of the feminine as distortion, and therefore, it leaves us only with the struggle for power within the pregiven hierarchy. But there is another, more subtle, danger in MacKinnon's unmodified feminism. That danger is the implicit privileging of "masculine" identified values—for example, freedom over love and the desire for intimacy—and a masculine concept of the self. Andrea Dworkin tells us that Emma Bovary, in Flaubert's novel, *really* wanted *freedom*. I want to leave aside for the moment the problem of the specificity of literary language which Dworkin ignores and to which I will return. For Dworkin, Emma Bovary is the symbol of an exemplary form of false consciousness. Dworkin is using Bovary to bolster her own horror story of the *truth* of intercourse against the dream that sexual passion might offer us the possibility of transcendence. "Romance was her suicidal substitute for action; fantasy her suicidal substitute for a real world, a wide world. And intercourse her suicidal substitute for freedom."[30] For Dworkin, Emma Bovary's death was the result of her supposed misunderstanding that what she wanted was love, let alone grand passion.

But what kind of freedom did she want, even under Dworkin's interpretation? The freedom "to be" Charles Bovary? The freedom to enter into the realm of the symbolic and by so doing assume her own castration? The message in Dworkin's fable of the fate of the literary figure, Emma Bovary, can be interpreted to be that *we*—women—would be better off if we stopped desiring intimacy. But would we, or for that matter would anyone be better off? (Indeed, *can* we even stop our desire in a system of gender in which the feminine as the phallic mother, and the intimacy she figures, is cut off by the order of the symbolic?)

But I do not want to emphasize the *can*, but the *should*. We *should* not want to cast off our desire for intimacy in the name of the freedom *supposed* of the masculine subject. I refer to Dworkin's use of Emma Bovary as a symbol of Woman's false consciousness only to reinforce the inevitable reinstatement of the masculine when the feminine is repudiated. If the choice is between suicide and the assumption of castration, of course then the very use of the word choice is *truly* a mockery.

The problem is not just the more general problem of false consciousness unless we can come up with a countervailing standard, sometimes loftily called truth, by which we can judge the actual consciousness of women as false. MacKinnon has the answer within her own framework to the more general problem. For MacKinnon, what women desire now under patriarchy is by *definition* false consciousness. So we think that we want love and intimacy? For MacKinnon, we only think that way because that's how they want and need us to think so that we will continue to be available to them. Women's expressed desire is only an ideology.

> First sexual intercourse is a commonly definitive experience of gender definition. For many women, it is a rape. It may occur in the family, instigated by a father or older brother who decided to "make a lady out of my sister." Women's sex/gender initiation may be abrupt and anomic: "When she was 15 she had an affair with a painter. He fucked her and she became a woman." Simone de Beauvoir implied a similar point when she said: "It is at her first abortion that a woman begins to 'know.' " What women learn in order to "have sex," in order to "become women"—woman as gender—comes through the experience of, and is a condition for, "having sex"—woman as sexual object for man, the use of women's sexuality by men. Indeed, to the extent sexuality is social, women's sexuality is its use, just as femaleness is its alterity.[31]

Because we think we want love and intimacy, we put up with "them" in a way we would not otherwise. We learn to accept our gender identity as the one who gets fucked because that is what we must learn to desire in order to survive. To become a woman is to be a "fuckee." So, under MacKinnon and Dworkin's analysis, no matter what I or any other woman says or writes about the legitimacy, and indeed value, of love, we do so only to the degree that we are deluded and, in spite of ourselves, complicit in our degradation. Once we are convinced that in "reality" we are just being fucked, we will cease to value what they supposedly desire that we desire. I do not want to underestimate the political and ethical problem of any group of women insisting that what other women desire is to be condemned because we do not know our minds, and therefore we need someone who thinks like a man—indeed, how else could we think when we think, because, for MacKinnon, there is no other structure of ideas except theirs—to straighten us out. Nor do I want to disagree with MacKinnon that sexual desire is intertwined with social constructs, inseparable from the social meaning given to gender difference, although I would argue that MacKinnon completely externalizes the power of desire because she pays no attention to the unconscious. As a result, her analysis of feminine desire, and desire more generally, is overly simplistic. Desire, for MacKinnon, is expressed by women in one way, because male power makes it so. Certainly, if psychoanalytic theory has taught us anything, it has taught us that the relationship between desire and politics is extremely complicated and, indeed, much more complicated than MacKinnon herself would have it.

I now want to emphasize another irony in MacKinnon and Dworkin's position, that when we insist on the value and importance of love, care, and sexual passion, rather than self-assertion (and indeed, I would suggest that although MacKinnon does not define freedom explicitly, her implicit appeal to freedom seems close to affirming a definition of freedom as self-assertion) we unfortunately betray our own interests. MacKinnon continually reminds us that one of the cultural wrongs to women is that we have been silenced.

> Further, when you are powerless, you don't just speak differently. A lot, you don't speak. Your speech is not just differently articulated, it is silenced. Eliminated, gone. You aren't just deprived of a language with which to articulate your distinctiveness, although you are; you are deprived of a life out of which articulation might come. Not being heard is not just a function of lack of recognition, not just that no one knows how to listen to you, although it is that; it is also silence of the deep kind, the silence of being prevented from having anything to say. Sometimes it is permanent.[32]

Yet MacKinnon, ironically, participates in that silencing through her refusal to recognize the legitimacy of speaking or writing from the side of the feminine. I use the phrase, "from the side the feminine," deliberately. MacKinnon, as we have seen, argues that any attempt to speak or write from the "side of the feminine" inevitably ends up denying the "truth" of the reality of women's suffering and oppression. Her position implicitly suggests that any writing or affirmation of sexual difference can only justify the way things are now. The problem with valuing what has been or what is for women, is that we see the "truth" of our oppression through rose-colored glasses.[33] Her implicit confusion is a failure to distinguish the feminine from actual women. As a result, she does not understand the difference between

Carol Gilligan and the French feminine writers. Ironically she also fails to realize what she and Gilligan have in common.

Her accusation against Carol Gilligan is precisely that Gilligan affirms the conditions of our oppression in spite of herself. Gilligan, in her book, *In a Different Voice*,[34] tried to trace the difference between the moral voice of women and the moral voice of men. She not only tried to demonstrate that there was a difference between men and women in how they considered moral problems, she also tentatively and speculatively explored the reason for the devaluation of women's own moral voice under Kohlberg's schema. She did not deny Kohlberg's findings that women and men did, and do, *reason* differently when confronted with moral dilemmas. Her explorations included putting Kohlberg's explorations and her own investigations into a different interpretative, normative grid in which it was not implicitly assumed that the way men reason was not only different from women, but better. Gilligan should not, then, be thought to simplistically argue that all women morally reason in one way. Her conclusion, if it can even be called that, was that there was a correlation between a certain kind of moral reasoning and gender identity. She obviously would not reject the "reality" that some women within patriarchy can learn to speak, reason, and write from the side of the masculine. But to argue that all women do not think in one way when confronted with moral problems does not mean that there is no correlation between gender and moral perspectives. As MacKinnon herself has rightly argued, in order to confirm that there is a correlation with gender, we do not need to show that *all women* think one way or that the difference is unique to one sex.

> One consequence of women's rejection of science in its positivistic form is that we reject the head-counting theory of verification. Structural truths about the meaning of gender may or may not produce big numbers. For example, to say "not only women experience that" in reply to a statement characterizing women's experience, is to suggest that to be properly sex specific, something must be unique to one sex. Similarly, to say "not all women experience that" as if that contraindicates sex specificity (this point is to Larry Grossberg) is to suggest that to be sex-specific, something must be true of 100 percent of the sex affected. Both of those are implicitly biological criteria for sex: unique and exclusive.[35]

But once we give her the benefit of the doubt, Gilligan's central contribution lies not so much in her attempted exposure of the *reality of* gender difference in moral reasoning. Instead, she tries to make us think again as to why this difference in moral reasoning, to the degree that it could be demonstrated as correlated with gender or sex, is relegated to level three under Kohlberg's scheme. This devaluation in Gilligan is just that, devaluation. With this attempt to make us "see" that the devaluation is not necessitated by a gender-neutral concept of reasoning, Gilligan is very close to MacKinnon. Her modest suggestion was not that the form of moral reasoning correlated with women's emphasis on care as opposed to rights thinking should be hailed as inherently better, but only that a woman's different voice should not be viewed as *inherently* inferior simply because it was/is "woman's." She, in other words, is challenging the ideal as well as the "reality" that the way men do things should be taken as a norm. So is MacKinnon.

Part of Gilligan's political and ethical project was, undoubtedly, to legitimate women's speech and experience as valuable. The silencing of the victim occurs because their experience as they interpret it is devalued, if it can be translated at all into the current norms. Difference from the norm has been defined as abnormal, and thus inferior, as in Kohlberg's conclusions about the hierarchy of moral reasoning. Communication studies have shown that it is precisely this devaluation that can lead to silencing. The speaker/writer anticipates the rejection and internalizes the judgment of inferiority. By valuing the women's voice, the norm that justifies the judgment of inferiority is challenged.

MacKinnon, in spite of herself, participates in the very devaluing of the "women's" voice she abhors, and by so doing is complicit in that silencing. MacKinnon has been vehement, even brutal, in her condemnation of other women for collaboration. My suggestion is that her own devaluation of the feminine, so evident in her debate with Gilligan,[36] is itself complicity in a gender system in which the feminine is repudiated by women, particularly professionally successful women, because of its taint of inferiority. For MacKinnon, a central aspect of feminism is that we learn to believe women. However, believing women cannot be reduced, as MacKinnon would do, to believing their accounts of their oppression. Believing involves *believing in*. Believing in, allowing us credibility, includes the recognition of the legitimacy, not just the accuracy of our account. MacKinnon, in the end, does not believe those who disagree with her. We are written off. As MacKinnon reminds us over and over again, the personal characteristics and norms of moral and individual success within patriarchy are those identified as masculine. So we value freedom as self-assertion over love because self-assertion, and not intimacy, love and care, are associated with a masculine identity. It is that privileging of the masculine as the only legitimate that Gilligan again asks us to question.

It should be noted, however, that Gilligan's affirmation of the feminine demands a *normative context* in which women's experience can be "seen" as valuable. Gilligan, like MacKinnon, can be understood to want to "capture reality," if this time to show the inherent normative perspective of feminine "reality." MacKinnon assumes that Gilligan's appeal to women's difference, based as it is on what is, is contaminated because it justifies our current condition. I do not want to deny that Gilligan tends to collapse the "is" and the "ought," precisely because her methodology is that of a cognitive psychologist who studies the "actuality" of moral development as it is differentiated between genders. But as we have seen, what is implicit in Gilligan's work is at least a moderate, ethical affirmation of female experience as valuable. She wants us to question why such experience is not valued as a legitimate form of moral reasoning. MacKinnon reduces Gilligan's project to its justification of what is, because it has a supposedly empirical basis in the way women are. But I have suggested that this is the least interesting way of interpreting Gilligan's project. MacKinnon misses Gilligan's normative critique of a context in which the masculine view is assumed as the norm.

In like manner, MacKinnon confuses the writing of French feminism and the work of Jacques Derrida with the support of existing sexual difference as it is represented within the current system of gender representation within our legal system. MacKinnon, as is well known, rejects the notion that the legal analysis of equality should turn on our difference from men, or likeness to them. For MacKinnon, any theory of sex or gender difference, any affirmation of sex or gender difference, legitimates this view of equality within legal doctrine. According to MacKinnon, if we can show that we are like them, we can legitimately claim to have access to those positions in society formerly only open to men. We have to show that we meet *their* standard, since they are *the* standard. If we can lift two hundred pounds, we should be able to apply to factory jobs that require us to lift two hundred pounds. The wrong in sex discrimination under this view of equality is that a universal, female identity is being wrongly imposed on women to whom it does not directly apply. All women are assumed to be alike and, then, different from men. The wrong of discrimination, in other words, is the imposition of the universal on the particular, on an individual who does not fit the generalization. Women, on this standard, should be able to show that they are not like the stereotypical Woman, i.e., that they can lift two hundred pounds. To the degree that women are *like* men, they can be considered equal.

For MacKinnon—and I agree with her—under our current Supreme Court, this view of equality in which we must demonstrate likeness to men has become dominant to the exclusion of other interpretations, although it clearly does not reign in philosophical or jurisprudential circles. MacKinnon, and again I agree with her, wants to challenge the idea that equality should be premised on the *empirical* demonstration that we are the same as they are for purposes of a particular case. Equality, in other words, should not be defined as likeness, because the question "Like whom?" will inevitably involve the projection of the norm as male-identified. Equality is unattainable if we see it as not involving the end of domination based on gender. To quote MacKinnon:

> What the sameness standard fails to notice is that men's differences from women are equal to women's differences from men. There is an *equality* there. Yet the sexes are not socially equal. The difference approach misses the fact that hierarchy of power produces real as well as fantasied differences, differences that are also inequalities. What is missing in the difference approach is what Aristotle missed in his empiricist notion that equality means treating likes alike and unlikes unalike, and nobody has questioned it since. Why should you have to be the same as a man to get what a man gets simply because he is one? Why does maleness provide an original entitlement, not questioned on the basis of *its* gender, so that it is women—women who want to make a case of unequal treatment in a world men have made in their image (this is really the part Aristotle missed)—who have to show in effect that they are men in every relevant respect, unfortunately mistaken for women on the basis of an accident of birth?[37]

As I have suggested in the last chapter, the messianic conception of justice rejects the reduction of justice to calculable proportion, and this is precisely why such a conception is in alliance with feminism. To identify justice as calculable proportion, which is precisely the standard of justice MacKinnon finds in the Supreme Court, disadvantages women, given the privileging of the masculine position as the norm. The messianic conception of justice, however, is different from the Marxist critique of the liberal state that MacKinnon offers. The emphasis is not on power and the struggle for power, although such struggles *against* injustice are obviously necessary. Indeed, such struggles are mandated in the name of justice and for justice. But these struggles are not, themselves, *justice*. Therefore, the differentiation between any politics and the struggle for justice is made as the divide between justice and law is kept open. Such a conception of justice, then, cannot be reduced to another "power-seeking ideology." But MacKinnon's rejection of calculable proportion as justice, on the other hand, is done, not in the name of justice, but in the name of the *revenge* which turns the tables. Thus, given the "reality" that we do not "now" have power, the affirmation of sexual difference can *seem* to be nothing but the reinforcement of the likeness doctrine of equality which subordinates us because of our supposed difference.

Put somewhat differently, MacKinnon would argue that the affirmation of sex difference also bolsters what I have called "the ideology of lesser expectations."[38] To pretend that there is value in femaleness *now* turns us away from our *real* project—the fight for equality—which in MacKinnon, as I have argued, is not truly a battle for equality, but a struggle for revenge. The battle under the slogan "Out Now" is freedom from them, not equality to them.[39] The castration rhetoric should be noted. But, more importantly, for MacKinnon, the affirmation of sexual difference lowers our aspirations and potential. "For women to affirm difference, when difference means dominance, as it does with gender, means to affirm the qualities and characteristics of powerlessness."[40]

The irony is that MacKinnon also, if differently, promotes "the ideology of lesser expectations." Women are fucked. And that is that. Any attempt to write from the side of the feminine, any attempt to celebrate feminine desire, our sexuality, is rejected. Feminine *jouissance*, with all of its disruptive force, is denied as the pretense that allows us to make peace with the world as it is. In its worst form, according to MacKinnon, it promotes the illusion that "we can fuck our way to freedom"[41] or worse yet, forsake the battle for freedom altogether in the name of our supposed pleasure. Put simply: every minute in bed getting fucked, is a minute away from the battlelines.

There are several dimensions involved in MacKinnon's mistaken rejection of the French feminine writing of sexual difference and feminine desire. But the most important is her failure to see, whether or not she thinks the effort is successful, that the attempt to evoke sexual difference involves the indication of the beyond to the replication of this current system of *gender* identity in which feminine difference is opposition and evaluated only in comparison with the masculine norm. To recognize that we must think sexual difference—including the specificity of feminine desire—if we are ever to disrupt the repetition of the same is not, as MacKinnon would have it, to advocate a *rule* of how sexual difference or gender identity should be calculated or evaluated within the current gender dichotomy. Indeed, the very difference as other than the same demands that we reject the making of rules that have defined any existing ethic of gender difference within the confines of current gender hierarchy.

In like manner, MacKinnon's reading of Derridean *différance* is also confused because she identifies her own understanding of *différance* with the significance of sex difference within legal ideology. *Différance*, as we have seen, is not reducible to either an empirical or a normative concept of relational difference. Nor is a *différance* meant to indicate the empirical difference between the sexes as they are now defined by the gender divide. We are once again returned to the question of style. The writing style of indication that Derrida adopts in his essay, "Différance," is not a coincidence. As Derrida himself explains his "style":

On the other hand, I will have to be excused if I refer, at least implicitly, to some of the texts I have ventured to publish. This is precisely because I would like to attempt, to a certain extent, and even though in principle and in the last analysis this is impossible, and impossible for essential reasons, to reassemble in a *sheaf* the different directions in which I have been able to utilize what I would call provisionally the word or concept of *différance*, or rather to let it impose itself upon me in its neographism, although as we shall see, *différance* is literally neither a word nor a concept. And I insists upon the word *sheaf* for two reasons. On the one hand, I will not be concerned, as I might have been, with describing a history and narrating its stages, text by text, context by context, demonstrating the economy that each time imposed this graphic disorder; rather, I will be concerned with the *general system of this economy*. On the other hand, the word *sheaf* seems to mark more appropriately that the assemblage to be proposed has the complex structure of a weaving, an interlacing which permits the different threads and different lines of meaning—or of force—to go off again in different directions. . . .[42]

Derrida shows us that the force of *différance* disrupts the claims to identity in the particular areas he discusses—linguistics, philosophy and psychoanalysis, amongst other examples. The "style" itself is brought to the fore, to show, as I argued earlier, that any claim of the real, let alone of the self-identity of the real, is caught up in the metaphors of its own justification and its assertion of its status. Thus the mechanism of deconstruction is always "present." Derridean *différance* as a "general economy" can only be demonstrated within the particular context, which is why *différance* can only be evoked through the metaphor of *sheaf*.

Within the context of gender identity, *différance* disrupts the rigid replication of the male and the female as unshakable biological entities, or within Lacanianism, frozen structures of meaning of the masculine and the feminine. *Différance*, then, is not given an unshakable meaning within the system of gender identity that MacKinnon describes. Thus, it is a complete misunderstanding to identify *différance* with the current concept of *sex difference* embodied in American constitutional law. MacKinnon, unlike Derrida, wants to "capture reality" so that we can expose the "truth" of women's condition. She offers us a *critique* which assumes that she has given us the foundation of the real. Derrida shows us instead that reality can never be completely enframed.

Ironically, MacKinnon makes the same mistake as Lacan by reducing the feminine and femininity to the endless masquerade of being the phallus so as to stand in as the signifier for their desire.[43] For both Lacan and MacKinnon, this is what we are, within this system of gender representation, which means that we are "not," because to be the phallus is an illusion. According to MacKinnon, to become a sex "for itself,"[44] to "be" at all, women must reject the masquerade of femininity. Of course, Lacan would argue that such an aspiration is impossible in a system of representation that divides the world vis à vis the transcendental signifier of the phallus. But the greater agreement between Lacan and MacKinnon is that the feminine and femininity can be *reduced* to the lack of the phallus, a lack that can be *known* as the nothing it is. The illusion of her "real" presence is just that, illusion.

MacKinnon herself reminds us of the relation between knowing and sex. By definition, the one who knows, for MacKinnon, can only be the fuckor. Knowledge as conquest. And yet she announces what woman *is*: fuckee. But how can MacKinnon, a fuckee, know at all? She is the object. Feminist knowledge is, by her definition, impossible. If *Spurs* shows us anything, it exposes the masculine underpinnings of such an assertion that woman can be known as lack. It is only the one who believes in the illusion that he actually has the phallus who can also believe in the illusion that he knows what Woman is and that she is the opposite to him, merely the mirror of his essence.

MacKinnon is, of course, right to note that we are "framed" by the social meaning of female identity that has restricted and contained us. If woman is defined hierarchically as the other to the masculine, as his opposite, non-essence to his essence, and if men have power, this conception of woman does take on a reality. It is, in that sense, "real." But the *real* is only "there" within a context which is, itself, enframed; and that frame is again enframed. Derrida's tracing of the frame also indicates the beyond to the masculine vision of reality and the infinite regress of the enframing of woman. MacKinnon denies the beyond to the current frame. We are framed. Our being framed is our only *reality*.

Sexual Difference Rethought

It is this obsession with the beyond to the current system of gender identity which privileges the masculine, that French feminine writing shares with deconstruction. It is not, therefore, the same as Gilligan's affirmation of a different voice, rooted in the way women are. As already suggested, it is instead an attempt to show that within the psychoanalytic structures and social frames that have developed, *Woman*, the feminine, is what cannot be captured, and therefore belies the absolute hold of this reality over us as it also denies that woman can be reduced to the "*pas tout*." This beyond, however, can only be glimpsed through the "reality" of gender identity. As Irigaray firmly reminds us:

The men and women of today who deny difference are, in my opinion, indulging themselves in a type of unbridled idealism, for difference exists and society has been constructed on it. To abolish difference is to forget that women are enclosed as in private property; that women are underpaid workers, the foreigners subjected to all kinds of mutilation. That reality exists. . . . The question remaining: How can we discover the positive characteristics of this difference?[45]

It is precisely the last question, and Irigaray's endless attempt to evoke the affirmative characteristics of sex difference, that separate her from MacKinnon. But it is also important to note the combination in Irigaray of the denunciation of the way in which sexual difference plays itself out now within our system of gender identity at the expense of women, and her indication and affirmation of the specific morphological characteristics of the feminine which allow us to give body to our experience differently from the way it has been seen: as just like theirs or as absolutely Other to it.

Up until now this residue has been offered up to or reserved for God. Sometimes a part of it becomes incarnated in a *child* or was thought of as being *neuter*. This neuter (like the child or God?) represents the possibility of an encounter that was endlessly deferred, even when it concerned an effect arising after the event. It always remained at an insurmountable distance, like a sort of respectful or deadly no-man's land. Nothing was celebrated, no alliance was ever forged.[46]

The striving for an alliance between the masculine and the feminine, between persons, and within each one of us, cannot be based on the repudiation of the feminine or the assumption that both sexes are the same. "One sex is never entirely consummated or consumed by another. There is always a *residue*"[47] unless one assumes that the neutered individual "is" "now." An alliance that is not an imposition, and therefore the same old story spun out again, demands this recognition of the feminine. In the same old story, the feminine is only the negation, the non-essence to their essence. But feminine sex specificity for Irigaray is only specifically feminine when it disrupts the oppositional structure. Only then can feminine specificity be other than as non-essence. As the force of disruption, the lack that cannot be captured and understood as nothing (as the "*pas tout*"), feminine *sex* specificity, as opposed to gender identity, is also not reducible to the established reality of the symbolic. To affirm the feminine is not to posit a countervailing essence that is *ours*, but to expose that the structure of masculine essence is itself in relationship to feminine lack. Its relational definition denies the essence of "man" as an independent substance. The intertwinement of the masculine and the feminine belies the very structure that would define one apart from the other as an ontological truth or one against the other, so that the masculine is privileged as the self-determining term that unites the pair. The feminine as *Other* remains. To write as the residue, as the remains, is to echo the thing or object that women are defined as within the economy of the masculine symbolic. But feminine writing also indicates that the remains of the current system of gender representation are feminine precisely as they are remains, outside the system. Derrida's *Glas* shows us that the writing of the remains is the stylized undermining of the claim of identity, because only in such undermining do we uncover the remains as the residual to established social reality. The frame of reality implies the remains. As Derrida reminds us:

> Objection: Where do you get that *there is* text, and after all, remain(s), for example this text here or this remain(s) here?
> *There is* does not mean (to say) *exists*, *remain(s)* does not mean (to say) *is*. The objection belongs to ontology and is unanswerable. But you can always let-fall-(to the tomb) {*laisser-tomber*}.[48]

But what is different is this recognition that what "remains," is not to say "is." To say "is," is to once again reinstate identity logic which, within gender context, reinscribes gender as opposition.

For Irigaray, this letting go of the significance of the phallus as the establishment of the identity of the One is also recognition of the feminine specificity, and of the significance of sexual difference in which one sex or gender can never stand in for the Other, even as the fantasy of the masculine imaginary. To heed the remains of the Other as remains, has implications for ethics and for politics. The Other remains Other.

> Who or what the Other is, I never know. But this unknowable Other is that which differs sexually from me. This feeling of wonder, surprise and astonishment in the face of the unknowable ought to be returned to its proper place: the realm of sexual difference. The passions have either been repressed, stifled and subdued, or else reserved for God. Sometimes a sense of wonder is bestowed upon a work of art. But it is never found in the *gap between man and woman*. This space was filled instead with attraction, greed, possession, consummation, disgust, etc., and not with that wonder which sees something as though always for the first time, and never seizes the Other as its object. Wonder cannot seize, possess or subdue such as object. The latter, perhaps, remains subjective and free?
> This has never happened between the sexes.[49]

The remains as Other, is also the beyond, to the symbolic; the "future" of Lacan's real, and the hope of the "past" of the feminine imaginary. The recognition of sex difference in Irigaray, then, also takes on a utopian perspective which attempts to evoke what has never been, a social world in which the sex difference is not limited to our difference from them. In this sense, a concept of difference which reduces to opposition is, for Irigaray as for MacKinnon, not the affirmation of difference at all, but the replication of gender identity in which the masculine is privileged. Such a concept of difference, whether it be found in psychoanalysis or in law, is the reduction of the woman to the complement of the man: she is what he is not, "there" only to mirror "him" as he wants to see himself.

> Woman herself is never at issue in these statements: the feminine is defined as the necessary complement to the operation of male sexuality, and, more often, as a negative image that provides male sexuality with an unfailingly phallic self-representation.[50]

But for Irigaray, the identification of Woman as the nothing that mirrors him turns in on itself. Nor is Irigaray's evocation of the ethical relationship of Other-Love—which, as she always writes, would involve a different relation, not only of man to woman but more generally, of subject to object, human to nature, because the *basis* of ethics in the identification we associate with *appropriation* would be undermined—simply a restatement of what I have called the non-erasable utopian moment inherent in deconstruction. Yes, Irigaray is ever attempting to evoke that which cannot be seen, the beyond as the limit to imagination, but she is also trying to refigure through the imagined and, specifically through the figure of the angels, a society in which human beings were not divided by gender.

Perhaps the angels give body to Derrida's dream of a new choreography of sexual difference. The angels are neither masculine nor feminine, but sexed differently. In Irigaray, the angels figure as the messengers of the possibility that cannot be wiped out, even within the stifling system of gender identity that marks each one of us. As Lacan reminds us, gender identity as opposition turns the sexual relation into non-sense, rather than a loving alliance.[51] Fucking cannot work[52] in a system in which feminine desire cannot be given expression, because woman can only be as his slave, or in MacKinnon's words the "fuckee." But to deny carnality as necessary is only a reaction, and more importantly, a reaction that would leave the system of gender identity in place. To fuck or not to fuck should not be the question, but rather how can "we," man to woman, woman to woman, man to man, ever hope to make love?

> A sexual or carnal ethics would demand that both angel and body be found together. This is a world that must be constructed

or reconstructed. A genesis of love between the sexes has yet to come about, in either the smallest or largest sense, or in the most intimate or political guise. It is a world to be created or recreated so that man and woman may once more or finally live together, meet and sometimes inhabit the same place. . . . As Heidegger, among others, has written, this link must forge an alliance between the divine and the mortal, in which a sexual encounter would be a celebration, and not a disguised or polemic form of the master-slave relationship.[53]

This dream of sex difference involves writing from the side of the feminine so as to express not only our sexuality, but our desire for an alliance beyond the master/slave dichotomy. The desire for this alliance is itself associated in Irigaray with the feminine, as the threshold located in the specificity of our desire for peace. To quote Irigaray:

Sexual difference is one of the important questions of our age, if not in fact the burning issue. According to Heidegger, each age is preoccupied with one thing, and one alone. Sexual difference is probably that issue in our own age which could be our salvation on an intellectual level.

But wherever I turn, whether to philosophy, science or religion, I find that this underlying and increasingly insistent question remains silenced. It is as if opening up this question would allow us to put a check on the many forms of destruction in the universe. . . .[54]

Irigaray does dream of such a world and hopes that some of us even now may try to live at the threshold and cherish the dream rather than remain cogs in the machine of the master/slave dialectic; or simply react to it, thereby merely confirming this world in which the sexual relation is identified with sado-masochism. It is this dream and indeed, the very language of dreaming, that again separates Irigaray from MacKinnon. The vision of women becoming a "sex for themselves" that MacKinnon advocates, once again legitimates the passing out of "sexual identity cards."[55]

But, more importantly, MacKinnon's reassertion of a "pure," uncontaminated identity for women, as the vision of what we might become, is ethically problematic since it would reconfine us rather than help us to dance free from rigid gender identities. As we will see, this desire for an uncontaminated gender identity, and a body kept free from what is other, outside, non-identical, can itself be understood as another example of MacKinnon's reconfirmation of the masculine position as that which is to be valued. We are returned again to the complexity of Irigaray's writing of the feminine, a complexity that MacKinnon herself fails to note, in the identification of the French feminine writing with Gilligan's affirmation of the different voice.

But let me summarize once more why this dream of a new choreography of sexual difference involves the affirmation of the feminine. In a social world characterized by the bipolarity of current gender identity, there is no way to achieve the third "position," even figured as the angel, except through the thinking and living of sexual difference. The repudiation of the feminine is, itself, part of this social order. The feminine is the underside of the hierarchy, with no "positive" value; the negation of the positive—the masculine—the non-essence to their essence, the nothing to their substance. The specificity of the feminine cannot "be" under "their" system in which we are completely enclosed in their projected image of femininity. MacKinnon totally accepts this vision of the feminine as the current stereotypes of femininity. Irigaray ultimately rejects that we are ever completely identified as the object of vision enforced as an established reality. The feminine, in Irigaray, "is" only as we evoke it through writing, a writing that constantly experiments with the limits of a discourse that shuts out our "reality" by delineating it within a masculine discourse. Irigaray distinguishes between an appeal to what women are as *the basis* for feminine difference, such as is done by Gilligan, and writing from the side of the feminine. What the feminine "is," is not the question. The first approach would once again turn us into an object of study within their discourse.

> In other words, the issue is not one of elaborating a new theory of which woman would be the *subject* or the *object*, but of jamming the theoretical machinery itself, of suspending its pretension to the production of a truth and of a meaning that are excessively univocal. Which presupposes that women do not aspire simply to be men's equals in knowledge. That they do not claim to be rivaling men in constructing a logic of the feminine that would still take onto-theo-logic as its model, but that they are rather attempting to wrest this question away from the economy of the logos. They should not put it, then, in the form "What is woman?" but rather, repeating/interpreting the way in which, within discourse, the feminine finds itself defined as lack, deficiency, or as imitation and negative image of the subject, they should signify that with respect to this logic a *disruptive excess* is possible on the feminine side.[56]

In order to evoke this disruptive excess, the remains, as feminine difference, we must work through the metaphors of the feminine; we cannot simply reject them. Yes, Irigaray also reminds us, Woman has been hemmed in by metaphors.

Stifled beneath all those eulogistic or denigratory metaphors, she is unable to unpick the seams of her disguise and indeed takes a certain pleasure in them, even gilding the lily further at times. Yet, ever more hemmed in, cathected by tropes, how could she articulate any sound from beneath this cheap chivalric finery? How find a voice, make a choice strong enough, subtle enough to cut through those layers of ornamental style, that decorative sepulcher, where even her breath is lost. Stifled under all those airs. She has yet to feel the need to get free of fabric, reveal her nakedness, her destitution in language, explode in the face of them all, words too. For the imperious need for her shame, her chastity—duly fitted out with the belt of discourse,—of her decent modesty, continues to be asserted by every man.[57]

But our hope of displacement of the metaphors, which are a disguise, lies in the slippage of meaning that metaphorical transference makes possible. We *cannot* simply reject the metaphors without repudiating the feminine once again.[58] To despise the metaphors of Woman, as MacKinnon does, is once again to despise ourselves as we have been "taught" to do.

The Hope of *Mimesis*

The disguise of the norm as male is ripped away by MacKinnon: neutrality is "their" ideology used to mask women's subordination. But this exposure is not enough if it only leaves us with their reality, the masculine, and correspondingly with the repudiation of the feminine as inferior to their superiority, abnormal to their norm, the lack to their presence. Instead, we must circle within the metaphors of the feminine. But this circling is not merely a repetition, because it affirms the feminine in a way foreign to patriarchy and, unfortunately, foreign to MacKinnon's own position. To understand what this circling from within entails, we must look to Irigaray's writing on *mimesis*. To quote Irigaray:

There is, in an initial phase, perhaps only one "path," the one historically assigned to the feminine: that of *mimicry*. One must assume the feminine role deliberately. Which means already to convert a form of subordination into an affirmation, and thus to begin to thwart it. Whereas a direct feminine challenge to this condition means demanding to speak as a (masculine) "subject," that is, it means to postulate a relation to the intelligible that would maintain sexual indifference.[59]

To write as Woman is to refute the hold of their discourse. But we cannot simply declare ourselves freed from prison. We are hemmed in.

Mimesis, in other words, is the way we can move within the gender hierarchy to engage with their metaphors of us, and give them new meaning, precisely because of the excess of what is not implicit in metaphor. *Mimesis*, however, is also a feminine "capacity" that helps us to evoke the disruptive excess, otherness, as feminine. In this unique sense, *mimesis* in Irigaray is doubly effeminate. First, *mimesis* allows us to circle within the feminine in order to live sexual difference differently, because this time *mimicry* is affirmative. *Mimesis* implies an evaluation of the feminine. Secondly, *mimesis* is also associated with the feminine positioning within the gender hierarchy, as "the speech" of the object. And why, exactly, is *mimesis*, as a mode of being in the world, correlated with the feminine as the speaking of the object? For Irigaray, women are, first of all, the source of masculine *mimesis*. "As guardians of 'nature,' are not women the ones who maintain, thus who make possible, the resource of *mimesis* for men? For the logos?"[60] As so defined, we are also objects. But how do the objects "speak"? We speak through "identification with" other objects. This "identification with" is also *mimesis*.

There is, then, another dimension beyond the turning of subordination into affirmation through the enhancement of *mimesis*. *Mimesis*, as Irigaray uses the word—as an ethical relation to otherness—is very close to Adorno's usage.[61] *Mimesis*, understood as a non-violent ethical relation to what is Other, and not as a mode of artistic representation that supposedly mimics, or more precisely mirrors, the real in art, is an expression of Adornian non-identity in which the subject does not seek to identify or categorize the object, but rather to let the object be in its difference. The subject, in other words, does not seek to know the object, in the sense in which knowledge is traditionally defined as identification—this is what the object *is*—through mirroring in the mind. Instead, *mimesis* identifies with, rather than identifying as. Identifying with, even as counter-pole, still does not fully express the mimetic capacity, but it does separate this understanding of *mimesis* from the conception of the subject or mind as mirror that appropriates the object in its own categories.

Mimesis involves the relinquishment of the rigid subject/object divide, a relinquishment associated with the feminine position in which the feminine is only defined as an object within the masculine symbolic. Mimetic identification involves letting the object come to the writer. The object takes over. The process of letting the object take over is beautifully described by Clarice Lispector in the engagement of the writer with a rose.

> The rose is the feminine flower that gives of itself all and so completely that the only joy left to it is to have given itself. Its

perfume is an insane mystery. When its scent is deeply inhaled it touches the intimate depths of the heart and leaves the inside of the entire body perfumed. The way it opens into womanhood is very beautiful; the petals taste good in the mouth—all you have to do is try them. But the rose isn't *it*. It is *she*.[62]

In the sense of letting one's self be taken over by the object, the writer loses control. Rather than as an active "knower," the writer becomes the receiver, but this reception is not passive. Identifying with demands the reception of the Other as other. The housewarming that Adorno's ethical understanding of *mimesis* implies is not a reaching out that seeks to appropriate so that the subject is still in control of what it seeks to touch. The Other is embraced, but not absorbed. I am using "feminine" language deliberately. *Mimesis*—as Adorno tries to evoke mimetic capacity as an attempt at an ethical relationship to otherness—is not easily, if at all, expressible in "phallic" language.[63] *Mimesis*, so understood, cannot easily be grasped in its so-called essence. The mistake of trying to grasp the truth of *mimesis* has been eloquently summarized by Phillipe Lacoue-LaBarthe:

> [The act of differentiating, appropriating, identifying, *verifying* mimesis] would without fail betray the essence or property of mimesis, if there were an essence of mimesis or if what is "proper" to mimesis did not lie precisely in the fact that mimesis has no "proper" to it, ever (so that mimesis does not consist in the improper, either, or in who knows what "negative" essence, but *ek-sists*, or better yet "de-sists" in this appropriation of everything supposedly proper that necessarily jeopardizes property "itself"). Which would betray its essence, in other words, if the "essence" of mimesis were not precisely absolute vicariousness, carried to the limit (but inexhaustible), endless and groundless—something like an infinity substitution and *circulation* (already we must again think of Nietzsche): the very lapse itself of essence.[64]

Mimesis as *de-sistance* is the "very lapse itself of essence" that makes the feminine, as *Other* than opposition, possible and yet allows us to affirm rather than repudiate the feminine. The very attempt to evoke rather than explain what *mimesis is*, demands the questioning of traditional "phallic" discourse. Adorno was very concerned with the development of a style that would allow for the expression of an interpellation of oneself with the other that is not an appropriation of the other by the subject.

But it is not *just* this shared need for the disruption of traditional discourse that allows Irigaray to write of the association of *mimesis* with the feminine. For Irigaray, the feminine, as we have seen, is connected to mimetic capacity because of the "identification" of the feminine as *itself*, Other, object. Feminine interpellation with the Other, as the object, is not reducible to subject/object relations precisely because we are defined as objects ourselves.[65] *Mimesis* indicates the relation of the feminine to the Other, in a social world in which the feminine Other is inexpressible as subject. "Subjectivity denied to woman: indisputably this provides the financial backing for every irreducible constitution as an object: of representation, of discourse, of desire. Once imagine that woman imagines and the object loses its fixed, obsessional character."[66] *Mimesis*, in other words, is the relationship to the object, imagined by the woman imagining her connection to Otherness, as an object.

But we now have to look at what exactly is the status of Irigaray's claim about the alliance of the feminine with *mimesis*. Is this association a claim about how all women are? The answer is no, and explicitly so. Here again we are returned to the difference between writing from the position of the feminine—even if to bring "feminine reality" into view, a revelation which is always more than just finding what is already "*there*"—and merely describing what women are. Indeed, the very methodology that attempts to identify what women *are* as the *basis* for the writing of the feminine is, itself, rejected as the very discourse in which the feminine can be again *grasped* as object, and therefore reduced to a knowable "thing." Positioned as objects, yes, but even within that positioning, we can slip out of their grasp. We cannot, in other words, be rigidly defined as subjects of examination.

> We can assume that any theory of the subject has always been appropriated by the "masculine." When she submits to (such a) theory, woman fails to realize that she is renouncing the specificity of her own relationship to the imaginary. Subjecting herself to objectivization in discourse—by being "female." Re-objectivizing her own self whenever she claims to identify herself "as" a masculine subject. A "subject" that would re-search itself as lost (maternal-feminine) "object"?[67]

We can, then, state the difference between Gilligan and Irigaray, at least to the degree that Gilligan roots her reevaluation of the feminine in a study of the way women supposedly *are*. To turn ourselves into subjects of study is still to turn ourselves into "their" objects, because the feminine cannot be positioned within the Lacanian gender hierarchy as a subject. Writing from the position of the feminine involves an explicit, ethical affirmation which in itself is a performative challenge to the devaluation of the feminine. We affirm the feminine, through *mimesis*, even as we recognize that the feminine cannot be reduced or identified with the lives of actual women, nor adequately represented as the elsewhere to masculine discourse.

For MacKinnon, on the other hand, we are fated to remain victims within patriarchal reality. When we perform the feminine, we only perform the masquerade for them. By definition, we cannot translate our feminine difference into the established masculine discourse, but we also cannot circle within to indicate the beyond through the affirmation of the threshold of sexual difference. We can, at the very best, in Lyotard's sense, become litigants.[68] Consciousness-raising, which, for MacKinnon, is the feminist method, involves the fundamental recognition of our victimization. We expand the boundaries of legal discourse in order to become litigants. MacKinnon's own writing on sexual harassment is a significant example of the legal creativity necessary for the wrongs to women to enter litigation. But in a more profound sense, the writing of feminine difference that allows for the remembrance, always provisional, of the excluded feminine, is rejected because the performative aspect of the re-metaphorization of the feminine, through *mimesis*, is denied.

Against her best intentions, MacKinnon reinforces the definition of femininity as complementarity which she associates with the standard of likeness as it has been incorporated into the ideal of equality. Femininity, as she understands "it," now is only as their complement, the object fashioned by their gaze.[69] On the level of the ideal, she also reinstates the privileging of the masculine, for the ultimate goal is that we become like them, in freedom from the condemnation of femininity. Superficially, of course, she rejects the old dream of symmetry, which measures us against the male norm. However, MacKinnon cannot but fall into that very old dream given the limits of her own theoretical discourse, which necessarily repudiates the feminine as femininity because she can only "see" from the masculine perspective.

There is a second reason, however, for why it is politically, and even legally, important to affirm the "other" dream of a new choreography of sexual difference, a dream which I have suggested involves the writing of sexual difference as the feminine, and not simply the postulation of a neutral person, no longer defined by the bipolarity of our current representations of gender identity. The psychoanalytic framework, particularly as it has been developed by Lacan, teaches us that the law and the legal system cannot be separated from the Law of the Father in and through which gender identity is established.[70] It also follows from MacKinnon's own position that we can only achieve legal equality if we challenge the very basis of gender identity as it perpetuates and justifies our subordination. But this subordination is mandated by the very gender divide which is defined as hierarchy. We are subordinated, in other words, by the definition of "our" gender imposed by the symbolic. This interdependence of law with the law of gender definition explains why we cannot just settle for changes in the legal system, because these reforms must themselves involve a challenge to gender identity. Otherwise—and we have certainly lived to testify to this reality—even the most modest legal reforms will be undermined at every stage by the reassertion of the law of gender in which the feminine is only our difference from them, and is devalued as inferior.

I do want to note that the idea that law cannot be separated from gender identity has implications for a debate that has recently been taking place between the groups that have been labelled communitarians and liberals. Thinkers like John Rawls, in an attempt to draw out constitutional essentials on which we can have at least hypothetical agreement, argue that we must not make constitutional law dependent on the resolution of the debate about the nature of the subject.[71]

The writing of the feminine—which insists that the polarity of gender has affected all aspects of our lives, including the concept of the subject—does challenge existing conceptions of subjectivity as masculine. But it also insists that such a challenge is necessary, not only for the law to open itself to feminine difference, but even for the reestablishment of the modest legal gains of the late Sixties and early Seventies. In this sense, I do not believe that a theory of constitutional essentials can escape the issue of the subject altogether. But to show just why this is the case, let me probe more deeply into the need and the significance of utopianism in feminism, and more specifically, into the connection between utopianism and the writing of the feminine.

The "Herethics" of Carnality

As we have seen, MacKinnon reminds us that *all* of our concepts are genderized. Under her *own* unmodified feminism, the idea of the self would have to be genderized as well. For MacKinnon, the feminine self is the one "who gets fucked." Again to summarize, femininity is the trap in which we ensnare ourselves in our distorted desire "to be fucked." To quote MacKinnon: "I'm saying femininity as we know it is how we come to want male dominance, which most emphatically is not in our interest."[72] The masculine self is defined as the "one who fucks," and "fucks over," the other. What is the worst imaginable disaster to this masculine self? To be fucked. The *man* is the one who penetrates, not the one who is penetrated. That's what, according to MacKinnon, makes him a man. But we now have to ask why is it the end of the world "to be fucked" if you're a man? The obvious answer is that this is what happens to women. Whatever happens to women is to be avoided in the name of "being" men. That is how he *knows* he is a man, he does not let *that* happen to him (which may provide a partial explanation of the homophobia directed toward gay men). But why is it the end of the world "to be fucked"? Why do we think of all forms of oppression in terms of "getting fucked"? Is the problem with "getting fucked," or is it with the system of gender representation that defines the masculine, and the self, correspondingly, as the one who does not "get fucked?"

MacKinnon, of course, has easy answers to these questions: to "be fucked" is to be turned into an object of masculine desire in which the woman, not the man, loses her subjectivity, her self. Yet, in all erotic passion, the boundaries of selfhood yield to the touching of the Other. Does MacKinnon successfully distinguish the vulnerability and risk to the self involved in eroticism from the specific feminine position of "being fucked"? Unlike Irigaray, Cixous and even the early Kristeva, she does not incorporate an affirmation of carnality into her political program. Indeed, she cannot affirm carnality as long as she recasts the subject as seeking freedom, not intimacy, in sex. If it is accepted that to be masculine, to be a self, is to not "be fucked," then if women are "fucked," we cannot be *individuals*. Therefore, women cannot be individuals until they give up "getting fucked." As we have seen, the only slogan that can follow from this acceptance of the definition of the self as the one who does not "get fucked" is MacKinnon's "Out Now." Here again, we see the implicit aspiration "to be" like a man.

I completely agree with MacKinnon that in a system of gender representation like our own, we do not choose heterosexuality. The reality of the sanction against those who attempt to define their sexuality differently makes meaningful choice impossible. (One also, then, *cannot choose* homosexuality. The ideology inherent in the words "sexual preference" is exposed as ideology.) MacKinnon remarks:

> Those who think that one chooses heterosexuality under conditions that make it compulsory should either explain why it is not compulsory or explain why the word choice can be meaningful here. And I would like you to address a question that I think few here would apply to the workplace, to work, or to workers: whether a good fuck is any compensation for getting fucked.[73]

I take MacKinnon's question with all the seriousness it deserves. Having done both, I do not simply want to insist that "getting fucked" and working in a factory do not yield the same experience of domination, although there is a distinction upon which I would insist, which is why I, in part, reject the transposition of the Marxist paradigm *without modification* into the realm of gender identity. Of course, we cannot escape the reality of the economics of sex, and the way exploitation affects, as MacKinnon has argued, the very definition of sex and sexuality. Yet when we go on strike against an employer we do not risk living mutilation in the same way we do when we cut ourselves off from the affective and, if we interpret ourselves as solely heterosexual, erotic relationships we have with men.

But I wish to ask an even more fundamental question: why should we endorse a view of selfhood and, more particularly, of the body, defined from the side of the masculine—as the one who does not "get fucked"? If this is what it means to be a self, why would a woman desire to become "it"? (I use the word "it" deliberately.) As a result, in order to challenge MacKinnon's apparatus of gender identification, we also need to challenge the two kinds of selves, rigidly designated as male and female, that are produced by it. Under MacKinnon's view of the individual or the subject, the body inevitably figures as the barrier in which the self hides and guards itself as the illusionary weapon—the phallus—in which "it" asserts itself against others. But why figure the body in this way? Why not figure the body as threshold or as a position of receptivity. As receptivity, the body gives access. To welcome accessibility is to affirm *openness* to the Other. To shut oneself off, on the other hand, is *loss* of sensual pleasure. If one figures the body as receptivity, then "to be fucked" is not the end of the world. The endless erection of a barrier against "being fucked" is seen for what it "is," a defense mechanism that creates a fort for the self at the expense of *jouissance*. It is not that a "good fuck" is not compensation for "being fucked," as MacKinnon would have it. It is not even that the economic rhetoric of the rational man is not adequate to feminine *jouissance*. My suggestion is, instead, that it is only if one accepts a masculine view of the self, of the body and of carnality, that "being fucked" *appears* so terrifying. Elizabeth Bishop, in her poem, "One Art," wrote: "It's evident / the art of losing's not too hard to master / though it may look like (*Write* it!) like disaster."[74] MacKinnon writes getting fucked as disaster.

Those of us, on the other hand, who have mastered the "One Art" know that there are more important things to do—like loving—than maintaining the self against all comers. I agree with MacKinnon that within patriarchy, gender is not just a matter of difference, but of domination. But from this insight MacKinnon concludes:

> I am getting hard on this and am about to get harder on it. I do not think that the way women reason morally is morality "in a different voice." I think it is a morality in a higher register, in the feminine voice. Women value care because men have valued us according to the care we give them, and we could probably use some. Women think in relational terms because our existence is defined in relation to men.[75]

MacKinnon's rhetoric gives her away. Men may well value getting hard because that is the example *par excellence* of masculine assertion, and maintains the illusion that having a penis is having the phallus. Why should we seek this form of impossibility for ourselves? MacKinnon argues that sex for women does not bring empowerment. If empowerment is defined as self-assertion, and if, in turn, self-assertion is identified with "getting hard," then clearly sex for women does not bring empowerment. But again, I would want to suggest that in the best of all possible worlds, empowerment should *not* be the goal in all relationships. Perhaps, if nothing else, the identification of empowerment as the sole practical goal of feminism shows how profoundly we remain under the sway of masculine symbolism. Furthermore, I disagree with MacKinnon that feminine desire can be completely identified with masculine constructs. I have already suggested that MacKinnon fails to note the power of the unconscious, identifying desire solely with external social structures. Moreover, for MacKinnon, feminine desire, at least as it is expressed in heterosexuality, can only be the desire to "be fucked." But is this anything other than the masculine fantasy of our desire which renders our desire symmetrical to theirs; because they want to fuck us, we want to fuck them? So they may fantasize, but that does not make it so. The writing of feminine desire not only expresses our pleasure beyond "the old dream of symmetry," in which we are only their complement, it also explicitly rejects the fantasy of symmetry as an adequate expression of feminine desire.

Of course, the writers of feminine desire recognize that any attempt to explicitly designate, and to thus hold down the feminine imaginary, let alone the uniqueness of the feminine unconscious, will fail if it is a failure to come up with a complete definition. So we try and try again, never pretending to have reached the end of the process. But the poetic evocation of the excess, of *jouissance*, that is the Other as feminine desire, is part of the bringing of our reality into "being," and of allowing our pleasure to be expressed.

Such writing, particularly in the case of Irigaray, is also an explicit rebellion against the psychoanalytic category of gender identity that makes feminine pleasure inexpressible. As we have seen, for Lacan, our pleasure, indeed, the feminine itself—as the beyond to masculine system of signification—can never find its expression in this world. It can be lived, but not written. When we write of feminine pleasure, we challenge their system and their discourse as the only way to articulate reality. But the effort is not, as MacKinnon would suggest, to find the "truth" values of woman in their society. It is, rather, to write on many planes at once through the evocation of motifs that are foreign to phallocentric discourse. Such motifs, which appear again and again in both Irigaray and Cixous, are the motifs of "self-touching" and "proximity" to the Other; these are tactile motifs, evoked from within the "dark continent" in which we touch ourselves rather than know ourselves as their object. But at the same time, all the difficulties of the evocation of motifs that "seem" feminine, because they have been identified as such within the phallogocentrism, are recognized. As Irigaray notes:

> And even the motifs of "self-touching," of "proximity," isolated
> as such or reduced to utterances, could effectively pass for an

attempt to appropriate the feminine to discourse. We would still have to ascertain whether "touching oneself," that (self) touching, the desire for the proximate rather than for (the) proper(ty), and so on, might not imply a mode of exchange irreducible to any *centering*, any *centrism*, given the way the "self-touching" of female "self-affection" comes into play as a rebounding from one to the other without any possibility of interruption, and given that, in this interplay, proximity confounds any adequation, any appropriation.[76]

Feminine style is this constant experimentation to write the unspeakable, knowing all the while the inherent contradiction in the effort. But without the effort, we can only have the wordless repetition of the same, in which the feminine is denied and repudiated, and our desire is rendered inexpressible, and therefore non-existent in its specificity. "If we keep on speaking sameness, if we speak to each other as men have been doing for centuries, as we have been taught to speak, we'll miss each other, fail ourselves. Again . . . . Words will pass through our bodies, above our heads. They'll vanish, and we'll be lost."[77] We will, in other words, be left in the state of *derelection*.

We can never know for sure that we have come out of their language. There is only the process of trying to write our pleasure differently. And since we are in this bipolar world of gender identity, we can only proceed to what is Other through *mimesis*. The other choice is to repudiate the feminine, as MacKinnon does, and by so doing to reduce our desire to the fantasy of symmetry. We are then left with the denial of *our* pleasure that their system demands. To quote Irigaray: "Feminine pleasure has to remain inarticulate in language, in its own language, if it is not to threaten the underpinnings of logical operations. And so what is most strictly forbidden to women today is that they should attempt to express their own pleasure."[78]

MacKinnon has joined with that prohibition. We have seen that the attempt to write "feminine" pleasure, rather to write *of it*, involves an appeal to tactile motifs. It also involves the reinterpretation of "figures" of women that have appeared in psychoanalysis, most notably the hysteric. It is precisely in the paralysis of desire that we "see" the excess implicit in the refusal to take on the status of normal femininity in which our desire is always and only for them. The hysteric does not adjust her desire; therefore, she is abnormal.

It is not the abnormality of the hysteric that is celebrated. Instead, the accounts of hysteria are reinterpreted through the trace, embodied in the symptoms of the excess of feminine desire, inexpressible in the masculine order except as illness. The symptoms themselves are real as "speaking as a woman" when there are no words to articulate feminine desire.

Hysteria: *it speaks* in the mode of a paralyzed gestural faculty, of an impossible and also a forbidden speech. . . . It speaks as *symptoms* of an "it can't speak to or about itself". . . . And the drama of hysteria is that it is inserted schizotically between that gestural system, that desire paralyzed and enclosed within its body, and a language that it has learned in the family, in school, in society, which is in no way continuous with—nor, certainly, a metaphor for—the "movements" of its desire. Both mutism and mimicry are then left to hysteria. Hysteria is silent and at the same time it mimes. And—how could it be otherwise—miming/reproducing a language that is not its own, masculine language, it caricatures and deforms that language: it "lies," it "deceives," as women have always been reputed to do.[79]

Hysteria, in other words, also "expresses" the inevitability of the "sufferance" of the feminine if "one" is defined as a woman within our own bipolar system of rigid gender identity. The hysteric's symptoms "announce" feminine desire as that which has been excluded, but even so and as such, leaves its mark. The traditional cure for the hysteric within psychoanalysis is to deny the legitimacy of the trace of the feminine elsewhere that is embodied in the symptoms. The cure is adjustment that must involve denial of the desire that is seeking voice. For the woman who refuses adjustment, who insists on the specificity of her desire, the hysteric is her sister. As Cixous writes:

> The hysterics are my sisters. As Dora, I have been all the characters she played, the ones who killed her, the ones who got shivers when she ran through them, and in the end I got away, having been Freud one day, Mrs. Freud another, also Mr. K . . . , Mrs. K . . .— and the wound Dora inflicted on them. In 1900, I was stifled desire, its rage, its turbulent effects. I kept the merry-go-round of bourgeois-conjugal pettiness from going around without squeaking horribly. I was everything. I sent each "person"/nobody back to his little calculations, each discourse to its lie, each cowardice to its unconscious, I said nothing but made everything known. I stole their little investments, but that's nothing. I slammed their door. I left. But I am what Dora would have been if woman's history had begun.[80]

The refusal to deny the specificity of her desire is also associated with the sorceress who takes the initiative and rides away on her broom, flies right away and denies the hold of their reality on us. But this expression of her own desire is so frightening because she is viewed as a castrator, the ultimate penis thief, who uses them for her own ends. The witch who refuses to be tied down expresses the masculine fear of the phallic mother. As Catherine Clément has written:

> Now she is a *penis thief*: the father's penis must certainly be in her belly. Let's return to *The Witches' Hammer*. "What [asks the Inquisitor] is to be thought of these witches who collect this way [by taking away the male organ], sometimes collecting a great number of them [20 or 30] and who then go around putting them in bird's [sic] nests or shutting them up in boxes, where they keep on moving like living organs, eating oats or other things as some have seen and as they are generally believed to do?" ("How witches can take the male organ from a man.") The sorceress takes men's penes, as, from the child's point of view, the mother takes the father's penis. . . . The fact remains that in this phantasmic mythology the sorceress and mother come together again.[81]

The figures of the hysteric and the sorceress express in their lives and—in the allegories in which they still exist as figures—the supposedly inexpressible, the specificity of female desire, as well as, in the case of the sorceress, masculine fear of uncontrolled female pleasure which appropriates the phallus for its own use. Hélène Cixous uses the woman writer, herself, as the figure of feminine difference expressed as a *jouissance* beyond calculation.

> To write—the act that will "realize" the un-censored relationship of woman to her sexuality, to her woman-being giving her back access to her own forces; that will return her goods, her pleasures, her organs, her vast bodily territories kept under seal; that will tear her out of the superegoed, over-Mosesed structure where the same position of guilt is always reserved for her (guilty of everything, every time: of having desires, of not having any; of being frigid, or being "too" hot; of not being both at once; of being too much of a mother and not enough; of nurturing and of not nurturing . . .). Write yourself: your body must make itself heard. Then the huge resources of the unconscious will burst out. Finally the inexhaustible feminine imaginary is going to be deployed.[82]

By writing our pleasure, we deny the hold of the taboo against the specificity of our desire, a taboo that MacKinnon insists is unbreakable. For MacKinnon, there is no breaking of the code until we actually have power. Not even in the figures of the writer, the hysteric or the sorceress. The woman writing, however, breaks the censorship against feminine pleasure that MacKinnon must inevitably maintain. Believing in the hysteric, believing in the sorceress, is not reducible to believing that they were actually abused. Believing the hysteric is believing in her thwarted desire as it indicates a feminine elsewhere irreducible to "their" construction of us. Believing in the sorceress is believing in her power through the refusal of adjustment. Believing in the writer is believing in Woman's new beginning. "I see her 'begin.' That can be written—these beginnings that never stop getting her up—can and must be written."[83]

Of course, MacKinnon could argue that the hysteric is the ultimate loser. Her desire is only her paralysis, a paralysis that keeps her from acting, from asserting herself. She could argue that feminine writing reinforces our oppression by reinforcing the pretense that our *jouissance* is possible now. MacKinnon would reminds us that, as women, we do not choose to be "losers." Within MacKinnon's analysis, if we recognize the hysteric or the sorceress, we should only do so by labelling her as the victim she "is." There is nothing in her desire to affirm. We must, she would argue, stop "losing," stop giving ourselves away. For Cixous, writing is itself a loss of the self, which is why writing is figured as feminine.

> Rare are the men able to venture onto the brink where writing, freed from law, unencumbered by moderation, exceeds phallic authority, and where the subjectivity inscribing its effects becomes feminine.
>
> Where does difference come through in writing? If there is difference it is in the manner of spending, of valorizing the appropriated, of thinking what is not-the-same. In general, it is in the manner of thinking any "return," the relationship of capitalization, if this word "return" (*rapport*) is understood in its sense of "revenue."[84]

We can now see just how and why MacKinnon misunderstood Gayatri Spivak's question to her in one of the lectures in *Feminism Unmodified*.[85] MacKinnon interprets Spivak to be suggesting that her unmodified feminism reinstates individualism. MacKinnon denies this, arguing that her definition of femaleness, and more specifically female desire, as complicity in their system is anti-individualistic at its core because it insists on the social construction of our sexuality. But on another level, as I have shown, her political program, as well as her condemnation of "getting fucked," reinstates not only a traditional concept of the individual, but pictures the self as masculine. When I engage with MacKinnon, I must take on the world of heterosexual male violence that MacKinnon makes us see. Certainly, exclusive engagement with other women potentially offers us release from this world. But as Irigaray reminds us:

> For women to undertake tactical strikes, to keep themselves apart from men long enough to learn to defend their desire, especially

through speech, to discover the love of other women while sheltered from men's imperious choices that put them in the position of rival commodities, to forge for themselves a social status that compels recognition, to earn their living in order to escape from the condition of prostitute . . . these are certainly indispensable stages in the escape from their proletarization on the exchange market. But if their aim were simply to reverse the order of things, even supposing this to be possible, history would repeat itself in the long run, would revert to sameness: to phallocratism. It would leave room neither for women's sexuality, nor for women's imaginary, nor for women's language to take (their) place.[86]

The very language of MacKinnon's either/or, "getting fucked" or casting "them" out, envisions feminine desire within the constraints of heterosexuality. If we are to open the space for feminine desire, we need to affirm our desire as other than the fantasy of symmetry, and it is precisely this affirmation that MacKinnon disallows. Once "they" are out, there is still no Other to "their" world, as offered to us by MacKinnon, in which we could speak from feminine desire. The vision of the body as a wall against, rather than as surface connection to, gives a very stark phallic image. The writing of the feminine has envisioned a different, feminine view of the body—and again let me stress that the body in Irigaray, Cixous and Wittig, should itself be understood as metaphor, not as the descriptive *basis* for femaleness. Irigaray imagines two women making love.

No surface holds. No figure, line, or point remains. No ground subsists. But no abyss, either. Depth, for us, is not a chasm. Without a solid crust, there is no precipice. Our depth is the thickness of our body, our all touching itself. Where top and bottom, inside and outside, in front and behind, above and below are not separated, remote, out of touch. Our all intermingled. Without breaks or gaps.[87]

Irigaray's prose poem should not be taken literally. To take it literally, as an essentialist appeal to the truth of the body, is to misunderstand the specificity of literary language. The image of the two lips evokes proximity, the nearness that is never collapsed into the identification of the phallic self. The two lips are near but not one. The prose poem, "When Our Lips Speak Together,"[88] proceeds through both metaphor and metonomy. But the two lips do give another motif for Other-Love, and for the nearness that is not self-possession through the illusion of having the phallus. The boundaries imposed by the phallus give way to touching. The solid ground gives way to the overflow of *jouissance*. Again to quote Irigaray:

How can I speak to you? You remain in flux, never congealing or solidifying. What will make that current flow into words? It is multiple, devoid of causes, meanings, simple qualities. Yet it cannot be decomposed. These movements cannot be described as the passage from a beginning to an end. These rivers flow into no single, definitive sea. These streams are without fixed banks, this body without fixed boundaries. This unceasing mobility. This life— which will perhaps be called our restlessness, whims, pretenses, or lies. All this remains very strange to anyone claiming to stand on solid ground.[89]

Monique Wittig's *The Lesbian Body*[90] also gives us a rhapsodic hymn to women's bodies and women's relationships even if she does so from within her own theoretical construct in which the lesbian loses her designation as woman through making love "outside" of heterosexuality.

For Wittig, sex and gender only become identified within the workings of the machine of heterosexuality. Very simply put, to "make love" differently is "to be" differently; and, more specifically, from within the constraints of heterosexuality, to break the shackles that imprison us in our femininity as "it" is cut out for masculine desire. Lesbian sexuality is no longer seen as passive, but as active desire with its own jubilation and modes of connection. More importantly, for Wittig, lesbianism is no longer feminine *being* at all. Feminine *being is* only feminine within heterosexuality. Lesbian love-making, in other words, tears down the edifices of woman and gender identity, constructed by the old dream of symmetry associated with heterosexuality. The phrases and expressions of sexuality are turned inside out in Wittig's hymn of what it *means* for sexuality when one woman loves, and finds the body of her Other as Woman. Our desire is only passive if we are seen as the one to be fucked. Between two lesbians, the rigid categories of "fuckor" and "fuckee" are re-enacted so as to be undone. The "bodies" of the two lovers are ripped apart as separate entities. The boundaries yield under the force of love and desire.

A tree shoots in m/y body, it moves its branches with extreme violence with extreme gentleness, or else it is a bush of burning thorns it tears the other side of m/y exposed muscles m/y inside m/y interiors, *I* am inhabited, *I* am not dreaming, *I* am penetrated by you, now *I* must struggle against bursting to retain m/y overall perception, *I* reassemble you in all m/y organs, *I* burst, *I* reassemble you, sometimes your hand sometimes your mouth sometimes your shoulder sometimes your whole body, when m/y stomach is affected your stomach responds when m/y lungs rattle your lungs rattle, finally *I* am without depth without place m/y stomach appearing between m/y breasts m/y lungs traversing the skin of m/y back.[91]

This sexual "reassembling" which breaks up the gender identity of woman of which Wittig sings, is irreducible to the subject fucking the object. The seduction is a descent in which the lovers both let their passion wash over them at the same time that they actively participate in their desire and seek each other out and turn each other inside/out. But this sexuality is also violent, indeed, filled with purportedly masculine metaphors. This filling in is, itself, deliberate. Wittig does not envision a sex for itself in which the masculine is, or indeed, can be, completely excluded. The absolute exclusion would, for Wittig, reinstate the very rigid gender identities she is trying to break down.

> We descend directly legs together thighs together arms entwined m/y hands touching your shoulders m/y shoulders held by your hands breast against breast open mouth against open mouth, we descend slowly. The sand swirls round our ankles, suddenly it surrounds our calves. It's from then on that the descent is slowed down. At the moment your knees are reached you throw back your head, *I* see your teeth, you smile, later you look at m/e you speak to m/e without interruption.[92]

Wittig's celebration of the "lesbian body" is obviously not just a description of all lesbian relationships as they take place within the dominant heterosexual norms. She celebrates the sexuality that disrupts gender identity. Hers is an explicitly utopian perspective but one that moves within the recitation of the "dark continent" from within. The lesbian body is being written so that lesbian *jouissance* can be affirmed as it is given voice. What is written "exists." It is, of course, important to note that Wittig would herself deny the possibility of feminine writing, because for Wittig the "feminine" "is" only within heterosexuality. The lesbian, therefore, is not a woman. To live sex differently is *to be* differently. Wittig shows that sex cannot be reduced to gender. The lesbian lives the possible disjuncture between sex and gender. My disagreement with her is that she argues for a pure model of heterosexuality in which the sexes are fully determined by their gender within heterosexuality. The repetition and the *mimesis* which are heterosexuality are also subject to *de-sistance*. On a theoretical plane, her materialism brings her closer to MacKinnon, at least in terms of her view of heterosexuality. But unlike MacKinnon, her fictional writings give us a very different view of sexuality, an engagement with the Other which breaks down the very boundaries and concepts of a self that MacKinnon would have us salvage. Certainly the ideal "here" is not that of the "unviolated" body implicit in the slogan "Out Now." Wittig is also only too well aware of the danger of reasserting the ideal of pure identity, of a "sex for itself."

Nor are Wittig's Amazons, in *Les Guérillères*,[93] identifiable as just another guise for traditional femininity. What is written exists, in the sense that it now stands before us as one "vision" of our reality. Wittig's island of women warriors involves the re-metaphorization and re-symbolization of the myth of Amazons. Wittig and Irigaray understand what MacKinnon does not—that "utopian" writing of the real as "fici-fact" is necessary if we are to avoid the denial and repression of our sexuality which inheres in the degradation of our reality to their construct. As a writer, Wittig breaks up the appeal to "reality" that inheres in her own "materialist," theoretical assertions about feminine identity within heterosexuality.

Utopian writing reaches out to the impossible in the flight from the enclosed reality of the symbolic.

> But we must make no mistake: men and women are caught up in a web of age-old cultural determinations that are almost unanalyzable in their complexity. One can no more speak of "woman" than of "man" without being trapped within an ideological theater where the proliferation of representations, images, reflections, myths, identifications, transform, deform, constantly change everyone's Imaginary and invalidate in advance any conceptualization.[94]

We cannot, however, simply assert that there is another way of living the feminine that is beyond the repetition of the same "old story." Given the "reality" of the bipolarity of gender identity, *mimesis* is the only choice. The "Art of Losing," even within heterosexuality, is what masochism, as defined, becomes when we interpret it as uncontainable within the oppositional structure of sado-masochism. The transformation of the masochism MacKinnon brilliantly describes into the "Art of Losing," which evokes the feminine as other than self-possession, cannot be separated from the writing, the fictions in which the feminine is reinterpreted. The difference between masochism and "The Art of Losing" is not obvious. Moreover, it cannot be when sadism seems to be the only alternative. Yet, the "Art of Losing" can only be simplistically identified with masochism if we continue to think within the hierarchy that privileges "the winners," as MacKinnon does. To think beyond the dialectic of sado-masochism, we have to transform from within. We have to dare to be out of step. MacKinnon tells us that we must give up collaboration. A crucial aspect of this collaboration is the attempt to succeed within their system.

> I'm evoking for women a role that we have yet to make, in the name of a voice that, unsilenced, might say something that has

never been heard. I will hazard a little bit about its content. In the legal world of win and lose, where success is measured by other people's failures, in this world of kicking or getting kicked, I want to say there is another way. Women who refuse to forget the way women everywhere are treated every day, who refuse to forget that *that* is the meaning of being a woman, no matter how secure we may feel in having temporarily escaped it, women as women will find *that way*.[95]

I am advocating that "The Art of Losing" is necessary if we are to find "that way" to indicate the specificity of the feminine desire as other than the longing to be like "them" in the illusion of their self-containment, the self-containment that Lacan so brilliantly shows us is a projection of the masculine imaginary.

I return to the beginning of this essay. If we do not bring the "feminine" reality from the "rere" to the front, we will be imprisoned in the genderized reality that MacKinnon so eloquently describes, in which everywhere we look, we find the man.

4

Feminine Writing, Metaphor and Myth

Introduction

But the project of bringing the "feminine" from the "rere" to the front carries within its own dangers. I have throughout this book warned against the reinstatement of "naturalist" or "essentialist" theories of Woman. Yet, even in my debate with MacKinnon, I have relied—at least in one interpretation—on myth to defend the feminine. As Barthes rightly describes myth: "We reach here the very principle of myth: it transforms history into nature."[1] Have I not, then, by defending the allegory of the feminine through myth, assumed the very position I rejected, a "naturalist" or "essentialist" theory, if even in the form of a myth of Woman? I am aware of the danger. But I would also argue with Barthes that "the best weapon against myth is perhaps to mythify it in its turn, and to produce an *artificial myth*: and this reconstituted myth will in fact be a mythology."[2] Even an allegory of Woman that protects the beyond *as* beyond can only express itself through an interchange with the mythology of the feminine. This coexistence is necessary if we are to give body to the figure Woman and mark the specificity of feminine sexual difference. The danger, as Kristeva has argued, is turning Woman into a religion. But, if Bataille is right, religion itself is an expression of the desire for intimacy we associate with Woman, and the primordial relationship to the mother. Religion and Woman may well go hand in hand, if both are understood to figure the desire for intimacy in the fantasy of symbiotic connection. However, the danger of turning Woman into religion is precisely the danger of feminism unmodified.

Thus, there is a tension in Kristeva's own writing between the attempt to locate the specificity of the feminine in the exploration of the experience of maternity as an instinct or drive,[3] and her "postmodern" concern with disrupting rigid gender identity structures so as to protect a subject in process. To quote Kristeva:

> What can "identity," even "sexual identity," mean in a new theoretical and scientific space where the very notion of identity is challenged? I am not simply suggesting a very hypothetical bisexuality which, even if it existed, would only, in fact, be the aspiration towards the totality of one of the sexes and thus an effacing of difference. What I mean is, first of all, the demassification of the problematic of *difference*, which would imply, in a first phase, an apparent de-dramatization of the "fight to the death" between rival groups and thus between the sexes. And this not in the name of some reconciliation—feminism has at least had the merit of showing what is irreducible and even deadly in the social contract—but in order that the struggle, the implacable difference, the violence be conceived in the very place where it operates with the maximum intransigence, in other words, in personal and sexual identity itself, so as to make it disintegrate in its very nucleus.[4]

The tension, simply put, is between the postmodern deconstruction of rigid identity structures and the very idea of identity itself, and the attempt to specify the feminine, even if only as a subversive force against the symbolic. As we have seen, this tension has led some feminists sympathetic to the postmodern critique of identity to conclude that the very attempt to embody the feminine through metaphor is a mistaken retreat to phallogocentrism. In spite of the best intent, so the argument goes, such efforts are metaphysical in that they reinstate the divide between masculine and feminine, and by so doing reinforce rigid gender identity. The second criticism is that any version of feminine writing rests on the "myth" of full presence by claiming to *show* us what the feminine *is*. Instead of this attempt to figure Woman or the feminine through metaphor, it is argued that we should adopt a strategy of showing her disfigurement within patriarchal society. MacKinnon's own work can, and to my mind should, be understood as the exemplar of this strategy of the exposure of disfigurement. We are disfigured because the feminine can only be given the body they see us to be. Woman as "fuckee," in all its supposed diversity, is in the end only their myth of Woman. Refigurement through metaphor, in other words, is not possible until the conditions of domination have been destroyed.

The Suspicion of Metaphor Restated

Unlike metaphorical refiguration, the primary role of metonomy is "exposure." In her excellent article, Domna C. Stanton puts it well. "A metonymic practice should/would displace focus from the utopian *arche* or future to the imperfect past/present in which all processes of exploration are located and all discoveries must begin."[5]

Metonomy, in other words, since it is inevitably bound up with contiguity, would show us the context-bound nature of our statements about Woman and thus show us how all such statements involve prejudice and limitation within the context of gender hierarchy. From within this understanding of feminism and of metonomy, metonomy is favored because it enacts the genealogical effort to uncover the structures of power that produce Woman. Genealogy unmasks, and indeed gives us a process of continual unmasking which would seem consistent with the postmodern critique of identity. This unmasking is done by exposing the power discourses that form woman, but not in the name of the authentic Woman, or done in the name of discourses beyond power. Feminism is this strategy of unmasking which, of course, can never come to an end in the discovery of Woman.

The counter-valorization of Woman associated with the re-metaphorization would risk the danger of essentialism and of claiming a special status of one vision of Woman. And yet, the metaphorization of the feminine in feminine writing, as I have suggested, has a "utopian" dimension in that such figures are irreducible to "their" vision of us or, indeed, to any one vision or representation. We should not, in other words, displace focus from the utopian "future" to the "present." This is my fundamental disagreement with Stanton. It is this utopian dimension that I have suggested is necessary if we are to affirm the feminine. Yet, in spite of the utopian dimension, the attempt at re-metaphorization does, of course, involve at least the preliminary location of the feminine, even if metaphoric transference also implies the relation of the "is" to the "not yet." Thus metaphor, or refiguration through metaphor, seems through transference to *establish*, as Stanton fears, the "proper place" for Woman.

Derrida's own "suspicion" of metaphor, an ethical suspicion, is that through Woman's re-metaphorization we will once again capture women in a new concept in which the very process of metaphorization will itself be erased.[6] As a result of the erasure of metaphoric transference, we would again reinstate one way of "seeing" Woman as her truth. The pretense that Woman has a "being" that can be known once and for all will be bolstered when it should instead be deconstructed. For Stanton, as already suggested, this danger should push us to prefer metonymic deferral, even though she knows that this strategy is not "phallogo-free."

> For metonymic deferral, postponement or putting off ironically represents the traditional feminine posture whenever a question of inter(dis)course arises. Nevertheless, in the present imperfect, that putting off, however offputting it may seem, is the more desirable

course for diverse female explorations than excessive, tumescent metaforeplay.[7]

I would like to suggest, on the contrary, that we need both writing "strategies," and, as Stanton herself recognizes, not the least because there can be no pure divide between metaphor and metonomy. Indeed, metonomy is always contaminated by the metaphors which allow continuity to be comprehensible. But more importantly, it is the "excessive, tumescent metaforeplay" that allows for the "mimetic" practice of feminine writing to be other than mere repetition of the pregiven stereotypes. As Kristeva herself has remarked, metaphor creates a "surplus of meaning"[8] which manages to open the surface of signs toward the unrepresentable. Thus, in Irigaray and Cixous, the practice of re-metaphorization—but without a replacement of the phallus as the primary metaphor of desire—is to mark the unrepresentable sexual difference that is erased by the current gender hierarchy.

This "spillover" capacity is associated with the paradoxical character of metaphorical truth. Paul Ricoeur has succinctly described this paradox. "The paradox consists in the fact that there is no other way to do justice to the notion of metaphorical truth than to include the critical incision of the (literal) 'is not' within the ontological vehemence of the (metaphorical) 'is.' "[9] The "is not" implied in metaphorical transference is what allows for the "surplus of meaning." But, of course, the other side of the paradox, and the one that Derrida emphasizes, is that Woman *as* still implies Woman *is*, even if what Woman is, her "being," can no longer be designated once and for all. Ricoeur also grasps the difficulty created by the paradox inherent in metaphorical truth.

> Can one create metaphors without believing them and without believing that, in a certain way, "that is"? So it is the relationship itself, and not just its extremes, that is at issue: it is still the correspondence concept of truth that rules between the "as if" of self-conscious hypothesis and the facts "as they seem to us." It is only modulated by the "as if," without being altered in its basic definition.[10]

Metaphor, the Imagination and Utopian Possibility

Ricoeur's study on metaphor and the way it "rules" the literal also led him to conclude that "utopianism" is essential to political and ethical theory. We are never simply working within what "is," because what is, is only "reachable" in metaphor, and therefore, in the traditional sense, not reachable at all. Thus, the conception of truth as adequation is rejected and with it, the commonsense realism of a certain conception of politics that appeals to what is. Utopianism, in other words, can no longer simply be pitted against "realism," in the colloquial sense of the word. The "as if" of the imagination is implicated in the very act of "seeing" the real. As a result, the divide between the imagination, and the so-called mind-set that pretends to have put aside utopian aspirations forever in the name of seeing things as they are, is undermined. Accommodation to what is "seen" as what "is" comes into view as an ethical and political positioning, and not as the necessity imposed upon one who "sees" accurately. It is, then, at least partially as a result of the supposed rule of the literal over the metaphoric, that so-called utopianism comes to be distinguished from "realism" and disfavored as out of touch with the "real world." Once we understand the role of metaphor in the constitution of "being" itself, the rigid divide between "realism" and utopianism is undermined. The dreamer may be a visionary, but that does not mean that she sees any less well. The possibility of the "as if" through which we construct reality is "there" to be seen, if by that we mean "presentable" in metaphoric transference.

Feminine writing, understood within this frame, does not so much try to reach the truth of Woman through metaphor. Instead we are trying to discover the possibility of the "way out" from our current system of gender identity in which "her" specificity opens up the unknown, in which sexual difference would not be re-appropriated. Through Irigaray's *mimesis*, we move within what has been prefigured so as to continually transfigure it. We not only affirm Woman, we continually re-metaphorize her through the "as if."

The necessary utopian moment in feminism lies precisely in our opening up the possible through metaphoric transformation. Earlier in this essay, I discussed "the unerasable trace of utopianism" of deconstruction. Derridean "utopianism" is structural and, as we saw, associated with his understanding of the disruptive force of temporalization of any site, or spatial enclosure. Here, I am using utopia in a more traditional way, but not in the sense of the establishment of a blueprint of an ideal society. Utopian thinking demands the continual exploration and re-exploration of the possible and yet also the unrepresentable. Deconstruction reminds us of the limits of the imagination, but to recognize the limit is not to deny the imagination. It is just that: the recognition of the limit. The political need to heed the limit, as well as to imagine, stems from the danger that any imagined scheme comes to be seen once again as the only truth. Without utopian thinking, however, feminism is inevitably ensnared in the system of gender identity that devalues the feminine. To reach out involves the imagination, and with imagination, the refiguration of Woman. As we have seen, this kind of shift in the presentation of Woman is particularly important in legal discourse if the wrongs to women are to appear at all.

But, of course, any new presentation will involve a refiguration, even if through metaphor, which once again would seem to tell us what or who Woman is and, by so doing, reinstate rigid gender identities. This is precisely why, as we have seen, Derrida questions the need for new "representations" of Woman. The disruptive power of the allegory of Woman ironically seems to depend on deferring any attempt to specify the feminine. The paradox of metaphor that Ricoeur describes would seem to lead us to privilege, even if cautiously, a metonymic strategy with its own danger of anti-utopianism. Yet it is precisely the "uneraseable trace of utopianism" inherent in deconstruction which makes Derrida himself suspicious of metaphor and wary of the productive imagination as it has been traditionally conceived. Put very simply, Derrida always reminds us that we cannot "see" what is truly "elsewhere." And yet, any context has an irreducible opening which Derrida refers to as "unconditionality." To quote Derrida:

> Now, the very least that can be said of unconditionality (a word that I use not by accident to recall the character of the categorical imperative in its Kantian form) is that it is independent of every determinate context, even of the determination of a context in general. It announces itself as such only in the *opening* of context. Not that it is simply present (existent) elsewhere, outside of all context; rather, it intervenes in the determination of a context from its very inception, and from an injunction, a law, a responsibility that transcends this or that determination of a given context. Following this, what remains is to articulate this unconditionality with the determinate (Kant would say, hypothetical) conditions of this or that context; and this is the moment of strategies, of rhetorics, of ethics, and of politics. The structure thus described supposes both that there are only contexts, that nothing *exists* outside context, as I have often said, but also that the limit of the frame or the border of the context always entails a clause of non-closure.[11]

The need for what Derrida calls "double writing" is based on this recognition that the very idea of the limit of context, its de-limitation, also implies its non-closure, and the possibility of the transformation of any context. Paraphrasing his recent essay on justice, if it is the deconstruction of law that protects justice, it is the deconstruction of gender hierarchy, and indeed, of any one unmodified concept of feminism, that allows for the opening of sexual difference as difference.[12] The tension between unconditionality and our situation within hypothetical conditions is what makes change possible. As Derrida himself explains, deconstructive writing "always makes this dual gesture, apparently contradictory, which consists in accepting, within certain limits—that is to say never entirely accepting it—the given-ness of context and its stubbornness. But how without this apparent contradiction would anything ever be done?"[13] It is the combination of the unconditional with the determinate that is key. Thus, it is a serious error, as Kristeva herself has done, to argue that deconstruction takes the position of "disinterestedness toward social structure." Deconstruction, instead, only shows us that any attempt to determine the hypothetical conditions of any given context is just that, hypothetical.

In like manner, the power of imagination is not denied, even if it is delineated. Imagining as imaging still rests on representation; representation is tied to the pregiven as representation. Images, in other words, are rooted in the pregiven world. Images, of course, and the imagination allow us to refigure the pregiven through metaphor. The imagination, in other words, does not just reflect. The process of refiguration through the imagination implies the slippage inherent in language that allows the defining of what is to give way, as well as to be reconsolidated. But even so, imagination as imagery remains within the field of vision and re-envisioning. Derrida exposes the limits of the imagination as the refiguration of hypothetical conditions. Refiguration, in other words, must not be confused with the final, "adequate" representation of Woman.

My contention then, is that the writing of the feminine, in spite of the "danger" of the reliance on metaphor, is perfectly consistent with the Derridean "double gesture" as long as the attempt to specify the feminine is understood as proceeding through a process of metaphorization that never fully captures Woman. There is always more to write. In writing, we do not just represent what can be imaged. Writing disrupts the field of representation through the strategies of both metaphor and metonomy. I understand that Derrida has been more hesitant to engage in this metaphorplay, because of the association of metaphor with metaphysics and indeed, with myth. But as I have argued throughout this essay, such "metaforeplay" is necessary if we are to avoid—if in a new postmodern form—the repudiation of the feminine, and thus again, the reinstatement of the privileging of the masculine. The feminist project as I have described it involves the demonstration of the irreducible opening of gender identity, the most stubborn of contexts, which in turn allows us to dream of a new choreography of sexual difference. The mimetic writing of feminine specificity, including the reworking of myth, can then be combined with the articulation of the determinate situation of women within our legal and political context, and with the genealogical exposure of how we are formed as objects within the masculine symbolic. *The mistake is to think that we cannot engage in all three aspects of the project, and worse, that one excludes the other.*

With this understanding of the role mimetic writing of the feminine plays within feminism more generally, we can again turn to the role of the myth in feminine theory. Indeed, Kristeva's own "Stabat Mater"[14] can be understood to exemplify the "double writing" as I have interpreted it. One side of the page analyzes the myth of the mother as it has played such an overwhelming role in religious traditions. Her particular focus is on the myth of the Virgin Mother, but her central concern is the way in which the mythology of the Mother obscures women's actual experience of maternity, and even more primordially, the very instinct or drive for motherhood. On the other side of the page, she disrupts her own account and working-through of the significance of these myths with a poetic evocation of her own experience of pregnancy and birthing. Yet the myths are not simply denied, nor can they be, because even as they are critiqued as the distortion of women's experience and the "instinctual" life of the mother, they retain a powerful hold over our imagination. We reimagine through these myths. But we also disrupt the images of our own refiguration. The status of these myths *as* myths is exposed as we also attempt to transfigure Woman as she is "presented" in them. Double writing, in turn, indicates the limit of refiguration. As Kristeva rightly warns, the danger of belief in Woman is that we re-establish a "new religion" which becomes its own edifice and does not allow for the continual exploration of new possibility, let alone the reaching out to the impossible. The only solution to this danger is to understand myth as artificial mythology so that the structure of "second nature" reinstated by myth will appear as our mythology. Nothing more, nothing less. There can always be other mythologies.

The Significance of Myth, and the Feminine as an Imaginative Universal

Moreover, the inability to simply escape our genderized context explains why the role of myth in feminist theory is essential to the reclaiming, and retelling, of "herstory" through the mimetic writing that specifies the feminine. I am again emphasizing the word "myth" deliberately, to emphasize the hold that myths of Woman and the feminine have over both individuals and cultures. They are remarkably unchanging. Hans Blumenburg has defined myth as follows:

> Myths are stories that are distinguished by a high degree of constancy in their narrative core and by an equally pronounced capacity for marginal variation. These two characteristics make myths transmissible by tradition: their constancy produces the attraction of recognizing them in artistic or ritual representation as well [as in recital], and their variability produces the attraction of trying out new and personal means of presenting them. It is the relationship of "theme and variations," whose attractiveness for both composers and listeners is familiar from music. So myths are not like "holy texts," which cannot be altered by one iota.[15]

Myth is one important way in which the feminine achieves what Blumenberg calls "significance." Significance is the deeper meaning we associate
with myth's capacity to provide our life-world with symbols, images, and
metaphors that not only give us a shared environment, but an environment
that matters to us and inspires us. It is the constancy of myth that allows us
to continue to recognize ourselves in the great myth-figures of the feminine,
and to engage with them as touchstones for a feminine identification, if not
identity. Hélène Cixous, for example, has powerfully evoked mythical figures
in order to give significance to the deliverance of the feminine writer, seeking
to find her way beyond a system of gender representation she finds crippling.
And, indeed, Irigaray has appealed to Ariadne to give mythic expression to
derelection. The appeal to the mythic heightens the intensity associated with
our own struggles to survive within patriarchal society and to find our ways
out, our *sorties*. It is precisely the shared sense that our struggle "really
matters" that is heightened through the engagement with mythical feminine
figures.

The reinterpretation and recreation of mythical figures can also help us to
give body to the dream of an elsewhere beyond patriarchy and the tragedy
imposed by a gender hierarchy which blocks the alliance between the sexes
of which Irigaray writes. In her *Sorties*, Cixous engages with mythical figures
to indicate the "way out" from the Lacanian tragic-comedy in which—as it
is beautifully evoked in Duras' allegory of thwarted desire, *Blue Eyes, Black
Hair*[16]—the two sexes are fated to miss one another. For Cixous, there has
to be an elsewhere in which love can be lived, in which lovers can meet in
an alliance.

> —There has to be somewhere else, I tell myself. And everyone
> knows that to go somewhere else there are routes, signs, "maps"—
> for an exploration, a trip. —That's what books are. Everyone
> knows that a place exists which is not economically or politically
> indebted to all the vileness and compromise. That is not obliged to
> reproduce the system. That is writing. If there is a somewhere else
> that can escape the infernal repetition, it lies in that direction, where
> *it* writes itself, where *it* dreams, where *it* invents new worlds.[17]

But this reinvention can only begin where we "are" and where we "have
been."

> If woman has always functioned "within" man's discourse, a
> signifier referring always to the opposing signifier that annihilates
> its particular energy, puts down or stifles its very different sounds,
> now it is time for her to displace this "within," explode it, overturn
> it, grab it, make it hers, take it in, take it into her women's mouth,

bite its tongue with her women's teeth, make up her own tongue
to get inside of it. And you will see how easily she will well up,
from this "within" where she was hidden and dormant, to the lips
where her foams will overflow.[18]

For Cixous, we can read and reread certain important myths, particularly
as they have been retold, as routes "out." For example, in her reading of
Penthesileia she finds signs that indicate the possibility of the elsewhere, a
woman's community not dominated by men. In Penthesileia, Cixous reveals
what first appears as "feminine" desire unleashed. The Law of the Father
does not seem to constrain the woman warrior. She lives as if she were free.
She acts as she pleases, indulges her own desire, fights back in the glory of
her own strength.

But the essence of Penthesileia is pure desire, frenzied desire,
immediately outside all law. She is absolutely unbridled: un-
bounded flight, panicked by any shadow of a boundary-stone. And
this pure desire, which has no other law than the need to reach its
object, is absolutely, with no uncertainty, the one she wants; she
saw it—like lightening she recognized it. A bolt of lightening itself.[19]

Yet the "law" catches up to her precisely because the code of reversal
demands that "[f]or a free woman, there can be no relationship with men
other than war."[20] The law of reversal only puts women where men have
been, in the role of domination. But the sado-masochist machine continues
to run. There is no place for love in the Amazons' code, only the war against
domination. MacKinnon's ideal of a "sex for itself" turns against its own
aspirations to be free of domination and ends in Penthesileia's death, the
death that is "the vengeance of castration." Under Cixous' interpretation of
the myth, Penthesileia had to die.

And Kliest-also-dies, from being Penthesileia, from not being
able to be Penthesileia without dying, as Penthesileia had to die
from being too close to the shadow of the law, from having been
afraid of the old ghosts, from having seen life itself get by within
reach, within sight, from having brushed against it, from having
felt the caress of its flaming hair, from not being able to hold onto
it.
How love a woman without encountering death? A woman who
is neither doll nor corpse nor dumb nor weak. But beautiful, lofty,
powerful, brilliant?
Without history's making one feel its law of hatred?
So the betrothed fall back into dust. Vengeance of castration,

always at work, and which the wounded poet can surmount only in fiction.[21]

The mistake of dreaming of a sex-for-itself in which the women are united against men is given mythical significance and played out in the lives of feminists who can only survive as the "warriors" responsible for keeping the boundaries intact so that men will not violate the border. The Law of the Father is reinstated at the same time that it is supposedly dominated. More precisely, to dominate the Law is to reinstate it. What is erected, according to Cixous' interpretation, is a barrier against the love which demands the new choreography of sexual difference, the multiplication of voices of lived sexuality.

Why obstacles to love? Accidents maybe. But anyway, in history, the first obstacle, always already there, is in the existence, the production and reproduction of images, types, coded and suitable ways of behaving, and in society's identification with a scene in which roles are fixed so that lovers are always initially trapped by the puppets with which they are assumed to merge.[22]

But sometimes, by playing, yet knowing we are playing, with the "role of the ideal woman," we unchain ourselves. This possibility is the hope of Irigaray's *mimesis*. Cleopatra, for Cixous, is the mythical figure for such a woman. Through her retelling of the story of Antony and Cleopatra, the couple in which history becomes myth, she gives body to the dream of love that evokes the elsewhere, indeed demands it, as she gives another figure of Woman, the woman who restyles herself playing with the role of being the phallus. Cleopatra, as read by Cixous, is the figure of feminine difference, complete stranger to "their" conventions which continuously restore the law of castration. She is the threshold that Antony must cross to find love. Nor for Cixous—herself Algerian—is it a coincidence that Cleopatra is from the "third world." She is the figure of the "other" woman who refuses to adjust to a culture which would deny her the life she seeks.

But in the Orient, the Impossible is born; she who is incomprehensible, who exceeds the imagination, who rewards the most powerful desire of the most powerful of men, she who has all, and who is more than all, no existence can contain her, no man has been able to equal her in radiance, in the length of ardor, in passion, yet the greatest ones have adored her, have approached her, she has not fled, it is herself in flesh and in reality who welcomes him, it is herself without making use of the glamour of absence who shows herself, unveiled, given to touch, to taste, but no man has ever equaled her. Except, at the end of her life, Antony.[23]

But she is also, for Cixous, the woman who knows that in order to survive, she must play her role as the signifier of their desire.

She is woman made Art: each moment of her story with Antony is created, at the same time ardently lived and immediately multiplied by incessant tensions, trans-formations, recreations that open and echo the thousands of scenes in which love can infinitely inscribe its need of no limit. All her art in the famous staging of her appearance to Antony's eyes. Entrance that has not ceased repeating itself over the centuries.[24]

But as she plays her role, she transforms it by affirming for herself the abundance and beauty of her flesh. She is not the distant object, the signifier of absence, she is "there," enacting in herself the art that makes love possible. The lovers, in Cixous' interpretation of the myth, meet and mingle their bodies.

Abundance of fantasies and metaphors that inscribe the dialectic of this desire in figures of nourishment—heavenly foods, meats, wines. Everything exchanged between the two boundless lovers is received as the child receives mother's milk: on Antony's word, Cleopatra's ear breakfasts, and that is the right way. We are far from object "a," from the fatality of its absence, from its evasions that only sustain desire by default.[25]

At the end of her quest Cleopatra "finds" a lover who does not demand that she be less, or so the story goes as Cixous dreams it. As Cixous writes, she consciously takes on the self-dramatization of expressing her own longing through myth. She knows that this is not the "real" story. Of course, she knows the danger of self-dramatization is the reinstatement of romanticism which glories in the self. Yet, what *matters* is to "preserve" her dream of a love beyond the machinery of sado-masochism. Cixous will not settle for the ideology of lesser expectations that would say such a love is "unrealistic." Of course, it is "unrealistic" in the world as it is. Nor is she afraid to write erotic love in all its chaos, as opposed to Kristeva's more cautious affirmation of caring love, or *agape,* as our hope. "Romantic" language is one rhetoric amongst others that Cixous plays with to evoke her Other-Love. Undoubtedly Cixous' seemingly "romantic" language can almost be embarrassing to the Anglo-American feminist, more cautious before the apparent pitfalls for women of such language and such longing. Isn't this dream of Other-Love what always got us in trouble? But from whose theory, whose vantage point is "it" trouble? Not Cixous'. She celebrates that trouble, a celebration that itself is transformation through mimetic enactment of the feminine.

> At the beginnings of *Other-Love* there are differences. The new love dares the other, wants it, seems in flight, be-leaves, does some stealing between knowing and making up. She, the one coming from forever, doesn't stand still, she goes all over, she exchanges, she is desire-that-gives. Not shut up inside the paradox of the gift-that-takes or in the illusion of onely uniting. She enters, she betweens—she mes and thees between the other me where one is always infinitely more than one and more than me, without fearing ever to reach a limit: sensualist in our be-coming. We'll never be done with it! She runs through defensive loves, motherings and devourings.[26]

Runs through, but does not merely repeat. "Elsewhere she gives," and what is given in Cixous' interpretation is precisely the elsewhere, ungovernable by the machine of sado-masochism.

> They have—from the moment Antony saw Cleopatra coming to him—abandoned the minuscule old world, the planet—the shell with its thrones and rattles, its intrigues, its wars, its rivalries, its tournaments of the phallus, so grotesquely represented by the game of penis-check played by the imperialist superpowers of the triumvirate, with the mean solemnity that makes history. And with a leap, it is toward the new land they go to look for an entirely different life.[27]

Cleopatra, in Cixous' rendering of the myth, refigures Woman as she who plays with the effects of her castration so as not to accept it. Cleopatra is already the Queen. Even Dido, for Cixous, is not a Woman within whom she can self-dramatize her own experience and find significance. But Cleopatra, as figured by Cixous:

> Profusion, energy, exuberance. That is what she is. To be sure, she has at her disposition material reserves from whose magnificence her generosity can draw. Absolute Queen of several countries, she can give more than anyone. But also, all the splendor of the life that Antony and Cleopatra make together is commensurate with the fabulous grandeur of their investments, material, fleshly, symbolic, spiritual: not only do they have everything, strength, power—almost absolute—but it is nothing. They do not take all this for

something, they reduce it, with a kiss, to the nothing that it has never ceased to be, save in the eyes of beings who know nothing of love, that is to say, everybody. At no moment do all these glories, all these treasures, for which men make peoples kill each other, make them bat an eye.[28]

Cixous' tone undoubtedly has a Nietzschean exuberance to it. With him, she celebrates through her retelling of myth the Woman of style. But the difference is that she tells the myth by emphasizing the side of the feminine from within and as the threshold that gives as "elsewhere." "And far from kingdoms, from caesars, from brawls, from the cravings of penis and sword, from the unnameable 'goods' of this world, far from show and self-love, in harmony with each other, in accord, they live still."[29] Cixous refuses the Lacanian lesson that love must be "banging your head against the wall."[30] Says who?

In Cixous, we remember the dream of living beyond castration by giving the dream expression and dramatic significance through the retelling of the myth. This memory is re-collective imagination. We re-collect the mythic figures of the past, but as we do so we reimagine them. It is the potential variability of myth that allows us to work within myth, and the significance it offers, so as to reimagine our world and by so doing, to begin to dream of a new one. In myth we do find Woman, with a capital letter. These myths, as Lacan indicates, may be rooted in male fantasy, but they cannot, as he would sometimes suggest, be reduced to it. The "reality" presented in myth cannot be separated from the performative capacity of language. This is why we can work within to create an artificial mythology. As a result, even in myth, "reality" is always shifting as the metaphors in which it is presented yield a different and novel interpretation of the myth's meaning. I want to suggest that the feminist reconstruction of myth, such as we find in Christa Wolf's *Cassandra*, and in Carol Gilligan's recent lectures on love, involve recovering the feminine as an imaginative universal, which in turn feeds the power of the feminine imagination and helps to avoid the depletion of the feminine imaginary in the name of the masculine symbolic.[31] This use of the feminine as an imaginative universal does not, and should not, pretend to simply tell the "truth" of Woman as she was, or is. This is why our mythology is self-consciously an artificial mythology; Woman is "discovered" as an ethical standard. As she is "discovered," her meaning is also created. In spite of Cixous' wariness of her defeat, better to love like Dido than found the Roman empire. In like manner, we have no doubt after reading Wolf's *Cassandra* that Achilles had his priorities all wrong, and that Cassandra should have been listened to because she saw the connection between destruction and masculine subjectivity. In this sense, the reconstruction of myth can bring the *differend* out of the shadows.[32] Moreover, the reconstruction of myth also involves making explicit the utopian aspiration which the reinterpretation expresses. As Wolf explains: "The Troy I have in mind is not a description of bygone days but a model for a kind of utopia."[33] That utopian Troy is Cassandra's Troy, not that of Achilles! But we also are given a different definition through the reinterpretation of the myth of feminine power.

The feminist visionary who sees the world differently and tells us of her world may be ignored, but her vision cannot be taken away from her, as MacKinnon would argue, because the only viewpoint available is male. Wolf's allegory of the feminine indicates that Woman is the *seer* precisely to the degree that she skirts castration by the symbolic order. Cassandra saw "the truth" of Troy. In the feminist retelling of the myth, she was not mad, only true to her "reality." Feminine power as defined in the myth is the gift and the burden of "seeing." Of course, we can enter, and indeed to some degree we are forced to enter, the realm of the symbolic as we write, and by so doing we undermine our power of seeing differently. The price we pay for seeing differently is great. We know what Wolf's *Cassandra* suffers.

But, of course, there is also an implicit retelling of Oedipus in Wolf's *Cassandra*. The ascension into the symbolic for the masculine subject is the acceptance of castration. Blindness is what follows, the price to be paid. The illusion that having the penis is having the phallus protects against "seeing." The price that has been paid is that *man* cannot see his own castration. But Cassandra *sees* that he does not have what he thinks he has. If there is a central mistake in Dworkin's *Intercourse*,[34] it is to accept the masculine illusion that having the penis is having the phallus. In the end, it's just a penis.

When we, as women, speak of Wolf's *Cassandra*, of her experience as reinterpreted, of her Troy as retold, we do not return to essentialism; we dream from the standpoint of the mythical figures who could redeem the feminine as the threshold to a life beyond castration. We are imagining, not describing.

The Critique of Strategic Essentialism

But this process of reinterpretation and reimagination should not be thought of as strategic essentialism. Gayatri Spivak has argued that, in spite of the postmodern deconstruction of gender identity, and more specifically of Woman, we need to speak and write of Woman, or in Spivak's case, the shared conditions of women, in order to promote the politics of feminism.[35] This writing and speaking of Woman, she refers to as strategic essentialism; strategic, because it is consciously directed toward a political goal, essentialism because it reinstates some version of the essence of Woman and the feminine, even if only temporarily and for a political purpose. To quote Spivak:

> To begin with, I think the way in which the awareness of strategy works here is through a persistent critique. The critical moment does not come only at a certain stage when one sees one's effort, in terms of an essence that has been used for political mobilization, succeeding, when one sees that one has successfully brought a political movement to a conclusion, as in the case of revolutions or national liberation movements. . . . It seems to me that the awareness of strategy—the strategic use of an essence as a mobilizing slogan or masterword like *woman* or *worker* or the name of any notion that you would like—it seems to me that this critique has to be persistent all along the way, even when it seems that to remind oneself of it is counterproductive. Unfortunately, that crisis must be with us, otherwise the strategy freezes into something like what you call an essentialist position.[36]

For Spivak, then, the very word strategy implies a critique of postures toward essentialism that attempt to give us more than strategy. As she explains, a strategy is not necessarily a position, which can too easily be frozen into a supposed explanation. As she also explains, "[a] strategy suits a situation; a strategy is not a theory."[37]

Therefore, embracing essentialism strategically need not lead necessarily to the normative injunction of a movement—in this case, identification as a woman, a worker, etc.—masquerading as a statement about ontology. Spivak emphasizes the appeal to essentialism as strategy and, therefore, as an explicitly political posture. If there were a "timeless" essence, it could not be strategically affirmed or rejected. It would remain. In a sense, the word strategy contradicts essentialism, if understood as "something" always "there," even if distorted in form.

For Spivak, the more profound point is that we cannot help but risk essence. For example, for the anti-essentialist, anti-essentialism becomes the essence of feminism. According to Spivak, deconstruction does not dismantle "essentialism" altogether as much as it shows us "the unavoidable usefulness of something that is very dangerous."[38] But she not only embraces "strategic" essentialism, she also distinguishes essentialism from an appeal to "context" and thus from attempts to write of the specificity of any particular group, including women. The debate over essentialism has become obstructionist for Spivak precisely because the anti-essentialists tend to identify all attempts to specify female national or class difference as essentialist. Her objection to the form in which this debate has recently taken place is political and explicitly so.

In a similar manner, in the sense of being inspired by a political positioning, Diana Fuss has argued that Irigaray's "essentialism" should be understood politically.[39] Her "essentialism" is necessary, in other words, within the gender hierarchy of Western philosophy that has reduced Woman to lack, the ground of man's essence.

> Irigaray's reading of Aristotle's understanding of essence reminds one of Lacan's distinction between *being* and *having* the phallus: woman does not *possess* the phallus, she *is* the Phallus. Similarly, we can say that, in Aristotelian logic, a woman does not *have* an essence, she *is* essence. Therefore to give "woman" an essence is to undo Western phallomorphism and to offer women entry into subjecthood. Moreover, because in this Western ontology existence is predicated on essence, it has been possible for someone like Lacan to conclude, *remaining fully within traditional metaphysics*, that without essence, "women does not exist." Does this not cast rather a different light on Irigaray's theorization of woman's essence? A woman who lays claim to an essence of her own undoes the conventional binarisms of essence/accident, form/matter, and actuality/potentiality. In this specific historical context, to essentialize "woman" can be a politically strategic gesture of displacement.[40]

My disagreement with Spivak and with Fuss is twofold. First, as I have argued, the writing of the feminine need not be essentialist or naturalist as these two terms are technically understood. Deconstruction shows us the limit of essentialism as one specific discourse in which the being of the thing is unveiled in its universal properties or grasped in its general form. But deconstruction shows the limit of essentialism as it is thought to encompass all attempts to write specifically of any group or context. Thus, there is a difference between an appeal to essence and the illumination of feminine specificity as an explicit ethical and political position. Spivak, in other words, is right to claim that not every appeal to "context" involves essence. Her mistake is that we should even adopt the word "essence" when we are indicating specificity. It is precisely the confusion of essentialism with any writing of the specificity of feminine difference that leads to the belief that we risk either "essentialism" or indifference to the suffering of women. The solution is precisely the one of deconstruction: to show the limit of essentialism through—at least in the case of Husserl—its self-contradictory positioning within language.

As Fuss herself reminds us, Irigaray directly states that what she seeks "is not to create a theory of woman, but to secure a place for the feminine within sexual difference."[41] Thus the thinking of feminine difference, as we have seen with Derrida, cannot be separated from the problem of thinking difference more generally. The difficulty, of course, is that to conceptualize difference is once again to reinstate the identity through its very determination as a concept. As a result, Derrida engages multiple rhetorical strategies— supplement, difference, etc.—to indicate the difference that cannot be conceptualized. In like manner, Irigaray does not want to conceptualize Woman, nor determine her essence, even as the basis for her subjecthood, precisely because this determination through the concept would inevitably reinstate the specific, phallogocentric structure of identification in which subjecthood had been defined. To define through the concept, and more specifically the concept of essence in which the thing is understood with its own negativity— as we learn from Hegel[42]—is still to define difference within a pregiven totality of ideality, even in the unique Hegelian sense of essence. The Derridean demonstration is that this reinstatement of difference within ideality is inadequate to difference.

Within Irigaray, the demonstration is also of the specific inadequacy of the relational ideality which has confined woman in her role as complement. Therefore, Irigaray does not write of woman as if she is to be reconceptualized as an essence or a subject; rather she writes from the side of the feminine, a positioning that has been imposed by the gender hierarchy. However, this being said, we cannot simply place ourselves outside of the ideality in which the masculine and the feminine have been defined.[43] We can't just drop out of gender or sex roles and pick them up again when we feel like it. Disruption takes place from "within." The writing of the feminine does not, then, displace through the reconceptualization of Woman's essence, but through *mimesis* as *de-sistance*. The feminine, through *mimesis*, is no longer repudiated as an imposition, but affirmed as a positioning. Such an affirmation is clearly both ethical and political.

This leads me to my second objection to Spivak and Fuss. In one sense, to write from the side of the feminine could be considered strategic, adopted for the purpose of achieving a political goal. But such writing is not simply strategic, in the sense that it is a *conscious* manipulation. We cannot escape the hold of the feminine on the unconscious, which is precisely why we work within myth to reinterpret and transform, rather than merely reject. Theoretically, identity may be deconstructed as pure form or structure, as the *de-sistance* of *mimesis*; but gender identity is, practically, very much in place and enforced by the law. *Mimesis* is our only other option if we are not to repudiate the feminine. More importantly, the affirmation of the feminine, and indeed, of the irreducibility of the feminine, is not simply strategic, goal-oriented, but also utopian in that it tries to keep alive an "elsewhere" beyond our current conception of the political as an instrumental struggle for power. As we have seen in Cixous, the feminine encompasses the possibility of Other-Love. The maternal, as one figure, embodies the utopian possibility of a different non-violent relation to otherness. In Irigaray the feminine as threshold is the limit to what is, while *as fantasy*, it is the overflow that cannot be contained. The recasting of immanence and transcendence is metaphorized by Irigaray's writing from the position of the feminine, and more directly from within the female "sex."

> We need both space and time. And perhaps we are living in an age when *time must re-deploy space*. Could this be the dawning of a new world? Immanence and transcendence are being recast, notably by that *threshold* which has never been examined in itself unto *mucosity*. Beyond the classic opposites of love and hate, liquid and ice lies this perpetually *half-open* threshold, consisting of *lips* that are strangers to dichotomy. Pressed against one another, but without any possibility of suture, at least of a real kind, they do not absorb the world either into themselves or through themselves, provided they are not abused and reduced to a mere consummating or consuming structure. Instead their shape welcomes without assimilating or reducing or devouring. A sort of door unto voluptuousness, then? Not that, either: their useful function is to designate a *place*: the very place of uselessness, at least on a habitual plane. Strictly speaking, they serve neither conception nor *jouissance*. Is this, then, the mystery of female identity, of its self-contemplation, of that strange word of silence: both the threshold and reception of exchange, the sealed-up secret of wisdom, belief and faith in every truth?[44]

Irigaray's Ethical Evocation of the Body of Woman

Is Irigaray, in her evocation of the language of the feminine body, writing literally of the characteristics of that body? Is this a description of what a woman's body *is*, and therefore an identarian logic: so the body is, so Woman is? Is she mapping the feminine on to femaleness, and therefore reverting to the essentialism of universal properties? Irigaray herself has explicitly distinguished between the anatomical and the morphological in her writing of the body, a distinction that many Anglo-American feminist theorists have found unconvincing. Beyond this distinction, however, should be the realization that Irigaray's evocation of the threshold in which difference could be lived differently is not a *description* at all. It is an attempt to give body to the threshold of the phallocentric order as feminine difference, to be sure. But such writing is explicitly *ethical* in that it tries to offer us an engagement with the Other that confounds the mirror symmetry that annihilates the difference in identity. The feminine body is no longer sentenced to confinement within their vision of "it" as lack. In other words, her writing does not give us a description of the woman's body as the essence of femaleness. Instead, she denies the truth of their description. Anatomy is *not* destiny, as essence or as imposed by the law of gender identity. The *feminine body* "figures" as an ethical relation that includes carnality and, indeed, is embodied as the woman sex that is not one. "The lips that touch" figure a connection to one's self that does not involve the illusory projection of the subject as one consolidated entity. When we try to envision a "new world," a destiny that is not the fate imposed upon us by the phallogocentric machine, we rely on literary techniques, here not the literality of the body, but the feminine body returned as the symbolization of the non-violatable relationship to difference, embodied in the sex that is not one.

(Superimposed, moreover, these lips adopt a cross-like shape that is the prototype of the crossroads, thus representing both *inter* and *enter*, for the lips of the mouth and the lips of the female sex do not point in the same direction. To a certain extent they are not arranged as one might expect: those "down below" are vertical.)
Approached in this light, where the edges of the body join in an embrace that transcends all limits and which nevertheless does not risk falling into the abyss thanks to the fertility of this porous space, in the most extreme moments of sensation, which still lie in the future, each self-discovery takes place in that area which cannot be spoken of, but that forms the fluid basis of life and language.[45]

For this love of the Other, that celebrates the love of oneself as Other, Irigaray evokes God—"or a love so scrupulous that it is divine"[46]—but God is embodied through the redeployment of space. The challenge to the traditional categories of immanence and transcendence—necessary to the redeployment of space to save the utopian possibility of Other-Lover—is done more specifically through the evocation of the "difference" of the female body. Certainly, this is an explicit challenge to the phallogocentric metaphors through which we can only conceive of difference through identification of the object as "for" the subject, Irigaray's "mirror symmetry." Fuss, for example, has argued that Irigaray's "two lips" is a metonymic figure deliberately opposed to the reigning metaphor of the phallus, and with the phallus, to the reign of metaphor itself. Fuss' reliance on the "two lips" as a metonymic figure, as against a metaphorical figure, is too neat, since the refiguration is inescapably metaphorical. When Irigaray evokes the threshold as feminine difference, and the proximity to difference in oneself as feminine and as figured by the two lips in contact, she relies on the power of metaphoric transference, i.e., the threshold "as." But Fuss is certainly correct in her interpretation of Irigaray's writing of the body as literary refiguration, not just description. My addition here is that this refiguration through the feminine body is necessary for a carnal ethics.

The sexualization of the ethical relation is deliberate and is a denial of the rejection of the flesh often associated with the very idea of a moral subject. We saw earlier that the writing of the maternal body "presented" a "subject of heterogeneity" in which the One is tied to the Other and, therefore, is not truly One. This writing is also explicitly ethical in that the "maternal body" presents us with an image of love through non-identity. But Irigaray's suspicion of the identification of the feminine as the maternal function has turned her away from this image of the One with the Other. Instead, we are presented with the carnality of the feminine "sex" as the embodiment of a proximity which is not appropriation, nor even an encompassing of the Other by the self. There is a broader theoretical point to be made here: the evocation of the ethical relation, as Other-Love beyond the current identity structures established by phallogocentrism, cannot rely on an appeal to what "is" either as mere description, or as a reality given to us in "the conversation of mankind." Difference is also differentiation in time, what is different from what is. The future is not conceived as an evolution of the present, which would be the perpetuation of the same, and in this case, the same old story of gender hierarchy. Feminine writing, in this sense, turns us toward the future.

The politics of difference demands that we think the new, the different. But, of course, whenever we think the new, we can only conceive of it within the pregiven ideality. The pregiven ideality, which undoubtedly establishes the intelligible, also serves as an undertow to repetition. The role of the aesthetic in the dreaming of the new, the different, beyond the current machine of sado-masochism, lies precisely in its power to evoke, and indeed to challenge, the very conventions of intelligibility which make us "see" the world from the viewpoint of the masculine. The explicit "use" of feminine language is one tool in undermining current conceptualizations in which the world, ethics and politics are perceived. It would be a mistake, then, to think that writing of the feminine is apolitical, or even that it replaces the political with the aesthetic. Rather, the politics of difference, and the difference of the feminine, demand the evocation of utopian possibility and, therefore, inevitably have an aesthetic dimension. Without the aesthetic evocation of utopian possibility of feminine difference, we are left with the politics of revenge to which MacKinnon calls us. Feminism becomes another power-seeking ideology, a reversal that inevitably reinstates the old economy. As Irigaray reminds us, on the contrary, "[t]he transition to a new age coincides with a change in the economy of desire, necessitating a different relationship between man and god(s), man and man, man and the world, man and woman."[47] Put very simply, the politics of feminism needs its poetry for the redefinition of the goal of feminist politics, and indeed, of the very content of politics itself. Politics is now not only the struggle for survival within patriarchy, as important as that struggle obviously is, but also the struggle through the dream for a new world, a different future.

We can now "see" how Catharine MacKinnon has obscured the real power of the celebration of the utopian potential of feminine difference. As we have seen in her debate with Gilligan,[48] MacKinnon challenged her opponent for affirming the conditions of women's oppression. MacKinnon was not concerned to challenge Gilligan's empirical findings over the question of whether this "ethic of care" was actually correlated with women. She argued that to the degree that women demonstrated different characteristics, it was because they had been subordinated. As a result these characteristics should be rejected as suspect. On the perspective I have offered here it is not important whether women have *actually* achieved a different way of loving that is superior and therefore to be valued. Gilligan and Wolf's narrations are a part of our artificial mythology. As we tell the story, we are in part creating the reality in which this is the case. What matters is that the retelling of the feminine as an imaginative universal gives body to the "elsewhere" which makes this one appear "fallen," and gives us the hope and the dream that we may one day be beyond it. But it also allows us to affirm the feminine.

Double Writing and Literary Language

The need to pay attention to the specificity of literary language, and to avoid a literal interpretation of feminine writing and mythology, also has been evidenced in another debate within feminist circles. Some literary critics have challenged the recent writing of Afro-American women for mistaken idealizations of that experience which reinstates the philosophy of full presence. The attempt is to give specificity and, indeed, mythological significance to the unique experience of Afro-American women. For example, Hortense Spillers challenged the author Toni Morrison for privileging speech—or, more specifically, a primordial, musical language—over writing, as she writes of the "lost origin" of the Afro-American mother-tongue.[49] "Nan," the woman who "mothered" Sethe and others, still spoke that language. She, in Sethe's memory, still lived with the mother-tongue.

> Nan was the one she knew best, who was around all day, who nursed babies, cooked, had one good arm and half of another. And who used different words. Words Sethe understood then but could neither recall nor repeat now. She believed that must be why she remembered so little before Sweet Home except singing and dancing and how crowded it was. What Nan told her she had forgotten,

along with the language she told it in. The same language her ma'am spoke, and which would never come back. But the message—that was and had been there all along.[50]

I use this quote deliberately. There are certainly other places in the novel where Morrison seems to appeal to a lost language that is different, and fundamentally so, from the white man's. There are many different levels on which the passage I have chosen can be interpreted. The first is that Sethe, the runaway slave forced ultimately to kill her own children in order to save them from slavery, is mourning her own lost possibility of a return to the mythical, "true" mother who knew the secret and could unlock the message. "Nan," on this reading, is the allegorical figure of the loss of the mother and with her, her magic to give counter-structures of identification, and with them a different language. "Holding the damp white sheets against her chest, she was picking meaning out of a code she no longer understood."[51] On this reading, Morrison's allegory of the lost mother who could provide the basis of identification, and thus of meaning, should not be identified with a statement about what Afro-American language *is*. Her language is the imaginary through which Sethe dreams of a different life whose possibility as a real alternative has now been forgotten. Sethe, herself, is the figure of the mother who had to kill her children to prevent their enslavement. Thus the tale of loss doubles in on itself. Sethe is left with the white man's language, which blocks her from recovering "the message."

Here we have a brilliant narration through the character of the Afro-American woman, Sethe, of how the loss of the "true" mother leaves only the white man's realm of the symbolic, in which the Afro-American woman cannot "find" herself. She can only remember herself through a future which is not yet. In Morrison's evocation of the lost or spectral mother, and with her a different language—what Kristeva has referred to as the semiotic—we also have the expression of one of the most profound tragedies imposed by racism and imperialism, the suppression of the Other's language and culture. Certainly, no one has written more sensitively than Derrida about the suppression of the Other's language and culture associated with imperialism and its racist justifications. The attempt to recover a language other than theirs, always an act of creation although frequently sought through the memory, motivated by loss, is part of the resistance of the imperialists' attempt to be the sole defining power of who the oppressed people are. To stress the difference of Afro-American speech can only be done through contrast with "theirs." This is a similar point to the one that Kristeva makes, that the semiotic is ultimately still dependent on the symbolic since it relies on its point of contact where break and resistance are defined.[52] Thus, when the "lost" language is given specification as different from theirs, it can only seem to take on characteristics reminiscent of the privilege of full presence, voice over writing, musical repetition over the distance of articulated language, etc. When we speak *of* the semiotic, we are not writing from within "poetic" language. When the women in *Beloved* hollered "[t]hey stopped praying and took a step back to the beginning. In the beginning there were no words. In the beginning was the sound, and they all knew what that sound sounded like."[53] The "lost" language escapes capture by the white man's imposed conventions. "They sang it out and beat it up, garbling the words so they could not be understood; tricking the words so their syllables yielded up other meanings."[54]

But it would be a mistake, since this is a novel, to quickly identify the fictional specification of the lost language—itself, as I have suggested, connected to the allegory of the spectral mother—as replicating the error of the "philosophy of presence." The technical interpretive danger is that such an interpretation potentially fails to take into account the distinctiveness of literary language. Such a language has the power to formulate itself as act. The performative aspect of this language creates its own reality. In the great "novel," *Finnegans Wake*, the reality of "fici-fact" which is written is constantly being undermined, put back into motion, by the very language in which it "is."[55] The language of the night blows apart the seemingly static articulations and conventions of day-to-day life. But such "night" language is not the only way to write which is consistent with "the double gesture." One must be careful of bringing the charge of reinstating "the philosophy of full presence" against a novelist who, as such, is engaging in the distinctive genre of literary discourse, but particularly in this case, where Morrison's "references" to the characteristic lost language should themselves be interpreted within the allegory of the unrepresentable "past" of the spectral mother. *Beloved* is best read as an allegory of the loss of identity of Afro-American women imposed by slave society. The dead baby, taken away from mother by a society which could give her no possibility of life, other than one of enslavement, returns as the ghost that keeps the past in the so-called identity of the escaped slave. But as such, the ghost allegorizes the disruption of that present identity. As an apparition, there can be no coming to a permanent identity which is fully present. *Beloved* is the allegory of this absence in the present. There can be no adequate account of her loss in their language, other than as allegory.

Everybody knew what she was called, but nobody anywhere knew her name. Disremembered and unaccounted for, she cannot be lost because no one is looking for her, and even if they were, how can they call her if they don't know her name? Although she has claim, she is not claimed. In the place where long grass opens, the girl who waited to be loved and cry shame erupts into her

separate parts, to make it easy for the chewing laughter to swallow
her all away.

It was not a story to pass on.[56]

To pass on the story would require its translation into a language inadequate to its expression. The Law of the Father cannot identify the Afro-
American woman, nor can she identify herself within the law.

In her powerful article, "Sapphire Bound!," Regina Austin has also shown
us that "the law" cannot conceive of the Afro-American woman other than
as a combination of "black" and "female" and, therefore, cannot think of
her at all.[57] In analysis of several legal cases she demonstrates how problems
of jurisdiction in employment discrimination and constitutional law cannot
be adequately resolved because judges have been incapable of thinking of
exactly what "quantities" of "blackness" and "femaleness" actually make
up a "black woman" for purposes of the law. Is she one-third "woman," two-
thirds "black"? Or is she instead, half and half? Or two-thirds "woman," one
third "black"? Is she, at least in some ways, more "black" than "woman,"
or more "woman" than "black"? Such questions *matter*. But courts go
around and around again. In "Sapphire," Austin shows that the very conception of the person used to analyze what it is to be "black" and "woman"—
cutting her into properties, and defining "blackness" and "femaleness" as
separate—fails, and inevitably so, to "represent" her. An Afro-American
woman is not divisible into her "blackness," and her "femaleness." It is not
that she is both "black" and "female." She is an Afro-American female,
whose purported property of "blackness" can in no way be separated from
who she is as woman. Woman is lived differently when one is an Afro-
American female. Austin brilliantly shows that the concept of "woman"
itself is thought to be primordially white, with "blackness" thrown in later.
When the courts, in other words, speak of "woman" as something separable
from Afro-American descent, they are postulating a kind of femaleness, as
a property or substance, that all women share. Femaleness is a universal that
can "be" shared. Then we add race or nationality. But as Austin demonstrates, it is precisely femaleness that is lived differently when the woman is
Afro-American. The specificity that must be sought is that unique to the
Afro-American woman.

Austin herself adopts an innovative style—certainly innovative for a law
review article—to give body to what cannot be conceived under the analytic
structure of the person. The figure of Sapphire exposes the impossibility of
finding her "reality" under their system of representation. As they struggle
to know her, to capture her in their categories, she remains beyond, figuring
herself in a way that cannot be grasped by them, and yet she is figured as
Sapphire. Austin's discourse, thus, avoids the danger of "indifference" in
which nothing is said or written about the specificity unique to Afro-Ameri-

can women, at the same time that she exposes the fallacy of the assumption that all women share femaleness as a property, in the same way.

To summarize, the "double gesture" as I have interpreted it, does not by definition have to belie any attempt to give body to the specificity, or more generally to the specificity of the feminine, as it is lived by women of color. If it did, it would be a necessary risk to "indifference."[58] Reliance on allegory can never be fully separated from the metaphorical attempt to give body to the figures of Woman who are evoked. Sapphire speaks for herself.

The Critique of Myth

The Appeal to Identity

The danger of reinstating the myth of full presence is only one objection to the affirmation of the need to interpret, rather than reject, the myths of the feminine. And, indeed, there are at least two different conceptions of what this objection involves, both with an explicitly ethical dimension. The two different conceptions should be kept separate, for one involves an appeal to individual identity, the other, at least on one level, to individual and social difference.

The first was made by Simone de Beauvoir in *The Second Sex*.[59] The myths of the feminine according to de Beauvoir reflect the refusal of the male to understand that woman is not his Other, but a being like him, given to transcendence. More specifically, myth reflects the social containment of women in a gender identity, which marks them as the Other. The identification of Woman as Other is what the myths justify. Yet it is precisely this structure of justification that prevents Woman from living out her singularity. Each woman becomes Woman. But Woman is nothing other than the projection of "their" fantasy of otherness that sustains "their" identity, "their" primacy. Once the role of myth in the perpetuation of the fantasy made reality of Woman as Other is exposed, it leads to de Beauvoir's conclusion that feminism must dethrone, rather than affirm, even if through reinterpretation, myths of the feminine. The myths, in other words, can only reinforce the conceptualization of Woman as Other, which in turn justifies femininity as the fate which undermines every woman's destiny as an individual human being.

> The women of today are in a fair way to dethrone the myth of femininity; they are beginning to affirm their independence in concrete ways; but they do not easily succeed in living completely the life of a human being. Reared by women within a feminine world, their normal destiny is marriage, which still means practically subordination to man; for masculine prestige is far from

extinction, resting still upon solid economic and social founda-
tions.[60]

Obviously de Beauvoir recognizes that the actual subordination of women
finds its basis in economic and social forms of oppression. But for de Beauvoir
it is not a coincidence that the justificatory apparatus of patriarchal society
demands the creation of myths of Woman. Men are the subjects; as subjects
they are the myth-makers. Therefore, there is a significant difference between
the mythologization of Woman and the celebration of masculinity through
heroes, even if done in myth. It is enough for a man to be a man. As man,
according to de Beauvoir, he is singular, himself. It is his uniqueness as an
actual subject that is celebrated.

> A myth always implies a subject who projects his hopes and his
> fears toward a sky of transcendence. Women do not set themselves
> up as Subject and hence have erected no virile myth in which their
> projects are reflected; they have no religion or poetry of their own:
> they still dream through the dreams of men. Gods made by males
> are the gods they worship. Men have shaped for their own exalta-
> tion great virile figures: Hercules, Prometheus, Parsifal; woman
> has only a secondary part to play in the destiny of these heroes. No
> doubt there are conventional figures of man caught in his relations
> to women: the father, the seducer, the husband, the jealous lover,
> the good son, the wayward son; but they have all been established
> by men, and they lack the dignity of myth, being hardly more than
> clichés. Whereas woman is defined exclusively in her relation to
> man. The asymmetry of the categories—male and female—is made
> manifest in the unilateral form of sexual myths. We sometimes say
> "the sex" to designate woman; she is the flesh, its delights and
> dangers. The truth that for woman man is sex and carnality has
> never been proclaimed because there is no one to proclaim it.
> Representation of the world, like the world itself, is the work of
> men; they describe it from their own point of view, which they
> confuse with absolute truth.[61]

In her description of the asymmetry between men and women embodied
in the mythological status that Woman as Other takes on in patriarchal
society, de Beauvoir comes very close to MacKinnon. As they represent the
world, so it is. Myth, with its deep hold on the unconscious, simply masks
that reality, that they are representing us as Other. As in Lacan, in de
Beauvoir we cannot find ourselves in the feminine embodied in myth. We
cannot identify with their fantasy of us. To dethrone myth is to expose the
fallacy—which preserves the illusion that their point of view is rightfully

identified as absolute truth—that their point of view deserves the status of myth. The only "truth" that is embodied in myth is precisely their fantasy projection of Woman as Other, which belies our singularity. Translated into de Beauvoir's existentialist idiom, we remain in our transcendence from the immanence that the species seemingly imposes upon us because of our femininity, even if it is undoubtedly the case as de Beauvoir sees it that femininity is the imposition of the species on us.

But in her next paragraph she concedes:

> It is always difficult to describe a myth; it cannot be grasped or encompassed; it haunts the human consciousness without ever appearing before it in fixed form. The myth is so various, so contradictory, that at first its unity is not discerned: Delilah and Judith, Aspasia and Lucretia, Pandora and Athena—woman is at once Eve and the Virgin Mary. She is an idol, a servant, the source of life, a power of darkness; she is the elemental silence of truth, she is artifice, gossip, and falsehood; she is healing presence and sorceress; she is man's prey, his downfall, she is everything that he is not and that he longs for, his negation, and his *raison d'etre*.[62]

At the heart of de Beauvoir's analysis of myth is her desire to return Woman to humanity. Men and women are to affirm "their brotherhood" as fellow human creatures, irreducible to their supposed divergent essences as males and females. As with MacKinnon, what sexual difference might mean in the future, freed from patriarchal ordering, is unimaginable now. The goal of feminist politics is to be like them, no longer burdened by the demands of the species and the constraints of a structure of gender identity in which "the male seems infinitely favored."[63]

> The free woman is just being born; when she has won possession of herself perhaps Rimbaud's prophecy will be fulfilled: "There shall be poets! When woman's unmeasured bondage shall be broken, when she shall live for and through herself, man—hitherto detestable—having let her go, she, too, will be poet! Woman will find the unknown! Will her ideational worlds be different from ours? She will come upon strange, unfathomable, repellent, delightful things: we shall take them, we shall comprehend them." It is not sure that her "ideational worlds" will be different from those of men, since it will be through attaining the same situation as theirs that she will find emancipation; to say in what degree she will remain different, in what degree these differences will retain their importance—this would be to hazard bold predictions indeed. What is certain is that hitherto woman's possibilities have been

suppressed and lost to humanity, and that it is high time she be permitted to take her chances in her own interest and in the interest of all.[64]

The dethroning of the myths of femininity is a necessary, even if not sufficient, step in dismantling patriarchy. In de Beauvoir, it is evident that women, once freed from their complicity in their perpetuation of their oppression and from economic subordination, will find their opportunity to achieve "full membership in the human race."[65] De Beauvoir must assume that women are like men; it is only their "false" projections of us that disguise this reality.

> Now, what peculiarly signalizes the situation of woman is that she—a free and autonomous being like all human creatures— nevertheless finds herself living in a world where men compel her to assume the status of the Other. They propose to stabilize her as object and to doom her to immanence since her transcendence is to be overshadowed and forever transcended by another ego (*conscience*) which is essential and sovereign. The drama of woman lies in this conflict between the fundamental aspirations of every subject (ego)—who always regards the self as the essential—and the compulsions of a situation in which she is the inessential.[66]

Thus, the first objection to the reinterpretation of the myths of the feminine postulates a universal human subject with certain characteristics, even if those characteristics be defined as the inevitability of transcendence and individual liberty. In that sense the objection appeals to identity. To make the feminine different is only to deny her the subjectivity she can still live up to. I use the words "live up to" deliberately. There is perhaps no greater example of the writer who constantly calls us "to be" like them than de Beauvoir. It is we who have to try harder. It is no coincidence that the relief that comes with the affirmation of feminine difference does so, at least in part, because we can at last stop trying so hard to be *like* them. As Irigaray reminds us, it is time for women to stop trying so hard. De Beauvoir's existentialist subject is masculine. Our femininity is our deficiency, an unfortunate imposition. I cannot describe in detail the way in which *The Second Sex* tragically reflects the repudiation of the feminine at the same time that it holds out the hope for emancipation. I only want to emphasize here that de Beauvoir's call to dethrone mythology is based on an underlying truth that, in spite of the imposition of femininity, we are still subjects *like them*. We must at last give up the "bad faith" which protects our difference, but only at the expense of denying our freedom. Part of giving up the "bad faith" involves dethroning the myths of the feminine, and with it the recognition of our shared status as "subjects."

The Appeal to National, Racial and Class Difference

If de Beauvoir's suspicion of the myths of the feminine rests on a postulated projection of a "universal" subject—at least in the sense that all subjects are marked by transcendence—the second criticism of the reinterpretation of the myths of the feminine turns rather on the danger inherent in myth to deny difference, to speak of Woman when there are only women. Myth, in other words, can never be "fair" to the extremely variegated nature of the lives of actual women. The word "fair" is not a coincidence, because the critique of any attempt to speak or write of women is ethical as well as methodological. Methodologically, the charge is that gender never exhibits itself in pure form, so that we can know the essence of Woman herself, but only as the feminine as expressed in the lives of actual women who, if they are women, are also women of a particular national, ethnic, cultural, and class background. To speak or write of Woman thus obscures these differences. Here we have the ethical critique. To write of Woman homogenizes, masking the differences. In its worst case, it simply validates the experience of white middle-class women as being that of Woman. If done in the name of creating solidarity through gender coherence, such theorizing, including through the reinterpretation of myth, would seem to risk racism, national chauvinism, and class privilege.

But let us reexamine the charge of homogenization by looking again at the retelling of the Medea Myth in Toni Morrison's *Beloved*. In *Beloved*, the mother decides to kill her children to protect them from slavery. There are, of course many interpretations of Medea. But there is certainly one interpretation that emphasizes the mother's protectiveness of her children. It is not her revenge on the Man, but her desire to protect her children from the vengeance of the Father that leads her to kill her children. This protectiveness can be interpreted as the most horrifying example of the over-protectiveness associated with the castrating mother, who denies, in the most graphic sense, the autonomous lives of her children.

In *Beloved*, however, the one life that the mother cannot give them, or at least guarantee them, is an autonomous life in even the most minimal sense. She cannot protect them from slavery. And so she protects them from the white patriarchal order in the only way she can. She takes their lives before they are turned over to him. The Man will not get these children. In *Beloved*, the myth is retold, and as it is retold, the "meaning," the deep significance of killing one's children, is problematized, by the slave "reality" in which the mother is allowed to bear the children but not to "raise" them. As we have seen, *Beloved* challenges on a very profound level the idealization of mothering as the basis for a unique feminine "reality." In the context of slavery, mothering (in the sense of bearing and raising children) tragically takes on its own meaning through the stark denial of maternal control or even of intervention into her children's lives. What does it mean to kill one's children when, by definition, they are denied full lives as human beings by the laws of the Father? Could we possibly understand this act, except within its own context, the context of slavery? The answer, I think, is no. But, at the same time, the reliance on one of our most profound myths, the "killing" mother, dramatically exposes the tragedy of slavery, and more generally, of the "impotence" of the mother to "raise," resurrect, her children, even if she could free herself. Her freedom cannot be guaranteed by a law and a social order from which she is excluded. She can leave no trace of herself behind. She erases her progeny.

Down by the stream in back of 124 her footprints come and go, come and go. They are so familiar. Should a child, an adult place his feet in them, they will fit. Take them out and they disappear again as though nobody ever walked there.

By and by all trace is gone, and what is forgotten is not only the footprints but the water too and what is down there. The rest is weather. Not the breath of the disremembered and unaccounted for, but wind in the eaves, or spring ice thawing too quickly. Just weather. Certainly no clamor for a kiss.[67]

Far from homogenizing the situation of Woman, the allegory of *Beloved* relies on myth to dramatize the very difference of the Afro-American mother's situation. In this sense, the "universals" expressed in myth are not and cannot be just the mere repetition of the same. Indeed, the "universal," the symbol of the "killing mother," cannot be known except as it is told in context. The "universal" in myth, in other words, is much closer to what Michael Walzer has called the "reiterative universalism."[68] The "universal" is only as it is told, in its difference.

The tragedy in *Beloved*, in other words, is symbolized as the tragedy of Medea. It is told through myth that brings forth the full weight of the oppression of the Afro-American woman in slavery. But, as the tragedy of the Afro-American mother, the meaning of this tragedy shifts. Sixty million and more. The story is that *significant*. In itself it is myth.

In this sense, to affirm that in a bipolarized society of gender identity, Woman signifies, particularly through myths, does not mean that the feminine can be reduced to a set of shared characteristics or properties. I am returned to Austin's allegory of Sapphire,[69] of the Afro-American woman who cannot be represented in the conception of the person as a collection of properties, including "black" and "woman." Sapphire is feminine, but as Woman she "is" differently. She "is" an Afro-American woman.

To say that we can simply escape myth, particularly myths of the feminine, is to once again reinstate the "neutral" conception of the person. As in de Beauvoir, myth can only be dethroned if we can finally raise the veil and "see" that women are *fully human*. But what does it mean for de Beauvoir "to see" that women are potentially fully human? It means, ultimately, that we "see" that they can be like men. The "myths" only disguise that "reality." Supposedly overcoming the gender divide only reinstates it. If de Beauvoir is right we can only escape "myth" completely once we have been freed from patriarchy. Walter Benjamin once said that as long "as there is one beggar there will be myth." Transposed into the gender hierarchy, I would argue that as long as there is the gender hierarchy there will be myth. We cannot simply erase myth. Nor can we dethrone myth altogether without a "neutral" concept of the person. Our only option is to work within myth to reinterpret it.

Of course, to recognize that we are operating within myth and not an "essential" female nature is already in one sense to dethrone "myth," for it denies the myth's claim to an atemporal universality. So it was, so it will be. As the myth is retold—think again of Wolf's *Cassandra* or Morrison's *Beloved*—"the so it was," as determinative of "the future" is itself called into question. Indeed, the "so it was" is "seen" differently once it is "seen" from the "feminine" perspective. There is always, of course, the danger that myth reifies through its very power to give significance. My only reminder is that this danger cannot be solved through the denial of myth's hold on us in a genderized society. The way beyond is to retrace the circle that seemingly encircles us. The retelling of myth begins—and perhaps we will always "be" so beginning—to specify the feminine, so that "herstory" can be told, in all its suffering and pain, as well as in all its glory.

"riverrun, past Eve and Adam's . . . ."[70]

Conclusion

"Happy Days"

Yes, tid. There's where. First. We pass through grass behush the bush to. Whish! A gull. Gulls. Far calls. Coming, far! End here. Us then. Finn, again. Take. Bussoftlhee, mememormee! Till thousandsthee. Lps. The keys to. Given! A way a lone a last a loved a long the[1]

Have we been given the keys to unlock the prison of gender identity so powerfully described by Lacan? Is the feminine the threshold through which we can open another possibility of Other-Love, evoked as a non-violative relation to difference, more generally? Is there even such a positioning as the feminine which already affirms the beyond to the *prison*, a prison in which "true" heterosexuality is both an impossibility, because the Other is never truly recognized as "hetero," and yet our fate? These are the questions around which this book has circled. As we have seen, for Lacan, sexuality is determined by gender structures. Of course, in Lacan, this determination is a social imposition, not a biological or an ontological necessity. Yet sexual difference is legislated in such a way as to reproduce its own categories, the most fundamental being the gender division itself. This division is into two, masculine or feminine. As Lacan explains, "[a]ny speaking being whatever is inscribed on one side or the other."[2] Thus, the possibility of access to the positioning of the other "sex" does not involve a challenge to the divide itself. In like manner, Lacan's exposure of the inevitable failure of "sexual" identity, precisely because there is no biological sequence that ultimately results in a normal, mature sexual identity, does not include the political undermining of the imposed structures of gender. The failure instead demands the fantasy of the Other that secures identity. In the case of the masculine subject, that fantasy is the psychical fantasy of Woman. But, of course, Lacan's central insight is that, given the gender divide, these projected fantasies of Woman define what women are allowed "to be" within the symbolic; her "being" is as their fantasy. To not take up the fantasy position is to not "be" a woman.

Unlike in Wittig, however, we cannot live our sexuality differently and, therefore, become "other" than one or the other, either male or female. In Lacan, the subject's entry into language secures the repetition of the law, which consolidates gender identity. Thus, the connection between the concept of *jouissance* and the concept of significance in Lacan's sense, as what shifts in language, does not promise a re-evolution—a re-evolution which might signal the beyond to our current gender hierarchy. We cannot, in other words, break through to the "elsewhere" of a new choreography of difference through the restylization of our sexuality. Thus, it is a mistake to argue that because, in Lacan, gender identity is only an effect of signification, not a fixed reality or a pre-discursive essence or nature, we have been given a key to freedom. As Kafka's parable "In the Penal Colony" so brilliantly reminds us, a sentence can be written in flesh.[3] In Lacan, we are sentenced to be signified in a gender. This sentence is truly written in our flesh, in our lived sexuality. Sexuality is not in and of itself a beyond to "sex," as determined by the law of gender. Here, we are returned to the "truth" of MacKinnon, gender is written in our sex as our sexuality. But is there "her sex" beyond or, more precisely, irreducible to the definition of the current gender hierarchy? As we have seen, the answer is yes, at least in the sense that "her sex" is only presented in language and, therefore, cannot be reduced to the unshakable reality, supposedly constructed by the male gaze, in which we are as they have made us. The political and ethical importance of the connection between *jouissance* and the inevitable shifts in language lies in this potential undermining of any given social order.

Yet, even if we rethink the ethical and political significance of Lacan's insight, it is still too easy to argue that, just because gender identity only signifies within a chain of signifiers that does not end in a biologically or ontologically given identity, we can just shake off our gender and live our sex and our sexuality differently. Philosophically, gender identity may be a parody if we understand that the assumption of gender identity involves "dressing up," a role, not an actuality just given. Gender identity never yields "perfect" identification, precisely because there is a phantasmatic dimension to the assumption of gender roles. As we have seen, gender identity cannot be reduced to sex, understood either as a biological reality, a sex that results necessarily from the body, or even as a conventionally accepted definition. To attempt to reduce it in this way is to forget that sex is lived in gender and that gender is performed in language. Sex "is" as performance.

Thus, I agree with Judith Butler that a crucial aspect of a feminist politics that seeks release from rigid gender identity plays with the possibility that inheres in the imperfection of repetition—what Derrida calls iterability—which "is" identity. As Butler explains:

> The critical task is rather, to locate strategies of subversive repetition enabled by those constructions, to affirm the local possibilities of intervention through participating in precisely those practices of repetition that constitute identity and, therefore, present the immanent possibility of contesting them.[4]

But I would specifically contrast the re-evolution of *mimesis* as *de-sistance* with the repetition compulsion of gender identity so brilliantly described by Lacan. Yet *mimesis* remains our only strategy precisely because displacement takes place within a location. Our space, in which we live sexually, is constrained by the imposition of gender identity.

Thus, to paraphrase the words of Hélène Cixous, the symbolic not only exists, it holds power. Its power is to enforce itself as truth. As Butler explains, to contest its supposed truth, we explore the phantasmatic dimension of gender identity that is disguised as biological or ontological necessity. This exposure is not an unveiling of another reality that belies the claim to truth, as much as it is a "shaking up from within," a different performance. But I would add that the contest to gender identity also involves the recognition of *derelection* that results from the gender hierarchy that pushes the feminine under. The tragedy is in the fate that is not necessary but which, at the same time, is imposed so that it appears as fate. We need not only "show" that what poses as ontological or natural necessity is a normative injunction; we also need to remember who and what is at stake in that imposition: ourselves as women.

Gender identity is a prison for both sexes, but given "the reality" of masculine privilege, the two genders do not suffer the same entrapment. As a result, *mimesis* tells us how to re-evolve with the definitions of the feminine. In that sense, it is explicitly ethical. The feminine is not an established set of properties of the female. The feminine, as continually re-metaphorized, does not demand that we reinstate a unified, identifiable subject, Woman. The feminine, through *mimesis*, is an affirmation, a valuation, but even so, is not a traditional, ethical concept that would identify the good of Woman with her fundamental properties. This approach to the truth of Woman, as we have seen in West's Aristotelian approach to the feminine, is ethical. Yet the affirmation I offer, as an affirmation, as valuation, is also ethical in that it recognizes the value of the Other of sexual difference. This is why I have adopted the expression "ethical feminism" to indicate that the affirmation of the feminine involves a positioning, not just a description. Given the gender hierarchy, in other words, the displacement of gender identity demands this affirmation, with its explicit utopian dimension. Otherwise we are returned to the devaluation of the feminine.

Furthermore, the recognition of the tragedy of *derelection* emphasizes that the performance of gender identity is not a role we consciously take on, a position consistent with the denial of a pre-genderized I. We are cast. This life of gender identity is not a stage we can simply walk off when we choose, even if we can always perform differently. To argue that it is, is to deny the unconscious, and its hold over us. Of course, we cannot directly speak *of* the unconscious. We can know "it" only as it *operates*. Lived within an enforced, yet hollow, heterosexuality—because never truly "hetero"—gender identity is a tragedy, even if seemingly only expressible as farce. But the lack of words and even the absence of the Other we can talk to, because we are separated by the gender divide, marks the Other of the unconscious as we reach out and find no way to touch the Other, and yet let her be Other. And yet, as Derrida reminds us with Samuel Beckett, the dream of the Other remains when we speak or write. The dream makes our "happy days" possible.

> Winnie: Do you know what I dream sometimes? (*Pause.*) What I dream sometimes, Willie. (*Pause.*) That you'll come round and live this side where I could see you. (*Pause. Back front.*) I'd be a different woman. (*Pause.*) Unrecognizable. (*Turning slightly towards him.*) Or just now and then, come round this side just every now and then and let me feast on you. (*Back front.*) But you can't, I know. (*Head down.*) I know.[5]

Played as a farce, lived as tragedy. As Beckett's play, *Happy Days,* proceeds, we see Winnie slowly sinking into the "same old shit." Yet she keeps speaking. She keeps talking as if her coming oblivion were not happening. She keeps hoping. As she hopes, she talks. As Winnie sinks, all the while trying to keep face, we cannot help but be returned to MacKinnon's critique of what it means for us to make ourselves up for them. MacKinnon always wants us to remember that we are being buried alive.

Winnie allegorizes the tragedy that is imposed upon women as their subordination. The feminine is pushed down and under. Slowly, slowly, she is buried. Our "reality" obliterated as what cannot be said. Silence, only, awaits us. Her "talk," translated into phallogocentric discourse, becomes foreign to her once again, which is why I have argued that consciousness-raising must involve creation, not just discovery. We need our poetry, our fantasies and our fables; we need the poetic evocation of the feminine body in Irigaray and in Cixous if we are to finally find a way beyond the muteness imposed by a gender hierarchy in which our desire is "unspeakable."

For someone like MacKinnon, the terrible reality of women's oppression, the horror that our lives are a slow burial, makes it obscene to argue the purportedly "postmodern" challenge to gender identity, and thus to her unmodified feminism. This challenge insists that we "always, already"[6] have the key to our freedom. For MacKinnon, the world is not the world of gender imprisonment in which everyone suffers, but the perpetuation of male power. As we have seen, for MacKinnon, only when we, women, have power, will we be able to free ourselves. For now, we must seek power. On this interpretation of our social world, men, as a rule, will not seek justice with us. As a power ideology, hers is also the politics of revenge against them. "Out Now." According to MacKinnon, we have only one real choice: to blow ourselves out of the shit which is slowly burying us. Yet, as we have seen, on Lacan's stage of wimps and ghosts the farce is played out differently, because it is not just at the expense of women as MacKinnon would have it. Here, again, we are returned to Beckett's allegory:

> Winnie: What is a hog exactly? What exactly is a hog, Willie, do
> you know, I can't remember. What *is* a hog, Willie,
> please!
> Willie: Castrated male swine. Reared for slaughter.[7]

Not much left in the life of a "castrated male swine reared for slaughter." Willie is on all fours. Castrated. Crawling. He can't even stand up. Hardly the tall, powerful Man who makes the world in his own image. He can't even engage in conversation. Now and again he intervenes. But that is not the back and forth we think of as conversation. If MacKinnon confuses man with God, it is because she buys into the fantasy compensation that identifies having the penis with having the phallus. In the allegory, it is Winnie who keeps talking. She has not yet been shut up. She speaks as she sinks. As she speaks, she belies her condition, that she is just "there" to be buried. As she insists that she can speak, she speaks of her "reality," a "reality" which includes her dream of the Other that affirms her life as *other* than just slow burial. Beckett's play is the allegory that lives only against that possibility of Irigaray's dream of a true alliance between "the sexes." In the war between the sexes imposed by the gender hierarchy, no one can win. MacKinnon, on the other hand, still thinks we can win, if we finally fight back, rather than deceive ourselves with false hopes.

In MacKinnon, it is *only* for them that we go on talking. Perhaps so.

> Winnie: Not that I flatter myself you hear much, no Willie, God
> forbid. Days perhaps when you hear nothing. But days

> too when you answer. So that I may say at all times, even
> when you do not answer and perhaps hear nothing,
> something of this is being heard, I am not merely talking
> to myself, that is in the wilderness, a thing I could never
> bear to do—for any length of time. That is what enables
> me to go on, go on talking that is.[8]

But is it just for man? Or is it for the Other we must at least dream is there, listening, if we are to go on talking or writing at all.

> Winnie: There is so little one can speak of. One speaks of it all.
> All one can. I used to think . . . I say I used to think that
> I would learn to talk alone. By that I mean to myself, the
> wilderness. But no. No no. Ergo you are there. Oh no
> doubt you are dead, like the others, no doubt you have
> died, or gone away and left me, like the others, it doesn't
> matter, you are there.[9]

We are now returned to Derrida's intervention which attempts to show us why Lacan's insight into the connection between sexuality and language can be turned against Lacan himself. Such a challenge involves the insistence that because gender is a role, we can play with ourselves differently. Derrida does not deny the hold of gender identity and the tragedy of the failure of love, and indeed, of "conversation" it brings in its wake. So he begins with Lacan.

Also, Derrida returns us to "Woman" as the undeniability of uncastratability.[10] It is the woman who dances differently, who promises the new beginning. Winnie: "Begin, Winnie. Begin your day, Winnie."[11]

So to begin to climb out, we return to Woman. Once again we have the connection between deconstruction and feminism. Deconstruction reminds us that we might yet fly away; it may not be our fate to forever "sink into the same old shit."

> Winnie: The earthball. I sometimes wonder. Perhaps not quite
> all. There always remains something. Of everything.[12]

By deconstructing the fate of gender identity, deconstruction keeps open the threshold to a different destiny. Yes, a world in which we might talk to one another face to face. Feminine writing embodies this dream through numerous and diverse writing stylizations. In the encoding of the dream, including the dream of the other way embodied in the feminine "sex," they move beyond Derrida. This dream of Other-Love is the focus for the alliance between the "sexes" that might make dialogue possible.

Is there anything inherent in deconstruction, then, that denies the desirability of dialogue? Certainly not. But Derrida and the Lacanian feminists also do not deny the hold of unconscious structures that weigh us down and ultimately threaten to silence us. We are reminded of the condition in which multiple voices, sexed differently, engage one another. That condition involves the break-up of the current gender prison. Dialogism, in other words, cannot skirt the issue of gender hierarchy by postulating persons who talk. The very condition of conversation is that we let the other be Other, and it is precisely this "reconciliation" with the Other that is rendered impossible by the gender hierarchy.

> Winnie: Oh I can well imagine what is passing through your mind, it is not enough to have to listen to the woman, now I must look at her as well. Well it is very understandable. Most understandable. One does not appear to be asking a great deal, indeed at times it would seem hardly possible—to ask less—of a fellow-creature—to put it mildly—whereas actually—when you think about it— look into your heart—see the other—what he needs— peace—to be left in peace—then perhaps the moon—all this time—*asking for the moon*.[13]

We have been sentenced. But even as sentenced one can still write differently. Derrida continues "to ask for the moon" precisely *through* deconstruction. But such writing demands the recognition of Woman, of the way in which the feminine is violently repressed in a phallogocentric world. Woman *is being* buried. But as she sinks she also remains, Other. Never entirely obliterated. "The Other, remains." As she remains she waits. The threshold between hope and ultimate silence can be protected if Woman is allegorized as the gatekeeper who continually calls to the Other. The writing of the feminine also celebrates Woman as threshold to Other-Love.

The feminine and, more particularly, the fantasy of the maternal and the writing of the maternal body, evokes this Other-Love in which the Other is welcomed as the Other. Nor is the explicit reliance on fantasy against the attempt to specify the actual conditions of women's suffering. Instead, I have advocated that it is the utopian "metaforeplay"[14] that provides the viewpoint, or more precisely a "redemptive perspective," by which we "see" this world as fallen. But to understand that we evoke Woman as fantasy, as utopian projection, is to understand her "metaforeplay" not as an unshakable *truth*. Understanding the feminine as myth and as allegory thus involves the recognition of the phantasmatic dimension of gender identity. But it allows for the re-engagement with these phantasms as they give shape to what gets called reality. Cixous' engagement with myth shows us one way to re-engage the phantasms. Phantasms also give us a process of identification as a performance which, as such, does not demand a conceptualization of an identity for Woman. But in like manner, it breaks the silence imposed by *derelection*, in which identification through Woman is denied or identified as phallic.

As we have seen, the suspicion of "metaforeplay" cannot be justified because such writing inevitably reinstates essentialism. For Irigaray, the writing of her "sex" is an explicit political act. Our bodies, our desire, have been buried by a discourse in which we cannot metaphorize our desire. Modern culture and its diseases—bulimia and anorexia, for example—can they not be understood as part of this burial? Is Irigaray saying this is what women are? Not at all. The very discourse that *this is what is*, is denied. Instead, the woman's voice is celebrated. The woman who speaks and writes against the never-ending process of burial is herself a threat to the system that would deny her existence, her otherness, the conditions of her continuing existence as otherness.

Otherness to what? To the system of gender hierarchy Beckett so beautifully allegorizes. The system in which a woman sinks into the shit, while a man crawls around behind unable to talk to her. Is this just a heterosexual reality? As we have seen, homosexuality cannot be so easily separated from heterosexuality as long as we understand the social and structural hold of our practice of sexuality by the gender hierarchy. It is only if we assume that gender can be dropped in sex, that we could argue that homosexuality can be completely separated from the meaning given to it by the dominant heterosexual matrix. The undermining of gender identity on which this matrix rests demands that we recognize the repudiation of the feminine as crucial to its functioning. Can this affirmation be engaged in by men, and as part of themselves? As we have seen, the answer is yes, even if their positioning *vis à vis* the feminine can never be exactly the same as a woman's. It is the engagement of "metaforeplay" with the exposure of genealogy that allows us to have it both ways, and without reinstating the repudiation of the feminine as the basis for feminism.

Daddy, "you do not do, you do not do"[15] is the voice only of rejection and, as Kristeva reminds us, all too easily leads to silence and even to suicide. But, as we have seen, Kristeva's rejection of the fantasy resurrection of the mother is also extremely threatening to women. In her later writing she can give us nothing but identification with the imaginary father as the only basis of a healthy identity. As a result, she leaves us in a state of *derelection*. Once again, the feminine is denied in the name of accommodation to this world. Winnie allegorizes the full price we pay for that accommodation. The voice of Woman evokes hope of a beyond, an Other in her very effort to talk. This is Cixous' mythical voice of the mother. The utopianism of feminine writing lies precisely in the rejection of this accommodation. But unlike MacKinnon, the repudiation of the feminine is also condemned as the fundamental "form" of accommodation.

The affirmation of the feminine may be impossible as other than the reversion to the old stereotypes. Undecidability cannot be wiped out in an appeal to knowledge if there is no ontological given to the feminine we can appeal to as our truth. We cannot know for sure, "Yes this is definitely different. Now we are affirming Woman as other than the signifier of their desire." But the possibility that we might be approaching a new choreography of sexual difference with every new step we take can also not be wiped out. The unexpected pleasure of the Other who remains with us, who keeps up the pace, is always a possibility. Affirmed as the feminine, the threshold might be the opening to a new alliance. This is what Irigaray seeks to protect: the possibility that feminine difference performs against phallogocentrism in the name of the Other. As we have seen, this performance is affirmed as performance, not as a mere description of what woman is. But as performance, its evocation is explicitly utopian. The utopia is precisely one in which the Other is other not just as male/female, but as singular, particular. The dream of a new choreography of sexual difference is not mere repetition of heterosexuality; it is instead the sexuality lived as love that must be premised on the truly "hetero," the Other, the beyond to our current system of gender identity in which difference is always reduced to the same gender divide with conventional "heterosexuality." Such a new choreography may be asking for the moon, but through asking for the moon, we speak and write.

Ontology of gender identity, then, has been deconstructed not just to expose the normative injunction that lies at its base, but to protect the possibility of a different destiny. Oh, happy day.

Notes

Introduction: Writing the Mamafesta:
The Dilemma of Postmodern Feminism

1. I use the word "postmodern" reluctantly. The very idea that periods of history can be rigidly separated is one I reject. More importantly, "postmodern" has become a catch-all phrase that defines very different philosophical positions as giving a similar message. As a result, we can potentially lose what is unique in the different positionings.

   That being said, I use the word anyway. It indicates both a longing—a longing certainly consistent with this book—that we not be fated to entrapment by the political and ethical concepts of feminism identified as modern. Those concepts fail to give significance to sexual difference as a philosophical question.

2. James Joyce, *Finnegans Wake* (New York: Penguin Books, 1939), p. 104.

3. Ibid., pp. 107–08.

4. As Luce Irigaray writes:

   > Woman never speaks the same way. What she emits is flowing, fluctuating. *Blurring*. And she is not listened to, unless proper meaning (meaning of the proper) is lost. Whence the resistances to that voice that overflows the "subject." Which the "subject" then congeals, freezes, in its categories until it paralyzes the voice in its flow.
   >
   > "And there you have it, Gentlemen, that is why your daughters are dumb." Even if they chatter, proliferate pythically in works that only signify their aphasia, or the mimetic underside of your desire. And interpreting them where they exhibit only their muteness means subjecting them to a language that exiles them at an ever increasing distance from what perhaps they would have said to you, were already whispering to you. If only your ears were not so formless, so clogged with meaning(s), that they are closed to what does not in some way echo the already heard.

> Outside of this volume already circumscribed by the signification articulated in (the father's) discourse nothing is: *awoman. Zone of silence.*

Irigaray, *This Sex Which is Not One*, pp. 112–13 (emphasis in original). See also, note 18 and accompanying text.

5. Marguerite Duras has recently addressed the issue of women's sorrow and silencing. As she has eloquently put it:

> I think that we women are all [affected], and not all men. Sorrow, for men, up to now, throughout time, throughout history, has always found its outlet, its solution. It was transformed into anger, into external events, like war, crimes, turning women out, in Moslem countries, in China, burying adulterous women with their lovers, both alive or disfiguring them. When I was five years old, in Yunnan they were still burying lovers alive, face to face in the casket. The deceived husband was the sole judge of the punishment. We have never had any other recourse but muteness. Even so-called liberated women, by their own declaration. One cannot compare women's experience of sorrow with man's. Man cannot bear sorrow, he palms it off, he has to get away from it, he projects it outside of himself in hallowed, ancestral demonstrations which are his recognized transfers—battle, outcries, the show of discourse, cruelty.

Marguerite Duras, *Green Eyes*, trans. Carol Barko (New York: Columbia University Press, 1990), p. 140. Originally published as *Les yeux verts* (Paris: Cahiers du Cinéma, 1980, 1987).

6. Martin Heidegger, *Being and Time*, trans. John Macquarrie and Edward Robinson (New York: Harper and Row, 1962).

7. Jean-François Lyotard, *The Differend: Phrases in Dispute*, trans. George Van Den Abbeele (Minneapolis: University of Minnesota Press, 1988). Originally published as *Le Différend* (Paris: Les Editions de Minuit, 1983).

8. Luce Irigaray, *Speculum of the Other Woman*, trans. Gillian C. Gill (Ithaca: Cornell University Press, 1985), p. 239 (italics in the original). Originally published as *Speculum de l'autre femme* (Paris: Les Editions de Minuit, 1974).

9. Susan Suleiman explores women's reappropriation of their identities as speaking, sexual, maternal, political subjects through writing, through what she calls in a chapter title, "Feminist Intertextuality." See Susan Rubin Suleiman, *Subversive Intent: Gender, Politics, and the Avant-Garde* (Cambridge: Harvard University Press, 1990), pp. 119–80. Specifically, she looks to Cixous' writing as an expression and affirmation of the heterogeneity of woman which does not deny any aspect—including motherhood.

> Heterogeneous, yes. For her joyous benefits she is erogenous; she is the erotogeneity of the heterogeneous: airborne swimmer, in flight, she does not cling to herself; she is dispersible, prodigious, stunning,

desirous and capable of others, of the other woman that she will be, of the other woman she isn't, of him, of you.

Hélène Cixous, "The Laugh of the Medusa," in *Signs* (Summer 1976), reprinted in *New French Feminisms: An Anthology*, ed. Elaine Marks and Isabelle de Courtivron (Amherst: University of Massachusetts Press, 1980), p. 260.

Suleiman notes how in pieces such as this Cixous "suggests, in a significant reversal of the avant-garde (and sometimes avant-garde feminist) stereotype, that a woman can be politically radical, artistically innovative and yet a mother." *Subversive Intent*, p. 166.

10. See Gayle Rubin, "The Traffic in Women: Notes on the Political Economy of Sex," in *Toward an Anthropology of Women*, ed. Rayna R. Reiter (New York: Monthly Review Press, 1975).

11. Catharine A. MacKinnon, *Feminism Unmodified: Discourses on Life and Law* (Cambridge: Harvard University Press, 1987), p. 54.

12. See Naomi Schor, "This Essentialism Which Is Not One: Coming to Grips with Irigaray," in *differences*, vol. 1, no. 2 (1989), p. 45.

13. Sylvia Plath, "Daddy," in *The Collected Poems* (New York: Harper and Row, 1981), pp. 222–23.

14. Alice Jardine, for example, has written of this "tension" within French feminine writing. See Alice Jardine, "Prelude: The Future of Difference," in *The Future of Difference*, ed. Hester Eisenstein and Alice Jardine (Boston: G.K. Hall and Co., 1980), p. xxvi.

15. See Gayatri Chakravorty Spivak with Ellen Rooney, "In a Word. *Interview*," in *differences*, vol. 1, no. 2.

16. Schor, "This Essentialism Which Is Not One," p. 45.

17. Domna C. Stanton, "Difference on Trial: A Critique of the Maternal Metaphor in Cixous, Irigaray and Kristeva," in *The Poetics of Gender*, ed. Nancy K. Miller (New York: Columbia University Press, 1986), p. 177.

18. Irigaray, *Speculum*, p. 237.

19. Schor, "This Essentialism Which Is Not One," p. 40.

20. Irigaray, *Speculum*, pp. 11–13.

21. See Jacques Derrida, *The Truth in Painting*, trans. Geoffrey Bennington and Ian McLeod (Chicago: University of Chicago Press 1987).

22. Toni Morrison, *Beloved* (New York: Penguin Books, 1987).

23. Jean-François Lyotard, *The Differend*.

1. The Maternal and the Feminine:
Social Reality, Fantasy and Ethical Relation

1. Robin West, "The Difference in Women's Hedonic Lives: A Phenomenological Critique of Feminist Legal Theory," *Wisconsin Women's Law Journal* (1987), p. 118 (emphasis in original).

2. Ibid., p. 82 (citations omitted, emphasis in original).

3. Robin West, "Jurisprudence and Gender," *University of Chicago Law Review*, vol. 55, no.1 (1988), p. 70.

4. West, "The Difference in Women's Hedonic Lives," p. 140, (emphasis in original).

5. West, "Jurisprudence and Gender," p. 71 (emphasis in original).

6. Naomi Schor, "This Essentialism Which Is Not One: Coming to Grips with Irigaray," in *differences*, vol. 1, no. 2 (1989), p. 38.

7. As we will see, I would include writers such as Hélène Cixous, Luce Irigaray, and Julia Kristeva who see in essentialist and naturalistic accounts a reinscription of the patriarchal structure.

8. Jacques Derrida, *Margins of Philosophy*, trans. Alan Bass (Chicago: University of Chicago Press, 1982), p. 164. Originally published as *Marges de la philosophie* (Paris: Les Editions de Minuit, 1972).

9. This is the title of a section of Derrida's book, *Margins of Philosophy*, p. 169.

10. Ibid., pp. 162–64.

11. Ibid., p. 160 (emphasis in original).

12. Ibid., pp. 171–72 (emphasis in original).

13. Ibid., p. 270 (emphasis in original).

14. Ibid.

15. Ibid., p. 249.

16. West, "Jurisprudence and Gender," p. 65.

17. See Jacques Derrida and Christie McDonald, "Choreographies," *Diacritics*, vol. 12 (Summer, 1982), reprinted in *The Ear of the Other: Otobiography, Transference, Translation*, ed. Christie McDonald, trans. Peggy Kamuf (Lincoln: University of Nebraska Press, 1985). Originally published as *L'oreille de l'autre* (Montreal: V1B Editeur, 1982).

18. Ibid.

19. Sigmund Freud, *Beyond the Pleasure Principle*, ed. and trans. James Strachey (New York: W. W. Norton and Co., 1961), pp. 8–11. See also, Luce Irigaray, "The Gesture in Psychoanalysis," in *Between Feminism and Psychoanalysis*, ed. Teresa Brennan, trans. Elizabeth Guild (London: Routledge, 1989); Jacques Derrida, "Roundtable on Autobiography," in *The Ear of the Other*, trans. Peggy Kamuf, pp. 69–71.

20. Jacques Lacan, *Feminine Sexuality: Jacques Lacan and the école freudienne*, ed. Juliet Mitchell and Jaqueline Rose, trans. Jaqueline Rose (New York: W. W. Norton and Company, 1985), p. 82.

21. Julia Kristeva, "La femme, ce n'est jamais ça" [Woman can never be defined], *Tel quel* (Autumn 1974), reprinted in *New French Feminisms: An Anthology*, ed. Elaine Marks and Isabelle de Courtivron, (New York: Schocken Books by arrangement with University of Massachusetts Press, 1980), p. 137.

22. Lacan, *Feminine Sexuality*, p. 82.

23. Ibid., p. 83.

24. Ibid., pp. 83–84.

25. See ibid., pp. 80–81.

26. Ibid., p. 144.

27. Ibid., p. 144 (emphasis in original).

28. *Jouissance* is a term which, as used by Lacan, lacks direct translation. In contemporary philosophical and psychoanalytic discourse, it is often taken to refer to women's specifically feminine, total sexual pleasure. For a more detailed and nuanced explication of this aspect, see Hélène Cixous and Catherine Clément, *The Newly Born Woman*, trans. Betsy Wing (Minneapolis: University of Minnesota Press, 1986), pp. 88–89. Originally published as *La jeune née* (Paris: Union Générale d'Éditions, 1975).

    However, *jouissance* is not limited either to sexual pleasure, which Lacan includes in the phrase "a *jouissance* of the body,"(*Feminine Sexuality*, p. 145), or to women. *Jouissance* also refers to the experience of perfect completion with the Other (Ibid., pp. 137–48), the lack of which is the source of desire (Ibid., pp. 116–17, 120).

29. Lacan, *Feminine Sexuality*, p. 144

30. Ibid., p. 145 (emphasis in original).

31. Julia Kristeva, "Women's Time," in *The Kristeva Reader*, ed. Toril Moi (New York: Columbia University Press, 1986), p. 206.

32. Julia Kristeva, "Motherhood According to Giovanni Bellini," in *Desire in Language: A Semiotic Approach to Literature and Art*, ed. Leon S. Roudiez, trans. Thomas Gora, Alice Jardine and Leon S. Roudiez (New York: Columbia University Press, 1980), p. 239.

33. It should be noted that the very idea of the mother/child dyad belies the masculine projection of symbolic unity.

34. Kristeva, "Motherhood According to Giovanni Bellini," p. 239.

35. Ibid., p. 240 (emphasis in original).

36. Kristeva, "Women's Time," p. 191 (emphasis in original, citations omitted).

37. Simone de Beauvoir, *The Second Sex*, trans. H.M. Parshley (New York: Random House, 1974). Originally published as *Le deuxieme sexe* (Paris: Alfred A. Knopf, Inc., 1952).

38. Kristeva, "Women's Time," p. 205.

39. Ibid., p. 206.

40. Kristeva, "Stabat Mater," in *The Kristeva Reader*, p. 161 (emphasis in original).

41. Ibid., p. 167.

42. Ibid., p. 177.

43. Ibid., p. 185.

44. Ibid., p. 185.

45. Kristeva, "Women's Time," p. 208.

46. Judith Butler, *Gender Trouble: Feminism and the Subversion of Identity* (New York: Routledge, Chapman and Hall, 1990), p. 91.

47. Carol Gilligan, *In a Different Voice: Psychological Theory and Women's Development* (Cambridge: Harvard University Press, 1982).

48. See Nancy Chodorow, *Reproduction of Mothering: Psychoanalysis and the Sociology of Gender* (Berkeley: University of California Press, 1978).

49. West, "Jurisprudence and Gender," p. 51 (emphasis in original).

50. See Jacques Lacan, *Ecrits: A Selection*, trans. Alan Sheridan (New York: W. W. Norton and Company, 1977). Originally published as *Ecrits* (Paris: Éditions du Seuil, 1966).

51. West, "Jurisprudence and Gender," p. 52.

52. Jaqueline Rose, "Introduction II," in *Feminine Sexuality*, p. 44, quoting unpublished typescript of Jacques Lacan, "Seminaire XVIII: L'envers de la psychanalyse," week 12, p. 4.

53. Marguerite Duras, *India Song*, trans. Barbara Bray (New York: Grove Press, 1976), p. 65. Originally published as *India Song* (Paris: Editions Gallimard, 1973).

54. Marguerite Duras, *The Vice Consul*, trans. Eileen Ellenbogn (New York: Grove Press, 1968). Originally published as *Le Vice-Consul* (Paris: Editions Gallimard, 1966).

55. Duras, *India Song*, p. 132.

56. Marguerite Duras, *The Ravishing of Lol Stein*, trans. Richard Seaver (New York: Pantheon Books, 1966), p. 38. Originally published as *Le ravissement de Lol V. Stein* (Paris: Editions Gallimard, 1964).

57. Marguerite Duras, *The Malady of Death*, trans. Barbara Bray (New York: Grove Press, 1986), p. 54. Originally published as *La maladie de la morte*, (Paris: Les Editions de Minuit, 1982).

58. Marguerite Duras, *Blue Eyes, Black Hair*, trans. Barbara Bray (New York: Pantheon Books, 1987). Originally published as *Les yeux bleus cheveux noirs* (Paris: Les Editions de Minuit, 1986).

59. Lacan, *Feminine Sexuality*, p. 158.

60. Ibid., p. 170.

61. Duras, *Blue Eyes, Black Hair*, p. 103.

62. I am borrowing the phrase "unavowable community" from Maurice Blanchot's extraordinary work of the same title. Maurice Blanchot, *The Unavowable Community*, trans. Pierre Joris (New York: Station Hill Press, 1988). Originally published as *La Communauté Inavouable* (Paris: Les Editions de Minuit, 1983).

63. Michéle Montrelay, "Inquiry Into Femininity," in *French Feminist Thought: A Reader*, ed. Toril Moi (New York: Basil Blackwell, 1987), p. 227.

64. See Kristeva, "Stabat Mater," p. 185.

65. In an interview, Kristeva did note that, on a political level, "there are still many goals which women can achieve: freedom of abortion and contraception, daycare centers for children, equality on the job, etc. Therefore, we must use 'we are women' as an advertisement or slogan for our demands." Kristeva, "La femme, ce n'est jamais ça" [Woman can never be defined], p. 137.

66. Toni Morrison, *Beloved* (New York: Plume Books, 1987).

67. Ibid.

68. I am using "intimacy" in the sense Bataille gives to the word. Intimacy is the fluid relationship between the self and the world that Bataille envisions as "water in water." In intimacy we experience the profound immanence of all that is, the soulful mingling of self and others. Intimacy cannot be expressed discursively. To quote Bataille:

> The swelling to the bursting point, the malice that breaks out with clenched teeth and weeps; the sinking feeling that doesn't know where it comes from or what it's about; the fear that sings its head off in the dark; the white eyed pallor, the sweet sadness, the rage and the vomiting . . . are so many evasions.
>
> What is intimate, in the strong sense, is what has the passion of an absence of individuality, the imperceptible sonority of a river, the empty limpidity of the sky. . . .

George Bataille, *Theory of Religion*, trans. Robert Hurley (New York: Zone Books, 1989), p. 50. Originally published as *Theorie de la religion* (Paris: Editions Gallimard, 1973).

69. West, "The Difference in Women's Hedonic Lives," p. 127 (emphasis in original, citations omitted).

70. See generally, Jean-François Lyotard, *The Differend: Phrases in Dispute*, trans. George Van Den Abbeele (Minneapolis: University of Minnesota Press, 1988), p. 141. Originally published as *Le Différend* (Paris: Les Editions de Minuit, 1983).

71. Ibid., p. 13.

72. Ibid., p. 9.

73. Roman Jakobson, "Two Aspects of Language and Two Types of Aphasic Disturbances," in *Fundamentals of Language* (The Hague: Mouton, 1956), pp. 76–82.

74. See Karen Barrett, "Date Rape—A Campus Epidemic?" *Ms.*, Sept. 1982, pp. 48, 50.

75. Hélène Cixous, "Sorties: Out and Out: Attacks/Ways Out/Forays," in *The Newly Born Woman*, pp. 88–89.

76. Ibid., p. 93 (emphasis in original).

77. Ibid.

78. Ibid., pp. 93–94.

79. Ibid., p. 86.

80. See Roy Schafer, *A New Language for Psycho-Analysis* (New Haven: Yale University Press, 1976).

81. Cixous, "Sorties," pp. 95–96.

82. Ibid., pp. 99–100.

83. Ibid., p. 82 (emphasis in original).

84. See Cynthia Chase, "Desire and Identification in Lacan and Kristeva," in *Feminism and Psycho-Analysis*, ed. Richard Feldstein and Judith Roof (Ithaca: Cornell University Press, 1989).

85. In a very thoughtful discussion, Madelon Sprengnether has argued that Kristeva's own writing could give us another alternative in which the mother could signify. Contrasting this alternative to Kristeva's position that women must accept the paternal function she argues that:

> A third possibility emerges, however, in Kristeva's reference to the condition of being divided, and the complexity of the "catastrophic-fold-of-'being.' " Although Kristeva remains hesitant about proclaiming this option as one that would revolutionize woman's place in respect to language, her maternal discourse provides a point of departure for theorizing along these lines.

Madelon Sprengnether, *The Spectral Mother: Freud, Feminism and Psychoanalysis* (Ithaca: Cornell University Press, 1990), p. 217.

86. Julia Kristeva, *Black Sun: Depression and Melancholia*, trans. Leon S. Roudiez (New York: Columbia University Press, 1989), p. 45. Originally published as *Soleil noir: dépression et mélancholie* (Paris: Editions Gallimard, 1987).

87. Ibid., pp. 13–14 (citation omitted).

88. Ibid., p. 53.

89. Ibid., p. 45.

90. Ibid., p. 27–28.

91. Ibid., p. 22.

92. Sylvia Plath, "Daddy," in *The Collected Poems* (New York: Harper and Row, 1981), p. 222.

93. Luce Irigaray, *This Sex Which Is Not One*, trans. Catherine Porter (Ithaca: Cornell University Press, 1985), pp. 203–04. Originally published as *Ce sexe qui n'est pas un* (Paris: Les Editions de Minuit, 1977) (emphasis in original).

94. Luce Irigaray, *Speculum of the Other Woman*, trans. Gillian C. Gill (Ithaca: Cornell University Press, 1985), p. 83. Originally published as *Speculum de l'autre femme* (Editions de Minuit, 1974).

95. Irigaray, *Speculum*, p. 84 (emphasis in original).

96. See Margaret Whitford, "Rereading Irigaray," in *Between Feminism and Psychoanalysis*.

97. Ibid., pp. 114–15.

98. Irigaray, *This Sex Which Is Not One*, p. 26 (emphasis in original).

99. Whitford, "Rereading Irigaray," p. 117.

100. Irigaray, *This Sex Which Is Not One*, p. 88 (emphasis in original).

101. Irigaray, *Speculum*, p. 237.

102. Ibid. p. 239.

103. Luce Irigaray, "And the One Doesn't Stir without the Other," *Signs: Journal of Women in Culture and Society*, vol. 7, no. 1 (1981), pp. 65–66.

104. Ibid., pp. 66–67.

105. Irigaray, *Speculum*, p. 134.

106. See Teresa de Lauretis, "The Essence of the Triangle or, Taking the Risk of Essentialism Seriously: Feminist Theory in Italy, the U.S., and Britain," in *differences*, vol. 1, no. 2 (1989).

107. Irigaray, *Speculum*, p. 229.

108. See Susan Rubin Suleiman, *Subversive Intent: Gender, Politics, and the Avant-Garde* (Cambridge: Harvard University Press, 1990), pp. 119–80. In her discussion of women's subversive reappropriation through writing of their multiplicitous identities, Suleiman specifically affirms the possibility of re-metaphorization, particularly of the mother, by which women may "play" with completion.

2. The Feminist Alliance with Deconstruction

1. Jacques Derrida and Christie McDonald, "Choreographies," *Diacritics*, vol. 12 (Summer 1982), reprinted in *The Ear of the Other: Otobiography, Transference, Translation*, ed. Christie McDonald, trans. Peggy Kamuf (Lincoln: University of Nebraska Press, 1985), p. 169. Originally published as *L'oreille de l'autre* (Montreal: V1B Editeur, 1982).

2. Jacques Derrida, *Glas*, trans. John P. Leavey, Jr. and Richard Rand (Lincoln: University of Nebraska Press, 1986). Originally published as *Glas* (Paris: Éditions Galilée, 1974).

3. Jacques Derrida, *The Post Card: From Socrates to Freud and Beyond*, trans. Alan Bass (Chicago: University of Chicago Press, 1987). Originally published as *La Carte Postale* (Paris: Flammarion, 1980).

4. Jacques Derrida, *Spurs: Nietzsche's Styles/Éperons Les Styles de Nietzsche* trans. Barbara Harlow (Chicago: University of Chicago Press, 1978).

5. Derrida, *The Post Card*, pp. 441–42.

6. Ibid., p. 426.

7. Luce Irigaray, *This Sex Which Is Not One*, trans. Catherine Porter (Ithaca:

Cornell University Press, 1985), pp. 86–105. Originally published as *Ce sexe qui n'est pas un* (Editions de Minuit, 1977).

8. Ibid., p. 88.

9. Jacques Derrida, "Deconstruction in America" (interview with James Creech, Peggy Kamuf, and Jane Todd), in *Critical Exchange*, no. 17 (Winter, 1985), p. 19.

10. Derrida and McDonald, "Choreographies," p. 169.

11. See, e.g., Marguerite Duras, *The Malady of Death*, trans. Barbara Bray (New York: Grove Press, 1986). Originally published as *La maladie de la morte*, (Paris: Les Editions de Minuit, 1982); Marguerite Duras, *India Song*, trans. Barbara Bray (New York: Grove Press, 1976). Originally published as *India Song* (Paris: Editions Gallimard, 1973); Marguerite Duras, *The Ravishing of Lol Stein*, trans. Richard Seaver (New York: Pantheon Books, 1966). Originally published as *Le ravissement de Lol V. Stein* (Paris: Editions Gallimard, 1964).

12. Derrida and McDonald, "Choreographies," p. 167.

13. Derrida, *Spurs*, p. 59 (italics in original).

14. Ibid., p. 55 (italics in original).

15. Gayatri Chakravorty Spivak, "Feminism and deconstruction, again: negotiating with unacknowledged masculinism," in *Between Feminism and Psychoanalysis*, ed. Teresa Brennan (London: Routledge, 1989), p. 215.

16. Derrida, *Spurs*, p. 51.

17. Ibid., p. 87 (emphasis in original).

18. Ibid., p. 133.

19. Ibid., p. 103, 105.

20. Derrida and McDonald, "Choreographies," pp. 170–71.

21. Ibid., p. 173.

22. Ibid., pp. 174–75.

23. Ibid., p. 169.

24. Jacques Lacan, *Feminine Sexuality: Jacques Lacan and the école freudienne*, ed. Juliet Mitchell and Jaqueline Rose, trans. Jaqueline Rose (New York: W. W. Norton and Company, 1985), p. 165.

25. Derrida, *Glas*, p. 229.

26. Derrida, *Spurs*, pp. 107, 109.

27. Derrida, *Glas*, p. 115.

28. Ibid., p. 117.

29. Ibid., pp. 116–17.

30. Ibid., p. 116.

31. Hélène Cixous, "Sorties: Out and Out: Attacks/Ways Out/Forays," in Hélène Cixous and Catherine Clément, *The Newly Born Woman*, trans. Betsy Wing

(Minneapolis: University of Minnesota Press, 1986), pp. 99–100. Originally published as *La jeune née* (Paris: Union Générale d'Éditions, 1975).

32. Sylvia Plath, "Daddy," in *The Collected Poems* (New York: Harper and Row, 1981), p. 222.

33. Derrida, *Glas*, p. 117.

34. Ibid., p. 65.

35. Ibid., p. 229 (italics in original).

36. Ibid., p. 135.

37. Derrida, *Spurs*, pp. 59, 61 (citation omitted).

38. Ibid., p. 61 (emphasis in original).

39. Derrida and McDonald, "Choreographies," p. 183.

40. Ibid., pp. 181–82 (emphasis in original).

41. Ibid., p. 178.

42. See generally, Luce Irigaray, *Speculum of the Other Woman*, trans. Gillian C. Gill (Ithaca: Cornell University Press, 1985), pp. 11–129. Originally published as *Speculum de l'autre femme* (Editions de Minuit, 1974).

43. Derrida and McDonald, "Choreographies," p. 175 (emphasis in original).

44. Ibid.

45. See Peggy Kamuf, "Introduction: Reading Between the Blinds," in *A Derrida Reader: Between the Blinds*, ed. Peggy Kamuf (New York: Columbia University Press, 1991) (forthcoming).

46. See Derrida and McDonald, "Choreographies," pp. 176–77.

47. Ibid., pp. 177–78.

48. Kamuf, *A Derrida Reader*, pp. 433–34.

49. Derrida, *Spurs*, p. 111 (emphasis in original).

50. I am, here, explicitly disagreeing with Jaqueline Rose's reading of Derrida. Jaqueline Rose, *Sexuality in the Field of Vision* (London: Verso, 1986), pp. 18–23.

51. Derrida and McDonald, "Choreographies," p. 180.

52. This is a deliberate reference to Hélène Cixous' essay, "Sorties: Out and Out: Attacks/Ways Out/Forays."

53. Derrida and McDonald, "Choreographies," p. 181.

54. Ibid., p. 172.

55. See generally, Robin West, "Jurisprudence and Gender," *University of Chicago Law Review*, vol. 55, no. 1 (1988); Robin West, "The Difference in Women's Hedonic Lives: A Phenomenological Critique of Feminist Legal Theory," *Wisconsin Women's Law Journal* vol. 3 (1987).

56. Derrida and McDonald, "Choreographies," p. 175.

57. Irigaray, *This Sex Which Is Not One*, p. 86–105.

58. Lacan, *Feminine Sexuality*, p. 84.

59. Derrida, *Glas*, p. 65.

60. See Jacques Derrida, *The Truth in Painting*, trans. Geoffrey Bennington and Ian McLeod (Chicago: University of Chicago Press 1987).

61. Jaqueline Rose has argued that feminine writing does appeal to a pre-linguistic libido. I am clearly disagreeing with her. See Rose, *Sexuality in the Field of Vision*.

62. Derrida, *Spurs*, pp. 95, 97.

63. Ibid., p. 97.

64. Joan Riviere, "Womanliness as a Masquerade," in *Formations of Fantasy*, ed. Victor Burgin, James Donald and Cora Kaplan (London: Methuen, 1986), p. 38.

65. Derrida, *Spurs*, p. 55.

66. Derrida, *Glas*, p. 188.

67. Derrida, *Spurs*, p. 67 (italics in original, citation omitted).

68. Seyla Benhabib, "On Contemporary Feminist Theory," *Dissent* (Summer 1989).

69. Derrida, *Spurs*, p. 139.

70. Derrida, *Glas*, p. 189.

71. Emmanuel Levinas, *Otherwise Than Being or Beyond Essence*, trans. Alphonso Lingis (The Hague: Martinus Nijhoff Publishers, 1981) p. 184.

72. See generally, Hélène Cixous, "Sorties," pp. 99–100.

73. Jacques Derrida, *Margins of Philosophy*, trans. Alan Bass (Chicago: University of Chicago Press, 1982), pp. 21–22. Originally published as *Marges de la philosophie* (Paris: Les Editions de Minuit, 1972).

74. Jean-François Lyotard, *The Differend: Phrases in Dispute*, trans. George Van Den Abbeele (Minneapolis: University of Minnesota Press, 1988). Originally published as *Le Différend* (Paris: Les Editions de Minuit, 1983).

75. I am borrowing this phrase from the work of John Rawls, "The Domain of the Political and Overlapping Consensus," *New York University Law Review*, vol. 64, no. 2 (1989) p. 233.

76. Lyotard, *The Differend*, p. 5.

77. Hélène Cixous, "Sorties," p. 83.

78. Alasdair MacIntyre, *Whose Justice? Which Rationality?* (Notre Dame: University of Notre Dame Press, 1988), pp. 368–69.

79. Jacques Derrida, "Force of Law: The 'Mystical Foundation of Authority,'" *Cardozo Law Review*, vol. 11, nos. 5–6 (1990), pp. 943, 945.

80. Ibid., p. 945.

81. Ibid., p. 955.

82. Ibid., pp. 969, 971.

83. Ibid., p. 959, (quoting Emmanuel Levinas, *Totality and Infinity: An Essay on Exteriority*, trans. Alphonso Lingis, [Pittsburgh: Duquesne University Press, 1969], p. 54.)

84. Derrida, "Force of Law," p. 949 (emphasis in original).

85. Ibid., p. 965.

86. Ibid., p. 951.

87. Ibid., p. 949 (emphasis in original).

88. Ibid., p. 965 (emphasis added).

89. Ibid., p. 957.

90. Ibid., p. 953.

91. See "Feminism Always Modified," ch. 3, infra.

92. Derrida, *Margins of Philosophy*, p. 21.

93. I want to be clear here that I am not suggesting that rights are not important. They are indeed important in and of themselves, and also under the messianic conception of justice, as a reminder that justice has not arrived.

3. Feminism Always Modified:
The Affirmation of Feminine Difference Rethought

1. Catharine A. MacKinnon, *Toward a Feminist Theory of the State* (Cambridge: Harvard University Press, 1989), p. 124.

2. Ibid., p. 219.

3. Catharine A. MacKinnon, *Feminism Unmodified: Discourses on Life and Law* (Cambridge: Harvard University Press, 1987), p. 149.

4. Ibid., p. 55.

5. Simone de Beauvoir, *The Second Sex*, trans. H.M. Parshley (New York: Random House, 1974), p. xviii. Originally published as *Le deuxieme sexe*, (Paris: Alfred A. Knopf, Inc., 1952).

6. MacKinnon, *Feminism Unmodified*, p. 55.

7. MacKinnon, *Toward a Feminist Theory of the State*, pp. 161–62.

8. Ibid., p. 162 (citation omitted).

9. Ibid., p. 163.

10. Ibid., pp. 163–64.

11. Ibid., p. 164.

12. MacKinnon, *Feminism Unmodified*, p. 148.

13. Ibid., p. 52.

14. Ibid., p. 172.

15. Ibid., p. 150 (italics in original).

16. Ibid., p. 51 (italics in original).

17. Carol Gilligan, *In a Different Voice: Psychological Theory and Women's Development* (Cambridge: Harvard University Press, 1982).

18. Luce Irigaray, "Sexual Difference," in *French Feminist Thought: A Reader*, ed. Toril Moi (New York: Basil Blackwell, 1987); Luce Irigaray, *Speculum of the Other Woman*, trans. Gillian C. Gill (Ithaca: Cornell University Press, 1985), pp. 142–143. Originally published as *Speculum de l'autre femme*, (Paris: Editions de Minuit, 1974); Luce Irigaray, *This Sex Which Is Not One*, trans. Catherine Porter (Ithaca: Cornell University Press, 1985), p. 70. Originally published as *Ce Sexe qui n'est pas un*, (Paris: Editions de Minuit, 1977).

19. Hélène Cixous, "Sorties: Out and Out: Attacks/Ways Out/Forays," in Hélène Cixous and Catherine Clément, *The Newly Born Woman*, trans. Betsy Wing (Minneapolis: University of Minnesota Press, 1986), pp. 88–89. Originally published as *La jeune née* (Paris: Union Générale d'Éditions, 1975).

20. MacKinnon, *Feminism Unmodified*, p. 39.

21. Ibid.

22. Ibid., p. 218.

23. Ibid., p. 219 (italics in original).

24. Ibid.

25. MacKinnon, *Toward a Feminist Theory of the State*, pp. 137–38.

26. MacKinnon, *Feminism Unmodified*, p. 59 (italics in original, except for last sentence).

27. Ibid., p. 54 (italics in original).

28. James Joyce, *Finnegans Wake* (New York: Penguin Books, 1939), p. 104.

29. Hélène Cixous, "Sorties," p. 88.

30. Andrea Dworkin, *Intercourse* (New York: The Free Press, 1987), p. 111.

31. MacKinnon, *Toward a Feminist Theory of the State*, p. 111, quoting Andrea Dworkin, *The New Woman's Broken Heart*, (Palo Alto: Frog in the Well, 1980), p. 3; de Beauvoir, *The Second Sex*, p. xviii.

32. MacKinnon, *Feminism Unmodified*, p. 39.

33. See Ronald Dworkin, *Law's Empire* (Cambridge: Belknap Press, 1986).

34. Gilligan, *In a Different Voice*.

35. MacKinnon, *Feminism Unmodified*, p. 55.

36. Isabel Marcus, et al., "The 1984 James McCormick Mitchell Lecture: Feminist Discourse, Moral Values, and the Law—A Conversation," *Buffalo Law Review*, vol. 34, no. 1 (1985), pp. 73–76.

37. MacKinnon, *Feminism Unmodified*, p. 37 (italics in original).

38. Drucilla Cornell, "The Ethical Message of Negative Dialectics," *Social Concept*, vol. 4, no. 1 (1987), p. 10.

39. " 'There is more than one kind of freedom,' said Aunt Lydia. 'Freedom to and freedom from. In the days of anarchy, it was freedom to. Now you are being

given freedom from. Don't underrate it.'" Margaret Atwood, *The Handmaid's Tale* (Boston: Houghton Mifflin Company, 1986), p. 24.

40. MacKinnon, *Feminism Unmodified*, p. 39.

41. MacKinnon, *Feminism Unmodified*, p. 219.

42. Jacques Derrida, *Margins of Philosophy*, trans. Alan Bass (Chicago: University of Chicago Press, 1982), p. 3. Originally published as *Marges de la philosophie* (Paris: Les Editions de Minuit, 1972).

43. See generally, Jacques Lacan, *Feminine Sexuality: Jacques Lacan and the école freudienne*, ed. Juliet Mitchell and Jaqueline Rose, trans. Jaqueline Rose (New York: W. W. Norton and Company, 1985); Jacques Lacan, *Ecrits: A Selection*, trans. Alan Sheridan (New York: W. W. Norton and Company, 1977). Originally published as *Ecrits*, (Paris: Éditions du Seuil, 1966).

44. See MacKinnon, *Toward a Feminist Theory of the State*, pp. 105, 271 note 25.

45. Irigaray, "How to Define Sexuate Rights" (unpublished MS, translated by Margaret Whitford), p. 6.

46. Irigaray, "Sexual Difference," p. 125.

47. Ibid.

48. Jacques Derrida, *Glas*, trans. John P. Leavey, Jr. and Richard Rand (Lincoln: University of Nebraska Press, 1986), p. 46. Originally published as *Glas* (Paris: Éditions Galilée, 1974) (italics in original).

49. Irigaray, "Sexual Difference," p. 124.

50. Irigaray, *This Sex Which Is Not One*, p. 70.

51. Lacan, *Feminine Sexuality*, p. 158.

52. In discussing the vicious circularity of male discourse, Irigaray quotes Lacan:

> There is no prediscursive reality. Every reality is based upon and defined by a discourse. This is why it is important for us to notice what analytic discourse consists of, and not to overlook one thing, which is no doubt of limited significance, namely that fact that in this discourse we are talking about what the verb 'fuck' expresses perfectly. We are speaking about fucking—a verb, in French *foutre*—and we are saying that it's not working.

Irigaray, *This Sex Which Is Not One*, p. 88, quoting Jacques Lacan, *Encore, Le Séminaire XX* (Paris, 1975).

53. Irigaray, "Sexual Difference," p. 127.

54. Ibid., p. 118.

55. Jacques Derrida and Christie McDonald, "Choreographies," *Diacritics*, vol. 12 (Summer 1982), reprinted in *The Ear of the Other: Otobiography, Transference, Translation*, ed. Christie McDonald, trans. Peggy Kamuf (Lincoln: University of Nebraska Press, 1985), p. 169. Originally published as *L'oreille de l'autre* (Montreal: V1B Editeur, 1982).

56. Irigaray, *This Sex Which Is Not One*, p. 78 (italics in the original).

57. Irigaray, *Speculum*, pp. 142–143.

58. I am aware that there is a reading of Irigaray that seemingly calls us to the "nakedness" that they have refused to see, insisting that we gussy ourselves up for them. That reading would insist that such rhetoric carries essentialist overtones. I would counter such a reading. Even "nakedness" is used as a metaphor against the masculine fantasy projection of the modest woman. Our pain, "our destitution in language," has been denied, covered in "eulogistic metaphors." Strip them away and the justifications for our oppression begin to fall. But such rhetoric need not imply that there is an ultimate truth of Woman that is "there" underneath all the metaphors. To read Irigaray's appeal to "nakedness" as a reversion to essentialism is to read her too literally. And yet, I am aware that the language I am using here is of restylization, rather than a stripping away. Such language, I am suggesting, is more invocative of feminine *mimesis*.

59. Irigaray, *This Sex Which Is Not One*, p. 76 (italics in original).

60. Ibid., p. 77.

61. See generally, Cornell, "The Ethical Message of Negative Dialectics."

62. Clarice Lispector, *The Stream of Life*, trans. Elizabeth Lowe and Earl Fitz (Minneapolis: University of Minnesota Press, 1989), p. 45 (italics in original).

63. See Cornell, "The Ethical Message of Negative Dialectics," p. 10.

64. Phillipe Lacoue-Labarthe, *Typography: Mimesis, Philosophy, Politics*, ed. Christopher Fynsk (Cambridge: Harvard University Press, 1989), p. 116. (The prefatory phrase comes from the Introduction, by Derrida.)

65. This non-reducibility of the relation of the feminine to the Other is all too easily identified as madness because the strict borders between subject and Other no longer hold. *Mimesis* demands the relinquishment of the rigid borders established to protect the subject's identification with itself against otherness. But *mimesis* is not the madness of a borderline even if it can be seen as such within phallogocentrism.

66. Irigaray, *Speculum*, p. 133.

67. Ibid.

68. Jean-François Lyotard, *The Differend: Phrases in Dispute*, trans. George Van Den Abbeele (Minneapolis: University of Minnesota Press, 1988). Originally published as *Le Différend* (Paris: Les Editions de Minuit, 1983).

69. Femininity, as I use it, is distinguishable from the feminine precisely because it rests on conventionally accepted conceptions.

70. Jacques Lacan, *Ecrits: A Selection*, trans. Alan Sheridan (New York: W. W. Norton and Company, 1977). Originally published as *Ecrits* (Paris: Éditions du Seuil, 1966).

71. John Rawls, "The Domain of the Political and Overlapping Consensus," *New York University Law Review*, vol. 64, no. 2 (1989).

72. MacKinnon, *Feminism Unmodified*, p. 54.

73. Ibid., p. 61.

74. "One Art"

> The art of losing isn't hard to master;
> so many things seem filled with the intent
> to be lost that their loss is no disaster.
>
> Lose something every day. Accept the fluster
> of lost door keys, the hour badly spent.
> The art of losing isn't hard to master.
>
> Then practice losing farther, losing faster:
> places, and names, and where it was you meant
> to travel. None of these will bring disaster.
>
> I lost my mother's watch. And look! my last, or
> next-to-last, of three loved houses went.
> The art of losing isn't hard to master.
>
> I lost two cities, lovely ones. And, vaster,
> some realms I owned, two rivers, a continent.
> I miss them, but it wasn't a disaster.
>
> —Even losing you (the joking voice, a gesture
> I love) I shan't have lied. It's evident
> the art of losing's not too hard to master
> though it may look like (*Write* it!) like disaster.

Elizabeth Bishop, "One Art," in *The Complete Poems: 1927–1979* (New York: Farrar, Straus, and Giroux, 1983), p. 178.

75. MacKinnon, *Feminism Unmodified*, p. 39 (citation omitted).

76. Irigaray, *This Sex Which Is Not One*, p. 79 (italics in original).

77. Ibid., p. 205.

78. Ibid., p. 77.

79. Ibid., pp. 136–37 (italics in original).

80. Cixous, "Sorties," p. 99.

81. Catherine Clément, "The Guilty One," in *The Newly Born Woman*, p. 52 (italics in original).

82. Cixous, "Sorties," p. 97.

83. Ibid., p. 88.

84. Ibid., pp. 86–87.

85. MacKinnon, *Feminism Unmodified*, pp. 54–58.

86. Irigaray, *This Sex Which Is Not One*, p. 33.

87. Ibid., p. 213.

88. Ibid., pp. 205–18.

89. Ibid., p. 215.

90. Monique Wittig, *The Lesbian Body*, trans. David Le Vay (Boston: Beacon Press, 1975). Originally published as *Le corps lesbien* (Paris: Les Editions de Minuit, 1973).

91. Wittig, *The Lesbian Body*, p. 98 (italics in original).

92. Ibid., p. 51 (italics in original).

93. Monique Wittig, *Les Guérillères*, trans. David Le Vay (Boston: Beacon Press, 1975; Paris: Les Editions de Minuit, 1969).

94. Cixous, "Sorties," p. 83.

95. MacKinnon, *Feminism Unmodified*, p. 77 (italics in original except for last line).

4. Feminine Writing, Metaphor and Myth

1. Roland Barthes, *Mythologies*, trans. Annette Lavers (New York: Noonday Press, 1972), p. 129.

2. Ibid., p. 135 (italics in original).

3. See Julia Kristeva, "Stabat Mater" in *The Kristeva Reader*, ed. Toril Moi (New York: Columbia University Press, 1986), pp. 160–86.

4. Kristeva, "Women's Time," in *The Kristeva Reader*, p. 209.

5. Domna C. Stanton, "Difference on Trial: A Critique of the Maternal Metaphor in Cixous, Irigaray and Kristeva," in *The Poetics of Gender*, ed. Nancy K. Miller (New York: Columbia University Press, 1986), p. 176.

6. Jacques Derrida, "Choreographies," in *The Ear of the Other: Otobiography, Transference, Translation*, ed. Christie McDonald, trans. Peggy Kamuf (Lincoln: University of Nebraska Press, 1985). Originally published as *L'oreille de l'autre* (Montreal: V1B Editeur, 1982).

7. Stanton, "Difference on Trial," p. 177.

8. Julia Kristeva, *Histoires d'amour* (Paris: Denoël, 1983), p. 254.

9. Paul Ricoeur, *The Rule of Metaphor: Multi-disciplinary Studies of the Creation of Meaning in Language*, trans. Robert Czerny (Toronto: University of Toronto Press, 1975), p. 255.

10. Ibid., p. 254.

11. Jacques Derrida, *Limited Inc.* (Evanston: Northwestern University Press, 1988), p. 152.

12. Jacques Derrida, "Force of Law: The 'Mystical Foundation of Authority,'" *Cardozo Law Review*, vol. 11, nos. 5–6 (1990).

13. Derrida, *Limited Inc.*, p. 116.

14. Kristeva, "Stabat Mater" pp. 160–86.

15. Hans Blumenberg, *Work on Myth*, trans. Robert M. Wallace (Cambridge: The MIT Press, 1985), p. 34. Originally published as *Arbeit am Mythos* (Frankfurt am Main, FRG: Suhrkamp Verlag, 1979).

16. Marguerite Duras, *Blue Eyes, Black Hair*, trans. Barbara Bray (New York: Pantheon Books, 1987). Originally published as *Les yeux bleus cheveux noirs* (Paris: Les Editions de Minuit, 1986).

17. Hélène Cixous, "Sorties: Out and Out: Attacks/Ways Out/Forays," in Hélène Cixous and Catherine Clément, *The Newly Born Woman*, trans. Betsy Wing (Minneapolis: University of Minnesota Press, 1986), p. 72. Originally published as *La jeune née* (Paris: Union Générale d'Éditions, 1975) (italics in original).

18. Ibid., pp. 95–96.

19. Ibid., p. 117.

20. Ibid., p. 116 (citation omitted).

21. Ibid., p. 122.

22. Ibid., p. 113.

23. Ibid., p. 126.

24. Ibid.

25. Ibid., p. 127.

26. Ibid., pp. 99–100 (emphasis in original).

27. Ibid., p. 128.

28. Ibid., p. 127.

29. Ibid., p. 130.

30. Lacan, *Feminine Sexuality*, p. 170.

31. Christa Wolf, *Cassandra: A Novel and Four Essays*, trans. Jan Van Heurck (New York: Farrar, Straus, and Giroux, 1984).

32. Jean-François Lyotard, *The Differend: Phrases in Dispute*, trans. George Van Den Abbeele (Minneapolis: University of Minnesota Press, 1988), pp. 150–51. Originally published as *Le Différend* (Paris: Les Editions de Minuit, 1983).

33. Wolf, *Cassandra*, p. 224.

34. Andrea Dworkin, *Intercourse* (New York: The Free Press, 1987).

35. Gayatri Spivak, "In a Word," *differences*, vol. 1, no. 2 (1989), p. 124.

36. Ibid., pp. 126–27.

37. Ibid.

38. Ibid., p. 129.

39. Diana J. Fuss, "Essentially Speaking: Luce Irigaray's Language of Essence," *Hypatia* vol. 3, no. 3 (1989).

40. Ibid., p. 76 (italics in original, citation omitted).

41. Irigaray, *This Sex Which Is Not One*, p. 159.

42. See generally, Georg W.F. Hegel, *Hegel's Science of Logic*, trans. A.V. Miller (Atlantic Highlands, N.J.: Humanities Press International, 1969).

43. Such is the status of women that the appeal to feminism is critical. As MacKinnon notes:

> Women's situation offers no outside to stand on or gaze at, no inside to escape to, too much urgency to wait, no place else to go and nothing to use but the twisted tools that have been shoved down our throats. There is no Archimedean point—or, men are their own Archimedean point, which makes it not very Archimedean. If Feminism is revolutionary, this is why.

Catharine A. MacKinnon, *Toward a Feminist Theory of the State* (Cambridge: Harvard University Press, 1989), p. 117.

44. Irigaray, "Sexual Difference" in *French Feminist Thought: A Reader*, ed. Toril Moi (New York: Basil Blackwell, 1987), p. 128 (italics in original).

45. Ibid. (italics in original).

46. Ibid.

47. Ibid., p. 120.

48. See, e.g., Isabel Marcus, et al., "The 1984 James McCormick Mitchell Lecture: Feminist Discourse, Moral Values, and the Law—A Conversation," *Buffalo Law Review*, vol. 34, no. 1 (1985), pp. 73–75.

49. See *Conjuring: Black Women, Fiction, and Literary Tradition*, ed. Marjorie Pryse and Hortense Spillers (Bloomington: Indiana Unversity Press, 1985).

50. Toni Morrison, *Beloved* (New York: Penguin Books, 1987), p. 62.

51. Ibid.

52. See generally, Kristeva, *The Kristeva Reader*, part I, "Linguistics, Semiotics, Textuality," pp. 23–136.

53. Morrison, *Beloved*, p. 259.

54. Ibid., p. 108.

55. James Joyce, *Finnegans Wake* (New York: Penguin Books, 1939)

56. Morrison, *Beloved*, p. 274.

57. Regina Austin, "Sapphire Bound!" *Wisconsin Law Review*, no. 3 (1989).

58. Naomi Schor, "This Essentialism Which Is Not One: Coming to Grips with Irigaray," in *differences*, vol. 1, no. 2 (1989).

59. Simone de Beauvoir, *The Second Sex*, trans. H.M. Parshley (New York: Random House, 1974). Originally published as *Le deuxieme sexe* (Paris: Alfred A. Knopf, Inc., 1952).

60. Ibid., p. xxxv.

61. Ibid., p. 161.

62. Ibid., pp. 161–62.

63. Ibid., p. 36.

64. Ibid., p. 795 (quoting a letter from Rimbaud to Pierre Demeny, May 15, 1871).

65. Ibid., p. xxxiv.

66. Ibid., pp. xxxiii–xxxiv.

67. Morrison, *Beloved*, p. 275.

68. Michael Walzer, "Two Kinds of Universalism" (1989), p. 9 of unpublished manuscript on file with the author.

69. Austin, "Sapphire Bound!"

70. Joyce, *Finnegans Wake*, p. 1.

Conclusion: "Happy Days"

1. James Joyce, *Finnegans Wake* (New York: Penguin Books, 1939), p. 628.

2. Jacques Lacan, *Feminine Sexuality: Jacques Lacan and the école freudienne*, ed. Juliet Mitchell and Jaqueline Rose, trans. Jaqueline Rose (New York: W. W. Norton and Company, 1985), p. 150.

3. Franz Kafka, "In the Penal Colony," in *The Penal Colony: Stories and Short Pieces*, trans. Willa and Edwin Muir (New York: Schocken Books, 1948), p. 197.

4. Judith Butler, *Gender Trouble: Feminism and the Subversion of Identity* (New York: Routledge, Chapman and Hall, 1990), p. 147.

5. Samuel Beckett, *Happy Days*, a play in two acts (New York: Grove Weidenfeld, 1961), p. 46.

6. Jacques Derrida, *The Post Card: From Socrates to Freud and Beyond* (Chicago: University of Chicago Press, 1987), p. 442. Originally published as *La Carte Postale* (Paris: Flammarion, 1980).

7. Beckett, *Happy Days*, p. 47 (italics in original).

8. Ibid., p. 21.

9. Ibid., p. 50.

10. Jacques Derrida, *Glas*, trans. John P. Leavey, Jr. and Richard Rand (Lincoln: University of Nebraska Press, 1986), p. 229. Originally published as *Glas* (Paris: Éditions Galilée, 1974).

11. Beckett, *Happy Days*, p. 8.

12. Ibid., p. 52.

13. Ibid., p. 29 (emphasis added).

14. I am echoing Domna C. Stanton's use of the term "metaforeplay". Domna C. Stanton, "Difference on Trial: A Critique of the Maternal Metaphor in Cixous, Irigaray and Kristeva," in *The Poetics of Gender*, ed. Nancy K. Miller (New York: Columbia University Press, 1986), p. 177.

15. This is a reference to Sylvia Plath's poem "Daddy." See Sylvia Plath, "Daddy," in *The Collected Poems* (New York: Harper and Row, 1981), p 222.

Bibliography

Atwood, Margaret. *The Handmaid's Tale*. Boston: Houghton Mifflin Company, 1986.

Austin, Regina. "Sapphire Bound!" *Wisconsin Law Review*, vol. 1989, no. 3 (1989), p. 539.

Barrett, Karen. "Date Rape—A Campus Epidemic?" *Ms.*, Sept. 1982.

Barthes, Roland. *Mythologies*. Trans. Annette Lavers. New York: Noonday Press, 1972.

Bataille, George. *Theory of Religion*. Trans. Robert Hurley. New York: Zone Books, 1989. Originally published as *Theorie de la religion*. Paris: Editions Gallimard, 1973.

de Beauvoir, Simone. *The Second Sex*. Trans. H.M. Parshley. New York: Random House, 1974. Originally published as *Le deuxieme sexe*. Paris: Alfred A. Knopf, Inc., 1952.

Beckett, Samuel. *Happy Days*, a play in two acts. New York: Grove Weidenfeld, 1961.

Benhabib, Seyla. "On Contemporary Feminist Theory." *Dissent* (Summer 1989).

Bishop, Elizabeth. *The Complete Poems: 1927-1979*. New York: Farrar, Straus and Giroux, 1983.

Blanchot, Maurice. *The Unavowable Community*. Trans. Pierre Joris. New York: Station Hill Press, 1988. Originally published as *La Communauté Inavouable*. Paris: Les Editions de Minuit, 1983.

Blumenberg, Hans. *Work on Myth*. Trans. Robert M. Wallace. Cambridge: The MIT Press, 1985. Originally published as *Arbeit am Mythos*. Frankfurt am Main, FRG: Suhrkamp Verlag, 1979.

Butler, Judith. *Gender Trouble: Feminism and the Subversion of Identity*. New York: Routledge, Chapman and Hall, 1990.

Chase, Cynthia. "Desire and Identification in Lacan and Kristeva." *Feminism and Psycho-Analysis.* Ed. Richard Feldstein and Judith Roof. Ithaca: Cornell University Press, 1989.

Chodorow, Nancy. *Reproduction of Mothering: Psychoanalysis and the Sociology of Gender.* Berkeley: University of California Press, 1978.

Cixous, Hélène. "The Laugh of the Medusa." *New French Feminisms: An Anthology.* Ed. Elaine Marks and Isabelle de Courtivron. New York: Shocken Books by arrangement with University of Massachusetts Press, 1980.

Cixous, Hélène and Clément, Catherine. *The Newly Born Woman.* Trans. Betsy Wing. Minneapolis: University of Minnesota Press, 1986. Originally published as *La jeune née.* Paris: Union Générale d'Éditions, 1975.

Cornell, Drucilla. "The Ethical Message of Negative Dialectics." *Social Concept,* vol. 4, no. 1 (1987).

Derrida, Jacques. "Force of Law: The 'Mystical Foundation of Authority.'" *Cardozo Law Review,* vol. 11, nos. 5–6 (1990).

———. *Limited Inc.* Evanston: Northwestern University Press, 1988.

———. *The Post Card: From Socrates to Freud and Beyond.* Trans. Alan Bass. Chicago: University of Chicago Press, 1987. Originally published as *La Carte Postale.* Paris: Flammarion, 1980.

———. *The Truth in Painting.* Trans. Geoffrey Bennington and Ian McLeod. Chicago: University of Chicago Press 1987.

———. *The Ear of the Other: Otobiography, Transference, Translation.* Ed. Christie McDonald, trans. Peggy Kamuf. Lincoln: University of Nebraska Press, 1985. Originally published as *L'oreille de l'autre.* Montreal: V1B Editeur, 1982.

———. *Margins of Philosophy.* Trans. Alan Bass. Chicago: University of Chicago Press, 1982. Originally published as *Marges de la philosophie.* Paris: Les Editions de Minuit, 1972.

———. *Spurs: Nietzsche's Styles/Éperons Les Styles de Nietzsche.* Trans. Barbara Harlow. Chicago: University of Chicago Press, 1978.

———. *Glas.* Trans. John P. Leavey, Jr. and Richard Rand. Lincoln: University of Nebraska Press, 1986. Originally published as *Glas.* Paris: Éditions Galilée, 1974.

Duras, Marguerite. *Blue Eyes, Black Hair.* Trans. Barbara Bray. New York: Pantheon Books, 1987. Originally published as *Les yeux bleus cheveux noirs.* Paris: Les Editions de Minuit, 1986.

———. *The Malady of Death.* Trans. Barbara Bray. New York: Grove Press, 1986. Originally published as *La maladie de la morte.* Paris: Les Editions de Minuit, 1982.

———. *India Song.* Trans. Barbara Bray. New York: Grove Press, 1976. Originally published as *India Song.* Paris: Editions Gallimard, 1973.

———. *The Vice Consul.* Trans. Eileen Ellenbogn. New York: Grove Press, 1968. Originally published as *Le Vice-Consul.* Paris: Editions Gallimard, 1966.

———. *The Ravishing of Lol Stein.* Trans. Richard Seaver. New York: Pantheon

Books, 1966. Originally published as *Le ravissement de Lol V. Stein*. Paris: Editions Gallimard, 1964.

Dworkin, Andrea. *Intercourse*. New York: The Free Press, 1987.

————. *The New Woman's Broken Heart*. Palo Alto: Frog in the Well, 1980.

Dworkin, Ronald. *Law's Empire*. Cambridge: Belknap Press, 1986.

Freud, Sigmund. *Beyond the Pleasure Principle*. Ed. and trans. James Strachey. New York: W. W. Norton and Co., 1961.

Fuss, Diana J. "Essentially Speaking: Luce Irigaray's Language of Essence." *Hypatia*, vol. 3, no. 3 (1989).

Gilligan, Carol. *In a Different Voice: Psychological Theory and Women's Development*. Cambridge: Harvard University Press, 1982.

Hegel, Georg W.F. *Hegel's Science of Logic*. Trans. A.V. Miller. Atlantic Highlands, N.J.: Humanities Press International, 1969.

Heidegger, Martin. *Being and Time*. Trans. John Macquarrie and Edward Robinson. New York: Harper and Row, 1962.

Irigaray, Luce. "The Gesture in Psychoanalysis." In *Between Feminism and Psychoanalysis*. Ed. Teresa Brennan, trans. Elizabeth Guild. London: Routledge, 1989.

————. *Speculum of the Other Woman*. Trans. Gillian C. Gill. Ithaca: Cornell University Press, 1985. Originally published as *Speculum de l'autre femme*. Paris: Les Editions de Minuit, 1974.

————. *This Sex Which Is Not One*. Trans. Catherine Porter. Ithaca: Cornell University Press, 1985. Originally published as *Ce sexe qui n'est pas un*. Paris: Les Editions de Minuit, 1977.

————. "And the One Doesn't Stir without the Other." *Signs: Journal of Women in Culture and Society*, vol. 7, no. 1 (1981).

Jakobson, Roman. *Fundamentals of Language*. The Hague: Mouton, 1956.

Jardine, Alice. "Prelude: The Future of Difference." *The Future of Difference*. Ed. Hester Eisenstein and Alice Jardine. Boston: G.K. Hall and Co., 1980.

Joyce, James. *Finnegans Wake*. New York: Penguin Books, 1939.

Kafka, Franz. *The Penal Colony: Stories and Short Pieces*. Trans. Willa and Edwin Muir. New York: Schocken Books, 1948.

Kamuf, Peggy. "Introduction: Reading Between the Blinds." *A Derrida Reader: Between the Blinds*. Ed. Peggy Kamuf. New York: Columbia University Press, 1991 (forthcoming).

Kristeva, Julia. *Black Sun: Depression and Melancholia*. Trans. Leon S. Roudiez. New York: Columbia University Press, 1989. Originally published as *Soleil noir: dépression et mélancholie*. Paris: Editions Gallimard, 1987.

————. *The Kristeva Reader*. Ed. Toril Moi. New York: Columbia University Press, 1986.

———— . *Histoires d'amour*. Paris: Denoël, 1983.

————. "La femme, ce n'est jamais ça" (Woman can never be defined). *Tel quel*

(Autumn 1974). Reprinted in *New French Feminisms: An Anthology*. Elaine Marks and Isabelle de Courtivron. New York: Schocken Books by arrangement with University of Massachusetts Press, 1980.

———. *Desire in Language: A Semiotic Approach to Literature and Art*. Ed. Leon S. Roudiez, trans. Thomas Gora, Alice Jardine and Leon S. Roudiez. New York: Columbia University Press, 1980.

Lacan, Jacques. *Feminine Sexuality: Jacques Lacan and the école freudienne*. Ed. Juliet Mitchell and Jaqueline Rose, trans. Jaqueline Rose. New York: W. W. Norton and Company, 1985.

———. *Ecríts: A Selection*. Trans. Alan Sheridan. New York: W. W. Norton and Company, 1977. Originally published as *Ecríts*. Paris: Éditions du Seuil, 1966.

———. *Encore, Le Séminaire XX*. Paris, 1975.

Lacoue-Labarthe, Phillipe. *Typography: Mimesis, Philosophy, Politics*. Ed. Christopher Fynsk. Cambridge: Harvard University Press, 1989.

de Lauretis, Teresa. "The Essence of the Triangle or, Taking the Risk of Essentialism Seriously: Feminist Theory in Italy, the U.S., and Britain." In *differences*, vol. 1, no. 2 (1989).

Levinas, Emmanuel. *Otherwise Than Being or Beyond Essence*. Trans. Alphonso Lingis. The Hague: Martinus Nijhoff Publishers, 1981.

———. *Totality and Infinity: An Essay on Exteriority*. Trans. Alphonso Lingis. Pittsburgh: Duquesne University Press, 1969.

Lispector, Clarice. *The Stream of Life*. Trans. Elizabeth Lowe and Earl Fitz. Minneapolis: University of Minnesota Press, 1989.

Lyotard, Jean-François. *The Differend: Phrases in Dispute*. Trans. George Van Den Abbeele. Minneapolis: University of Minnesota Press, 1988. Originally published as *Le Différend*. Paris: Les Editions de Minuit, 1983.

MacIntyre, Alasdair. *Whose Justice? Which Rationality?*. Notre Dame: University of Notre Dame Press, 1988.

MacKinnon, Catharine A. *Toward a Feminist Theory of the State*. Cambridge: Harvard University Press, 1989.

———. *Feminism Unmodified: Discourses on Life and Law*. Cambridge: Harvard University Press, 1987.

Marcus, Isabel, et al. "The 1984 James McCormick Mitchell Lecture: Feminist Discourse, Moral Values, and the Law—A Conversation." *Buffalo Law Review*, vol. 34, no. 1 (1985), p. 11.

Montrelay, Michéle. "Inquiry Into Femininity." *French Feminist Thought: A Reader*. Ed. Toril Moi. New York: Basil Blackwell, 1987.

Morrison, Toni. *Beloved*. New York: Penguin Books, 1987.

Plath, Sylvia. *The Collected Poems*. New York: Harper and Row, 1981.

Rawls, John. "The Domain of the Political and Overlapping Consensus." *New York University Law Review*, vol. 64, no. 2 (1989), p. 233.

Ricoeur, Paul. *The Rule of Metaphor: Multi-disciplinary Studies of the Creation of Meaning in Language.* Trans. Robert Czerny. Toronto: University of Toronto Press, 1975.

Riviere, Joan. "Womanliness as a Masquerade." *Formations of Fantasy.* Ed. Victor Burgin, James Donald and Cora Kaplan. London: Methuen, 1986.

Rose, Jacqueline. *Sexuality in the Field of Vision.* London: Verso, 1986.

Rubin, Gayle. "The Traffic in Women: Notes on the Political Economy of Sex." *Toward an Anthropology of Women.* Ed. Rayna R. Reiter. New York: Monthly Review Press, 1976.

Rubin Suleiman, Susan. *Subversive Intent: Gender, Politics, and the Avant-Garde.* Cambridge: Harvard University Press, 1990.

Schafer, Roy. *A New Language for Psycho-Analysis.* New Haven: Yale University Press, 1976.

Schor, Naomi. "This Essentialism Which Is Not One: Coming to Grips with Irigaray." *differences,* vol. 1, no. 2 (1989).

Spillers, Hortense. *Conjuring: Black Women, Fiction, and Literary Tradition.* Ed. Marjorie Pryse and Hortense Spillers. Bloomington: University of Indiana Press, 1985.

Spivak, Gayatri Chakravorty. "Feminism and deconstruction, again: negotiating with unacknowledged masculinism." *Between Feminism & Psychoanalysis.* Ed. Teresa Brennan. London: Routledge, 1989.

―――― with Rooney, Ellen. "In a Word. *Interview." differences,* vol. 1, no. 2 (1989).

Sprengnether, Madelon. *The Spectral Mother: Freud, Feminism and Psychoanalysis.* Ithaca: Cornell University Press, 1990.

Stanton, Domna C. "Difference on Trial: A Critique of the Maternal Metaphor in Cixous, Irigaray and Kristeva." *The Poetics of Gender.* Ed. Nancy K. Miller. New York: Columbia University Press, 1986.

Walzer, Michael. "Two Kinds of Universalism" (1989). Unpublished manuscript on file with the author.

West, Robin. "Jurisprudence and Gender." *University of Chicago Law Review,* vol. 55, no. 1 (1988), p. 1.

―――― . "The Difference in Women's Hedonic Lives: A Phenomenological Critique of Feminist Legal Theory." *Wisconsin Women's Law Journal,* vol. 3 (1987), p. 81.

Wittig, Monique. *Les Guérillères.* Trans. David Le Vay. Boston: Beacon Press, 1975; Paris: Les Editions de Minuit, 1969.

―――― . *The Lesbian Body.* Trans. David Le Vay. Boston: Beacon Press, 1975. Originally published as *Le corps lesbien.* Paris: Les Editions de Minuit, 1973.

Wolf, Christa. *Cassandra: A Novel and Four Essays.* Trans. Jan Van Heurck. New York: Farrar, Straus and Giroux, 1984.

Index

Abjection of the Mother 68–69, 72
Abortion 23–24, 58–60, 213, n. 65
Accommodation 12
Adorno 1, 149
Affirmation of Sexual Difference 134, 139
Affirmation of the Feminine 2, 12–14, 21,
    33–34, 75, 77, 100–102, 111, 125, 132,
    146, 199, 205
Allegory 18–19, 67, 79–88, 101–102, 117–
    118, 165, 170, 188, 201
Antony and Cleopatra 175–177
Aporia 113
Appropriation 144
Ariadne 173
Aristotle 31–32
Asymmetry 191
Austin, Regina 189, 195
Autonomy 51, 53

Barthes, Roland 165
Bataille, George 165
Beckett, Samuel 197–205
Benjamin, Walter 195
Biology 24, 26, 42, 61, 124, 198
Birth 23, 48
Bishop, Elizabeth 154
Blumenburg, Hans 172–173
Bovary, Charles 132
Bovary, Emma 132–133
Butler, Judith 49, 199

Ca 89
Call of the Other 113

Carnal Ethics 144
Carnality 152–164, 184–185
Cassandra 178–179, 195
Castration 37, 53, 73, 77, 80, 84, 86–87,
    89, 91, 103, 105, 131, 157, 179, 201
Chase, Cynthia 68
Child-Rearing 46, 50
Chodorow, Nancy 50–51
Cixous, Hélène 8, 21–22, 57, 59, 64–67,
    91, 94, 101, 104, 108, 110, 125, 153,
    155, 157–160, 168, 173–178, 199–204
Class 59, 194–195
Clément, Catherine 158
Collaboration 163
Conference of Critical Legal Studies 51, 128
Consciousness-Raising 4–5, 32–33, 62, 151
Context 109
Contraception 213, n. 65
Counter-valorization 167
Critique of Myth 190–194

Daddy 11–12, 72, 91
Dasein 97–99
de Beauvoir, Simone 11, 44, 120, 182,
    190–193
De-sistance 149, 162, 199
Deconstruction 4, 18, 26, 28–29, 33, 49,
    67, 71, 79–118, 141, 166, 169, 171,
    180–181, 202–203
Depression 7, 69
Dérèlection 7–8, 22, 34–35, 41, 60, 73–78,
    101, 156, 199–200, 204

235

Derrida, Jacques 3, 11, 18, 26–31, 35, 79–118, 137, 139–144, 167, 170–171, 187, 199, 202–203
Desire 36, 38, 68, 71, 73, 76–77, 125, 161
Despair 57
Devaluation 114, 136, 152, 200
Dialogue 202
Dido 177
Différance 85, 98, 100–101, 108–109, 118, 125, 139–140, 185
Differend 6, 60–61, 63, 178
Differentiation 50
Discourse 29, 53, 89, 115, 146–148, 200
Domination 12–13
Double Writing 170, 186–190
Duras, Marguerite 54–57, 71, 74, 83, 173
Dworkin, Andrea 132–134, 179

Ego-Ideal 73
Empowerment 154
Equality 122, 126, 137–138
Erasure 5, 167
Eroticism 42, 153, 176
Essentialism 4–5, 7, 13–15, 21, 25–26, 34–35, 49, 73–74, 126, 165–167, 181–183, 210, n. 7
Ethical Feminism 131–132, 199
Ethical Relation 148
Ethics 8, 13, 31–32, 84, 94–95, 97–98, 101, 110, 116–118, 126, 136, 169, 181, 185

False Consciousness 133
Fantasy 30, 36–37, 40, 46, 81, 91, 143, 165, 183, 198
Fantasy of the Maternal 64–67, 203
Feminine 107, 129, 130; Body 93; Desire 16–17, 62, 103, 134, 139, 144, 155–160; Difference 14, 17, 21, 34, 36–50, 119, 158; Identity 57, 83; Imaginary 57, 64, 66–67, 71, 77, 88, 73, 104, 144; Language 149; Pleasure 156; Power 179; Reality 2–3, 5, 9, 24, 26, 34, 52, 56, 59–62, 82–83, 93, 130, 150; Restylization 92–107; Sexuality 4, 119; Solidarity 52–57, 83; Specificity 33, 36, 52, 61, 78, 142, 165, 189; Subjectivity 43; Symbolic 77–78; Voice 3; Writing 2–4, 8, 18–19, 22, 66, 71, 81, 96, 143, 148–152, 158–159, 165–196, 202, 215, n. 108, 218, n. 61

Femininity 10, 16, 31, 47, 72, 79, 99, 102–107, 129–130, 146, 151–152, 193
Feminism 4–5, 33–34, 37, 44, 50, 55–59, 62, 79–118, 119–164, 167, 225, n. 43
Feminist Jurisprudence 20, 23–24, 34–35, 56, 60, 111, 115; Politics 82; Theory 171
Fiction 129
Finnegans Wake 1, 188
First Amendment 123
Freedom 44, 132, 136, 153, 201, 220, n. 39
French Feminine Writers 135, 139–141, 146
Freud, Sigmund 22, 36, 46, 58, 63, 70, 73
Full Presence 101, 111, 187, 190
Fuss, Diana 181–184

Gender Difference 103, 128, 137; Divide 93; Hierarchy 4, 6–7, 9–11, 17–18, 20, 22, 35, 87, 94, 99, 107, 110, 118, 121, 124, 129, 139, 148, 150, 167, 182, 185, 195, 198–200, 204; Identification 99, 154; Identity 2, 63, 72, 79–80, 84, 93, 130, 133, 135–142, 151, 157, 162, 166, 170–171, 179, 198–202, 205; Representation 141
Genealogy 18, 116, 167
Genesis 97
Gilligan, Carol 50, 125, 135–137, 141, 146, 150, 178, 186
God 184
Gush 15

Hegel, Georg W.F. 11, 15, 182
Heidegger, Martin 5, 85, 97–98
Herethics 7, 21, 48, 58, 152–164
Heterogeneity 8, 22, 35, 43, 185, 208, n. 9
Heterosexual Norm 73
Heterosexuality 19, 69, 126, 132, 153–155, 161–163, 197, 200, 204–205
Hierarchy 95, 123, 132
Homophobia 152
Homosexuality 153, 204
Husserl, Edmund 15, 26–28, 32, 181
Hysteria 156–159

Identification 69, 75, 77, 100, 148, 198
Imaginary 88, 130
Imaginary Father 68, 70
Imaginative Universal 172–179
Incest 23

Individualism 33
Internalization 43, 66
Intimacy 132–133, 136, 153, 165, 213, n. 68
Irigaray, Luce 1, 8–10, 15–17, 19, 73–77, 94–96, 101, 104, 125, 142–147, 153, 155, 160, 163, 173, 175, 181–186, 201, 205
Irreducibility 102–104, 89
Iterability 199

Jakobson, Roman 62
Jewish Humanism 113
Jouissance 2 ,16–17, 40, 42, 44, 48, 65, 67, 75, 77, 139, 154–162, 198, 211, n. 28
Joyce, James 1
Justice 109, 112–114

Kafka, Franz 198
Kennedy, Duncan 51
Kohlberg 135
Kristeva, Julia 7, 12, 21–22, 35, 36–50, 54, 56–57, 62, 64, 66–73, 88, 90–91, 103, 117, 153, 165, 168, 171, 187, 204

Lacan, Jacques 2, 7, 16–18, 22, 36, 38–41, 49, 53, 55, 58, 63,68–69, 75, 79–81, 86–88, 92, 98, 103, 140–144, 151, 164, 178, 191, 197–198, 202
Lack 38–39, 141–142
Lacoue-Labarthe, Phillipe 149
Language 26, 34, 42–43, 47, 64, 69, 86, 88, 90, 93–94, 101, 104, 131, 171, 178, 186
Language 198, 214, n. 85, 222, n. 58
Law 6, 9, 37, 53, 60–61, 63, 68–69, 113–116, 121–122, 138, 144, 151
Law of the Father 7, 41–42, 52–53, 56, 64, 88–89, 93, 103, 108, 151, 174–175, 189
Legal Doctrine 137
Lesbianism 161
Levinas, Emmanual 97–98, 107, 113
Lispector, Clarice 148–149
Literary Language 186–190
Loss of the Mother 52–57
Love 45, 55, 58–59, 136, 161, 175, 178
Lyotard, Jean-François 6, 19, 60, 109–110, 151

MacDonald, Christine 87
MacIntyre, Alisdair 110–111

MacKinnon, Catharine 4, 6, 10–11, 17, 21, 116, 119–164, 174, 179, 185–186, 191, 192, 198, 200–201, 204–205
Madness 54
Male Discourse 221, n. 52; Domination 128; Gaze 120, 124, 198, 33, 139; Norm 137–138, 151; Power 120, 122; Privilege 53, 199; Reality 52–53, 56; Sexuality 124
Marxism 122, 126, 132, 138, 153
Masculine Desire 63; Discourse 47, 66; Domination 130; Fantasy 34, 53–55, 124, 155; Identity 53; Imaginary 64, 78, 88, 143; Projection 39; Subjectivity 39, 52–57, 178; Symbolic 48, 80, 109, 171, 178; Temporality 43; View 94, 137; See also, Male Gaze
Masochism 163
Masquerade 105–106, 130, 140
Master-Slave Dialectic 145
Materialism 3, 6, 162
Maternal 7–8, 21–22, 25, 36–51, 57, 59, 63, 182; Body 41–42 47–51, 57; Ideal 58; Signification 214, n. 85
Maternity 171
Matricide 70–71, 74, 90–91
Medea 194
Melancholia 69
Mère/Mehr 2, 84, 94
Messianic Conception of Justice 113–114, 138, 219, n. 93
Metaforeplay 15, 168, 203–204, 227, n. 14
Metaphor 3, 27, 29–31, 58–59, 63, 65, 68, 82–83, 87–88, 101, 107, 131, 140, 146–147, 162, 165–196
Metaphoric Transference 31, 100–101, 147, 167, 169
Metaphorization 73–74, 77–78, 81, 101; See also, Re-metaphorization
Metonomy 15, 62–63, 82, 166–168, 171
Metonymic Deferral 167
Mimesis 30, 147–52, 156, 162–163, 175, 182, 199, 222, n. 65
Misogyny 85
Mommy 40
Montrelay, Michéle 57
Moral Reasoning 135–137
Morrison, Toni 19, 59, 186–188, 194–195
Mother 38, 67–73, 89, 92
Mother/Child 7, 211, n. 33
Mother/Daughter 22, 76–78

Mothering 6, 63, 72
Mourning 53, 57, 70–71, 88–92
Myth 19, 39, 81, 86, 94, 102, 163, 165–196

Nakedness 222, n. 58
Nationality 194–195
Naturalism 7, 21, 25, 33, 35, 49, 63, 73, 165, 210, n. 7
Negation 69–70, 91
Negativity 48
Neuter 142
Nietzsche 85–86, 98, 104–106
Nominalism 85
Norm Legal 23

Object of Desire 39
Object Relations Theory 6, 50–52, 55–57, 74
Objectification 5, 10, 119–120
Oedipal Complex 36
"One Art" 154, 223, n. 74
Ontology 99
Oppression 134
Other-Love 65–67, 72, 91, 108, 144, 160, 176–177, 182, 184–185, 197, 202–203

Palleonomy 85
Paternal 69, 72
Patriarchy 12, 54, 76, 102, 133, 151, 154, 166, 173, 210, n. 7
Penal Colony 198
Penis 37, 103, 154, 158, 179, 201
Penthesileia 174
Performance 151, 198–199
Performative 17, 85, 92, 131, 176
Phallic Discourse 149
Phallic Image 160
Phallic Mother 36–37, 41, 43, 46, 55–56, 59, 63–64, 68–69, 71, 133, 158
Phallocentrism 96, 183
Phallogocentrism 9–10, 16, 66, 86, 103–104, 155, 182, 200, 205, 222, n. 65
Phallus 16, 36–38, 40, 49, 55–56, 65, 68, 71, 79–80, 82, 87–88, 103, 105, 140–141, 154, 160, 175, 179, 201
Phenomenology 22, 26, 29, 34, 61–62
Poetic Language 188
Point of View 131
Politics 56, 84, 98, 101, 136, 138, 159, 169, 181, 185–186

Politics of Revenge 11
Pornography 10, 23, 123–125
Postmodern Critique 73
Postmodern Philosophy 5–6, 18, 26, 35
Postmodernism 201, 207, n. 1
Power 130, 201
Power-seeking Ideology 138
Pregnancy 41, 46–47, 58, 63, 171
Privileging 7, 58, 34, 95, 100
Privileging of the Masculine 136, 144, 151
Psychical Fantasy 58–59
Psychoanalysis 144, 156
Psychoanalytic Framework 49, 51

Race 59, 194–195
Rape 23–24, 63, 127, 130
Rawls, John 152
Re-collective Imagination 178
Re-metaphorization 2, 17, 100, 102, 118, 163–167, 169, 215, n. 108; See also, Metaphorization
Re-symbolization 163
Real 88
Reality 20, 103, 117, 119, 135–136, 141, 143, 200–201
Reappropriation 208, n. 9
Reduplication 44, 75
Religion 44, 47, 165
Repression 36, 57, 71, 95
Repression of the Mother 90
Reproduction 43
Reproductive Capacity 51
Repudiation of the Feminine 12, 19, 72–74, 91, 105, 126, 136, 151, 156, 171, 205
Repudiation of the Maternal 44, 64
Resistance 110
Restylization 106, 198
Revenge 138
Rhetoric 126
Rich, Adrienne 60
Ricoeur, Paul 168–170
Rights 126
Riviere, Joan 105–106
Romance 132
Romanticism 56
Romanticization 14

Sameness 138
Schafer, Roy 66
Schor, Naomi 11, 15–16
Semiotic 7, 41, 46

Sensual Pleasure 154
Sex 15–17, 94, 127, 130; Difference 120,
   125, 139; Discrimination 137
Sexism 126, 128
Sexual Desire 134
Sexual Difference 2, 4, 6, 9, 11–12, 16, 18,
   35, 38, 52–53, 67, 73, 79, 81, 84, 86–
   87, 89, 96–110, 118, 129, 139, 141–147,
   151, 169, 171, 175, 199, 205;
   Harassment 23, 61–63, 151; Identity 13;
   Norms 62–63; Preference 99, 153;
   Relation 55; Repression 102
Sexuality 62, 81, 143, 153, 162–163,
   198
Signifier of Desire 36, 40, 176
Signifier(d) 68
Silence 3, 33, 55, 72, 207, n. 4–5
Silencing 134–136
Slavery 195
Slippage 13, 100, 131, 147, 171
Sorceress 158
Spectral Mother 188
Spillers, Hortense 186
Spivak, Gayatri 13–14, 85, 159, 179–182
Stanton, Domna C. 166–168
Stereotype 85, 93, 93
Strategic Essentialism 179–180
Style 105–106, 140, 178, 202
Stylization 85
Subjectivity 150

Subordination 44, 123
Suicide 69
Supreme Court 138
Symbolic 36–38, 41, 46, 65, 70–72, 79, 84,
   86, 91–92, 108, 144, 163, 166, 187
Symbolic Order 39, 179
Symmetry 10, 17, 55, 95, 151, 155–156,
   161, 183, 193

Temporalization 108, 117, 169
Time 43, 104, 108, 185
Transcendence 192–193
Transcendental Signifier 37, 88, 141

Universalism 195
Utopian Moment 45–46
Utopianism 152, 168–172

Valuation 199
Violence 23, 123, 131

Walzer, Michael 195
West, Robin 4–6, 9, 21–36, 51–52, 56–57,
   59, 62, 109, 117
Whitford, Margaret 74–77
Wife/Mistress 38
Wittig, Monique 160–163, 198
Wolf, Christa 178–179, 186, 195
Womanliness 105